Preventing Prenatal Harm

CLINICAL MEDICAL ETHICS

Editors

H. TRISTRAM ENGELHARDT, JR., The Center for Ethics, Medicine and Public Issues, Baylor College of Medicine, Houston, Texas

KEVIN WILDES, S.J., Department of Philosophy, Georgetown University, Washington, D.C.

Editorial Advisory Board

GEORGE J. AGICH, School of Medicine, Southern Illinois University, Springfield, Illinois

DAN W. BROCK, Department of Philosophy, Brown University, Providence, Rhode Island

BARUCH A. BRODY, Center for Ethics, Medicine and Public Issues, Baylor College of Medicine, Houston, Texas

ALLEN E. BUCHANAN, School of Medicine, University of Wisconsin at Madison, Madison, Wisconsin

ANTONIO M. GOTTO, JR., Department of Medicine, Baylor College of Medicine, Houston, Texas

ANGELA R. HOLDER, School of Medicine, Yale University, New Haven, Connecticut

JAY KATZ, Yale Law School, Yale University, New Haven, Connecticut

LORETTA M. KOPELMAN, Department of Medical Humanities, School of Medicine, East Carolina University, Greenville, North Carolina

EDMUND D. PELLEGRINO, Director, Center for Clinical Bioethics, Georgetown University, Washington, D.C.

STEPHEN WEAR, Department of Philosophy, State University of New York at Buffalo, Buffalo, New York

Previous Books in the Series

Competence to Consent
BECKY WHITE

Balancing Act: The New Medical Ethics of Medicine's New Economics
E. HAAVI MORREIM

Preventing Prenatal Harm
Should the State Intervene?
Second Edition

Deborah Mathieu

GEORGETOWN UNIVERSITY PRESS / WASHINGTON, D.C.

Georgetown University Press, Washington, D.C.   20007
© 1996 by Georgetown University Press. All rights reserved.
Printed in the United States of America.
10   9   8   7   6   5   4   3   2   1   1996
THIS VOLUME IS PRINTED ON ACID-FREE OFFSET BOOKPAPER.

Library of Congress Cataloging-in-Publication Data

Matthieu, Deborah.
    Preventing prenatal harm : should the state intervene / Deborah
Mathieu.   —   New rev. ed.
        p.   cm.   —   (Clinical medical ethics)
    Includes bibliographical references.
    1. Prenatal care—United States—Moral and ethical aspects.
2. Fetus—Legal status, laws, etc.—United States.   3. Pregnant
women—Legal status, laws, etc.—United States.   I. Title.
II. Series: Clinical medical ethics (Washington, D.C.)
RG960.M33   1996
176—dc20
ISBN 0-87840-600-X   (pbk.   :   alk. paper)
                                                                    95–36923

To Hank, with love and thanks

Contents

Preventing Prenatal Harm

1

The Problem

During her pregnancy Adrienne Robinson subsisted on potato chips and used her federal pregnancy-related food supplies to purchase cocaine. "I knew I was killing my baby," Ms. Robinson said, "But I couldn't stop."[1] Her son was born with syphilis and addicted to cocaine. If he is like other children born to cocaine addicts, then he is also tiny for his age and underdeveloped, he cries constantly, and he rarely meets his mother's gaze. Another cocaine addict, Traci Jackson, was less fortunate than Adrienne Robinson. Jackson delivered a still-born baby in the bathroom of a crack house. The infant, autopsy reports revealed, had "enough cocaine in its liver to kill some adults." Ms. Jackson was convicted of possessing cocaine and sentenced to twelve years in prison.[2]

It is natural to feel sympathy for these infants. It is natural also to feel outrage on their behalf; if their mothers had behaved differently, these children could have been born healthy. It is natural to feel, even, that these children were wronged, and that their mothers are culpable. After all, the children's chances for leading independent lives were destroyed through their mothers' actions, and now one of them has no future and the other's future is in jeopardy.

But how far should we take our sympathy and our outrage? Do we want the state to intervene and seek to prevent these kinds of misfortunes? Do we want the state to use its coercive force to require pregnant women to behave in certain ways? Do we want the state to punish women whose behavior while pregnant caused devastating harm to their children?

The choice is between respecting a pregnant woman's right to decide what happens to her own body and protecting an innocent child from avoidable damage. In other words, whose interests should

1

the state protect: a woman's interest in remaining free from certain forms of state control or the child's interest in having a decent quality of life?

This book explores situations that have come to be known as "maternal–fetal conflicts." While catchy, the phrase is misleading. It places the emphasis on the fetus instead of on the born child (who will bear the burden of any harm done prenatally); it assumes a conflict between the pregnant woman and her offspring (while the issue is usually considerably more complex); and it incorrectly implies that all pregnant women are appropriately regarded as mothers. For these reasons I have chosen to avoid the phrase "maternal–fetal conflict" altogether, and will instead speak in terms of "preventable prenatal harm." I mention this at the outset for those of you familiar with "maternal–fetal conflicts" who might be wondering if I am addressing the same issues. Yes. But I am trying to look at them in a more fruitful way.

Some commentators have suggested that the issues at stake can readily be resolved by a straightforward appeal to individual rights. One view is that the state's recognition of a woman's right to decide what happens to her own body is inconsistent with a policy of encouraging or requiring fetal therapy. A very different position is that a fetus has a right to be born healthy and the state should be empowered to act to protect this right, even if it means overriding a woman's right of self-determination. Obviously, the espousal of one of these rights rather than the other leads to a very different conclusion regarding the proper role of the state and the culpability of the pregnant woman.

Such a simple rights-based approach, however, provides no adequate resolution of these problems. Instead, the rights principles must be refined, weighed against one another, and applied within a complex framework of moral values, legal considerations, practical issues, and attention to consequences. In what follows, then, I will offer a pluralistic approach to the problems. This approach does not rest upon a single moral value and does not attempt to solve subtle moral issues by exclusively focusing on rights principles, much less on one right, but instead reflects an intricate mixture of moral, legal, and practical concerns. My hope is not to offer the perfect solution to the dilemmas at hand; such a solution does not exist. Nor do I attempt to offer a grand theory about the proper relationship between the individual and the state in all matters; that ambition is beyond the scope of this

essay. My goal, instead, is to analyze the problem of preventable prenatal harms and to offer good reasons—rather than political slogans
or emotional reactions—for determining which alternatives are superior to others.

AFFECTING THE OUTCOME OF A PREGNANCY

A pregnant woman's actions and omissions, and those of her physician, take on moral significance when the actors have a choice, when
there are alternatives available to them. If only one course of action is
possible, then their pursuit of that course cannot be construed as morally problematic. Likewise, interventions into pregnant women's
activities are rationally justified only when it is possible to affect the
outcome of the pregnancy. No one is obligated to make futile efforts
to prevent or ameliorate a harm.

Lifestyle Choices

The outcome of a pregnancy can be affected by a variety of interventions, and one approach is to seek to influence a pregnant woman to
change her lifestyle in some particular way. Such changes could benefit a great many children, since a wide array of lifestyle choices of
pregnant women may have deleterious effects on their offspring.
There is some evidence, for instance, that ingesting such seemingly
innocuous substances as caffeine and quinine could result in birth
defects. And using some common over-the-counter medications—
such as aspirin and cough syrup—may also cause fetal damage.[3]
Even the pregnant woman's diet can have severely harmful effects on
the fetus. Maintaining a diet low in nutrition may cause congenital
malformations, brain impairments, and growth retardation.[4]

Other lifestyle choices of the pregnant woman can also jeopardize
the health of the fetus. Many studies have indicated that consuming
alcohol during pregnancy substantially increases the risk of serious
harm to the future child, including growth retardation, mental retardation, central nervous system abnormalities, and craniofacial abnormalities.[5] The reason for this is straightforward:

> Ethyl alcohol, or ethanol, passes freely across the placenta. There-
> fore, whatever a pregnant woman drinks, the baby she is carrying
> drinks, too. It is that simple. Moreover, the fetus cannot eliminate
> alcohol nearly as quickly as the adult body can; when a woman

drinks, the concentration of alcohol *in utero* is higher than in the rest of her system, and it persists twice as long. By the time the woman feels pleasantly relaxed or euphoric, the fetus may be comatose.[6]

The relationship between smoking cigarettes during pregnancy and growth retardation of the child has been demonstrated in studies conducted since the 1950s. The growth retardation is generally symmetrical; the newborn weighs less (because of a reduction in lean body mass, not just fat) and is smaller from head to foot. Some physicians consider this symmetrical growth retardation to be a "fetal tobacco syndrome." In addition, smoking during pregnancy increases the risk of premature birth and perinatal death, and may cause serious placental complications.[7]

The damaging effects of the use of narcotics (codeine, morphine, heroin, and methadone) during pregnancy have been noted for decades. Neonatal drug dependence, for instance, has been well-documented since the turn of the century, and a variety of other risks to the child also have been noted: low birthweight, hyaline membrane disease, and sudden infant death syndrome.[8] Cocaine and crack (a less expensive and more potent form of cocaine) also have negative effects on the children born to addicted mothers; premature birth, low birthweight, emotional and developmental problems, central nervous system disorders, and a variety of malformations (e.g., to the genitals, kidneys, head, intestines, and spinal cord) have been reported.[9]

It has been demonstrated, however, that a woman who ceases these activities during pregnancy greatly improves the health of her future child and its chances for survival.[10] This, for some people, is reason enough to conclude that women who engage in these activities should be required to change their lifestyles while they are pregnant. The harm to a woman would be minor, it is contended, compared with the great benefits to her future child. One proposal is to use the threat of criminal prosecution to coerce pregnant women into changing their lifestyle. Legislators could pass laws mandating that women behave in certain ways while pregnant (e.g., refrain from smoking cigarettes and/or drinking alcohol) or face criminal charges.

Fetal Therapy

A related area of growing concern involves techniques of fetal therapy. One of the oldest means of fetal therapy is the cesarean section, which is employed to save the life and/or health of the term fetus in a variety of circumstances: cases of myelomeningocele, respiratory distress, abnormal presentation, maternal herpes infections, AIDS, and placenta previa, among others. And since the early 1960s, physicians have been able to treat a wide assortment of other fetal conditions which would have resulted, had they been left untreated, in serious impairments after birth.

The first few successful fetal interventions—blood infusions (to ameliorate hydrops fetalis associated with maternal Rh sensitization) and the administration of steroids (to mitigate respiratory distress syndrome)—have been expanded to include the administration of a wide assortment of other medications and vitamins to the fetus (through the mother). A fetus who cannot properly metabolize biotin (vitamin H), for example, can be given large doses of the vitamin to control this potentially fatal genetic disorder.[11] Even premature birth, one of the major causes of morbidity and mortality in the newborn period, can be prevented in many instances. A panel of the National Institute of Child Health and Human Development estimated that widespread use of corticosteroid therapy could save the lives of over 6,000 premature babies each year.[12]

Medical researchers have also made significant progress in their ability to intervene surgically in the development of potentially devastating genetic defects, thus preventing the harmful effects of these defects from being fully realized. Among these defects are hydronephrosis (obstruction of the urinary tract), hydrocephalus (excessive cerebrospinal fluid), congenital diaphragmatic hernia, and a variety of tumors.[13] It is anticipated that advances in the ability to treat anatomic defects of fetuses will continue, and that genetic etiologies of severe disabilities will increasingly come under control. For instance, techniques to correct neural tube defects (such as spina bifida) and limb bud malformations (which impair growth and differentiation of the extremities) are continually being developed.

A dramatic extension of this type of therapy is gene surgery, which involves replacing a defective gene with a normally functioning one. Researchers are hopeful that, in the not-too-distant future, a fetus who carries the gene for sickle-cell anemia, for example, could be treated in this manner, and a healthy child would be born in place of a sick one. In addition, the recent genome sequencing project promises even more elegant interventions. By mapping the chemical sequences of human genes, scientists hope to learn more about the fundamental mechanism that governs subcellular life, such as how we develop from a single egg, how we age, and why we succumb to certain diseases. The knowledge gained from this research may lead to simpler and more effective treatments for diseases (such as sickle-cell anemia, cystic fibrosis, and hemophilia) than gene replacement, which involves surgery.

The physician who wishes to administer a therapy which would alleviate a severe impairment of the fetus will clash with the pregnant woman who—although she intends to bring the fetus to term—refuses to undergo the treatment. Four factors form the basis of the dilemma in this case: (1) A variety of existing fetal therapies can alleviate seriously deleterious conditions; (2) some pregnant women refuse the administration of these therapies, even though the women intend to carry their pregnancies to term; (3) competent adults must give their informed, competent, and voluntary consent before medical treatment can be administered to (or through) them; and (4) women have the legal right to seek abortion.

These factors do not imply any particular moral, legal, or policy imperatives, but they raise important questions that must be answered before the legal and policy issues can be fully addressed. Why, for instance, would we even consider coercing a pregnant woman to accept medical treatment against her will when she has the power to make our efforts futile by having an abortion? What are the grounds for thinking that medical treatment should be administered to a fetus despite its mother's objections? Does a fetus have a right to medical care? Does the state (or the mother, or the physician) have an obligation to provide medical care to the fetus? And what are the grounds for thinking that a pregnant woman is free to refuse medical treatment for her fetus? Does she have a legal (or moral) right to be left alone? Would the harm of interfering with her decision outweigh the benefits of interfering?

The use of fetal therapy techniques is of special significance because it requires us to reexamine old debates that many believed had been settled long ago. It even calls into question an almost sacred tenet of Anglo-American law and contemporary medical ethics: that a competent adult (in this case, the pregnant woman) has an overriding right of self-determination with respect to medical treatment. One of the major thrusts of medical ethics in the past has moved steadily toward reinforcing this right and defending it against what many saw as a rather pervasive medical paternalism. But new developments in fetal therapy call this legal right into question. We are now confronted with the apparently inescapable conflict between respect for a pregnant woman's right of self-determination and prevention of serious harm to the child she will bear.

Reproductive Hazards in the Workplace

A third method of affecting the outcome of a pregnancy is by removing women from (or prohibiting fertile women from working in) jobs involving the use of substances believed to cause fetal damage. There are two types of reproductive health hazards in the workplace: Some substances cause damage directly to the developing fetus (teratogenic damage); others cause damage to the parents' reproductive systems, and thus indirectly affect their offspring (mutagenic damage). Several substances commonly found in the workplace—such as lead, ethylene oxide, and vinyl chloride—cause both kinds of damage.[14]

Goodyear, Eastman Kodak, Dow, DuPont, American Cyanamid Company, B.F. Goodrich, Johnson Controls, Olin Corporation, General Motors, and other major corporations responded to evidence concerning reproductive hazards in the workplace by barring women from certain jobs. Although some companies prohibited only pregnant women from working with specific substances, another common exclusionary policy prohibited all females between the ages of sixteen and fifty from working with substances believed to be reproductive hazards, unless the women could prove that they were sterile. Proponents of these exclusionary policies argue that they are necessary to protect future generations from serious harm, while critics charge that they unfairly discriminate against women.

The issue of reproductive hazards in the workplace, then, highlights a tension between economic interests (companies want to make profits, women want to have well-paying jobs) and moral interests (women want equal employment opportunities, everyone wants healthy children). Although these interests are not necessarily incompatible, they conflict in those cases in which the risk of reproductive harm is uncertain and/or the cost involved in cleaning up the work environment appears prohibitive. In these instances it simply is not feasible to meet all of the interests at stake, and so the policy issue becomes a choice of whose interests will prevail. As with the imposition of fetal therapies, the choice is between two unfortunate outcomes:

causing harm to some women in order to seek to prevent harm to their offspring, or permitting harm to befall newborn children in the hope of avoiding harm to their mothers.

Other Methods of Affecting the Outcome of a Pregnancy

Perhaps, though, prenatal harm could best be dealt with after the fact. Rather than intervening in the lives of pregnant women in order to prevent prenatal harm, we might do better to permit the children who had been harmed *in utero* to sue their mothers and/or the responsible health care providers. The child would still be harmed, to be sure, but at least he or she could seek compensation for it. Tort law, then, might be the best method for dealing with these situations. Or we may prefer to punish women who caused serious prenatal harm by jailing them and/or removing their children from their custody.

There are other alternatives as well. We can maintain the status quo: At present, most pregnant women are free to behave however they wish, no matter how injurious their actions are to their future children, and the state offers few inducements to act otherwise. On the other hand, perhaps it is time to develop incentive structures to encourage women (but not to require them) to behave in certain ways during pregnancy.

Discussion

The newly gained options for fetal benefit seriously challenge the traditional view of pregnancy as a personal matter, and challenge as well society's depth of commitment to freedom of choice in general. Indeed, these situations raise fundamental ethical, legal, and social policy questions: Should pregnant women be coerced into giving up damaging substances such as alcohol, tobacco, and narcotic drugs? Should fetal therapy ever be forced on an unconsenting pregnant woman? Should a woman be punished for having caused serious prenatal harm? Should she be required to pay damages to the child to compensate for the harm she caused or could have prevented? What role should the law courts, legislatures, and health care professionals play? What are the legal and moral rights at stake here, and the obligations? Which ones are most compelling?

It is fair to say that the new techniques for recognizing and responding to prenatal harm generate a variety of troubling issues which, in turn, pose fundamental challenges to the fields of medicine, biomedical ethics, law, and public policy. And even more questions regarding the appropriate treatment of a pregnant woman and her fetus will arise as new procedures for fetal intervention are developed and perfected. Many of these dilemmas exist because we are uncertain how best to utilize our new technologies. It is difficult sometimes to perceive how time-honored methods of dealing with difficult moral choices can come to our aid, when we are faced with new issues for which there are no widely accepted conventions or clearly legitimate expectations. Nor is there any general agreement about our goals—except perhaps for some consensus regarding a few abstract ideals, such as the general value of healthy babies. We need to be more explicit about our purposes here; what are we trying to accomplish? And, of course, we must not forget the most frequently asked question in bioethics: Who should decide whose interests will predominate?

LEGAL CASES

U.S. law courts have already confronted many questions regarding the appropriate treatment of pregnant women who act in ways that are detrimental to the life and/or health of the children they intend to bear, but no consensus has emerged. What is clear, however, is that these cases raise in a new and vivid way some of the most basic issues about rights, duties, the moral limits of the law, and the scope of legitimate state action.

Some courts of law have ruled against the women. In one of the earliest cases, the Supreme Court of New Jersey ordered a twenty-three-year-old Jehovah's Witness, who was eight months pregnant, to undergo a blood transfusion for the sake of her "unborn child." The attending physician had determined that the woman was in danger of severe hemorrhaging, and the court acted because it believed that "the unborn child is entitled to the law's protection."[15] The woman left the hospital, however, before the blood transfusion could be administered.

Since then, other pregnant women have been ordered by courts to undergo medical treatments—some of them considerably more invasive than a blood transfusion—for the sake of the children they were planning to bear. Some women have even been ordered to undergo major surgery—cesarean sections—believed necessary to save the lives of their term fetuses. In one case, a woman in the thirty-ninth week of pregnancy was diagnosed as having complete placenta

previa, a condition which portended, the attending physician
claimed, that neither she nor her fetus would survive a vaginal delivery. She refused a cesarean section, however, for religious reasons.
The judge who heard the case ruled that the state legislators had
intended the juvenile statutes to apply to viable fetuses, and so concluded that this fetus was a "deprived child" within the meaning of
the state juvenile code. The judge then ordered that "all medical procedures deemed necessary by the attending physician to preserve the
life of the defendant's child" be performed.[16] Ironically, a cesarean section was ultimately unnecessary; the woman's condition seemed to
correct itself and the child was delivered alive vaginally (prompting
many people to question the accuracy of the original diagnosis).

In Colorado, a thirty-three-year-old morbidly obese woman who
was near term found herself immersed in a judicial proceeding shortly
after admission to the hospital. Her attending physician had recommended a cesarean section because of indications of fetal hypoxia (lack
of oxygen), but the woman refused to undergo the operation because
of her fear of surgery. In response to a telephone call from the physician, a judge held a hearing at the woman's bedside. The judge ruled
that the fetus was a "dependent and neglected child" within the meaning of the Colorado juvenile code, and ordered the woman to undergo
the operation in order to safeguard the life of the term fetus. The
woman accepted the judge's decision and permitted the operation to
proceed. On hindsight, this surgery may have been unnecessary as
well. The child to whom she gave birth was much healthier than the
physicians had expected, leading them to suspect that their fetal monitoring devices had given them inaccurate information.[17]

Courts have sanctioned other sorts of limitations on pregnant
women's liberty as well. A judge in Maryland, for instance, ordered a
pregnant woman who was addicted to narcotics to enter a drug treatment program and to submit to weekly urinalysis until the birth of
her child. The physician who brought the suit against the woman
claimed that her ingestion of a variety of drugs—morphine, cocaine,
and valium—would "retard, inhibit, and prevent [the child-to-be's]
further growth and development" to a life-threatening degree.[18] In
Wisconsin, a judge ordered a near-term teenager to be placed in
secure detention until the birth of her child because she lacked "moti-
vation or ability to seek prenatal care."[19] And a District of Columbia
Superior Court judge ordered a thirty-year-old pregnant woman, who
was convicted of second-degree theft for passing $721.98 in bad

checks, to 180 days in jail in order to protect her fetus from her alleged drug use. Acknowledging the harshness of a six-month sentence for this kind of first offense, the judge explained, "I'm going to keep her locked up until the baby is born because she tested positive for cocaine when she came before me. She's apparently an addictive personality and I'll be darned if I'm going to have a baby born that way." Not only would the child benefit, the judge argued, but so would the "taxpaying public who would undoubtedly have to pay for . . . a child who could have severe and expensive problems." The woman received regular prenatal care while in jail and her child was born healthy.[20] In a different use of the criminal sanction, over 200 women in more than two dozen states have been prosecuted for exposing their fetuses to illegal drugs.[21] The charges have varied from child endangerment to child abuse to assault with a deadly weapon to manslaughter. Many of the women either pleaded guilty or accepted plea bargains.[22]

The most well-publicized recent case involving a pregnant woman who ingested illegal drugs, however, had a different outcome: The court ultimately ruled in favor of the woman. The state of Florida brought criminal charges against twenty-three-year-old Jennifer Johnson, who had ingested cocaine while pregnant with two children. One was born in 1987, the other in 1989. Although both children tested positive for cocaine exposure and Ms. Johnson admitted having smoked crack while pregnant, both deliveries were normal and neither child appeared damaged. Given the clear evidence of Ms. Johnson's drug use during pregnancy, however, the prosecution tried a novel approach. They charged Ms. Johnson with delivering a controlled substance to a minor, arguing that she had passed cocaine through the umbilical cord to her child in the minute after birth, before the umbilical cord was cut. A lower court convicted her on two criminal counts and the District Court of Appeal affirmed her convictions.[23] The Florida Supreme Court, however, overturned the ruling. Stating that there was no evidence that Florida legislators ever intended the statute prohibiting delivering a controlled substance to a minor to be used this way, the court added that it "declines the state's invitation to walk down a path that the law, public policy, reason and common sense forbid it to tread." [24] Interestingly, among the parties who filed briefs on behalf of Ms. Johnson were the American Medical Association, the American Public Health Association, and the American Society of Law and Medicine.

Courts in other states have concluded similarly. In Connecticut, Ohio, New York, North Carolina, and Michigan, for instance, courts refused to rule against women who had ingested illegal drugs while pregnant on the grounds that state statutes do not apply to fetuses.[25] Other courts have reached this same resolution for a different reason: to uphold the rights of the mother. In releasing a woman who had been accused of child neglect for having ingested cocaine while pregnant, a Bronx judge averred that, "By becoming pregnant, women do not waive the constitutional protections afforded to other citizens."[26]

Some courts have also sided with the pregnant woman on decisions involving medical treatment. The Illinois Appellate Court, for instance, refused to order a cesarean section for a pregnant woman whose placenta was failing and whose fetus, her physicians believed, would die or suffer severe mental retardation if not delivered immediately. The young woman transferred to another hospital, where she gave birth naturally to a four-pound twelve-ounce boy.[27]

THE PLAN OF THE BOOK

There are four stages during which the state can act to prevent prenatal harms: (1) before the woman becomes pregnant (e.g., by forbidding fertile women to work in certain jobs known to cause genetic damage); (2) during pregnancy (e.g., by requiring that pregnant women refrain from engaging in certain activities known to be hazardous to the fetus, such as imbibing alcohol); (3) during delivery (e.g., by requiring her to undergo a cesarean section); and (4) after the child is born (e.g., by allowing the injured child to sue his mother and/or others for damages, or by prosecuting the mother for having caused harm to her child). Should the state use its power to impose on any woman any of these (or other) methods of affecting the outcome of her pregnancy?

Three very different responses to these questions will be examined: (1) A pregnant woman has both moral and legal obligations to act in the interests of her child-to-be, obligations which the state should uphold; (2) the state should uphold *some* of a woman's moral obligations to her future child; and (3) while a pregnant woman may have moral obligations to act in the interests of the child she intends to bear, these obligations should *not* be backed by the coercive power of the state. Each of these stances raises profound and perplexing ethical, legal, and public policy issues, and all will be examined here.

The next chapter provides the background information and analyses of basic issues that are essential for understanding the arguments for and against state intervention to prevent prenatal harm explored in the following chapters. Using the conclusions drawn in Chapter Two, Chapters Three and Four will explore arguments for and against coercing pregnant women to behave in certain ways. Chapter Three analyzes the reasons in favor of limiting individual liberty in order to prevent prenatal harm, whereas Chapter Four discusses reasons against such policies. These chapters are fairly abstract, focusing on general moral and legal principles and on public policy issues, and hence they are inconclusive. Although various arguments are explored, no final adjudication is made as to which position is strongest. This is the goal of Chapters Five and Six, which are much more concrete. They apply the arguments presented in the earlier chapters to specific cases and argue for particular conclusions. Chapter Seven explores an alternative response to preventable prenatal harms which involves limited state interference with individual decision making, and summarizes the arguments and conclusions of the book.

NOTES

1. S. L. Nazario, "High Infant Mortality Is a Persistent Blotch On Health Care in U.S.," *Wall Street Journal*, Oct. 19, 1988.

2. "Mother Sentenced for Exposing Fetus to Cocaine," *Washington Post*, July 2, 1991, p. A4.

3. C. C. LoBue, "Effects of Drugs on the Fetus," in K. R. Niswander (ed.), *Manual of Obstetrics*, Boston: Little, Brown, pp. 281–304, 1983; C. S. Catz and S. J. Yaffee, "Environmental Factors: Pharmacology," in National Institutes of Health, *Prevention of Embryonic, Fetal and Perinatal Disease*, Washington, D.C.: Government Printing Office, pp. 119–45, 1976.

4. American College of Obstetricians and Gynecologists Committee on Nutrition, *Nutrition in Maternal Health Care*, Chicago: American College of Obstetricians and Gynecologists, 1974; C. Phillips and N. Johnson, "The Impact of Quality of Diet and Other Factors on Birth Weight of Infants," *American Journal of Clinical Nutrition* 30, pp. 215–21, 1977; R. Rosso, "Nutrition and Maternal–Fetal Exchange," *American Journal of Clinical Nutrition* 34, pp. 744–81, 1981.

5. E. L. Abel, *Fetal Alcohol Syndrome and Fetal Alcohol Effects*, N.Y.: Plenum Press, 1984; S. B. Blume, "Is Social Drinking During Pregnancy Harmless? There is Reason to Think Not," *Advances in Alcohol & Substance Abuse* 5,

pp. 209–19, 1986; S. K. Clarren and D. W. Smith, "The Fetal Alcohol Syndrome," *New England Journal of Medicine* 298, pp. 1063–67, 1978; American Medical Association Council on Scientific Affairs: "Fetal Effects of Maternal Alcohol Use," *Journal of the American Medical Association* 249, pp. 2517–21, 1983; J. W. Hanson et al., "The Effects of Moderate Alcohol Consumption During Pregnancy on Fetal Growth and Morphogenesis," *Journal of Pediatrics* 93, pp. 457–60, 1978; R. E. Little, "Moderate Alcohol Use During Pregnancy and Decreased Infant Birth Weight," *American Journal of Public Health* 67, pp. 1154–56, 1977; R. E. Little et al., "Fetal Alcohol Effects in Humans and Animals," *Advances in Alcohol & Substance Abuse*, pp. 103–25, 1982; M. Nadel, "Offspring with Fetal Alcohol Effects," in D. Cook et al. (eds.), *Psychosocial Issues in the Treatment of Alcoholism*, Haworth Press, N.Y., 1985; R. Olegard, "Alcohol and Narcotics: Epidemiology and Pregnancy Risks," *International Journal of Technology Assessment in Health Care* 8 (Supplement 1), pp. 101–05, 1992; J. Olson et al., "Alcohol Use, Conception Time and Birthweight," *Journal of Epidemiology and Community Health* 37, pp. 63–75, 1983; M. L. Plant and M. A. Plant, "Family Alcohol Problems Among Pregnant Women: Links with Maternal Substance Use and Birth Abnormalities," *Drug & Alcohol Dependence* 20, pp. 213–19, 1987; J. L. Sphor et al., "Prenatal Alcohol Exposure and Long-Term Developmental Consequences," *Lancet* 341 (8850), pp. 907–10, 1993.

6. M. Dorris, "The Tragedy of Fetal Alcohol Syndrome," *1994 Medical and Health Annual*, p. 122.

7. S. Cnattingius, "Smoking During Pregnancy," *International Journal of Technology Assessment in Health Care* 8 (Supplement 1), pp. 91–95, 1992; S. Cnattingius et al., "Smoking, Maternal Age, and Fetal Growth," *Obstetrics and Gynecology* 66, pp. 449–52, 1985; L. M. Longo, "Health Consequences of Maternal Smoking," in the National Research Council, *Alternative Dietary Practices and Nutritional Abuses in Pregnancy*, Washington, D.C.: National Academy Press, 1982; Z. Stein and J. Kline, "Editorial: Smoking, Alcohol and Reproduction," *American Journal of Public Health* 73, pp. 1154–56, 1983; P. H. Shiono et al., "Smoking and Drinking During Pregnancy," *Journal of the American Medical Association* 255, pp. 82–84, 1986.

8. L. G. Alroomi et al., "Maternal Narcotic Abuse and the Newborn," *Archives of Disease in Childhood* 63, pp. 81–83, 1986; S. Deren, "The Children of Substance Abusers: A Review of the Literature," *Journal of Substance Abuse Treatment* 3, pp. 77–94, 1986; L. P. Finnegan, "Outcome of Children Born to Women Dependent upon Narcotics," *Advances in Alcohol and Substance Abuse*, pp. 55–101, 1982; A. A. Flandermeyer, "A Comparison of the Effects of Heroin and Cocaine Abuse upon the Neonate," *Neonatal Network*, pp. 42–48, 1987; R. Olegard, "Alcohol and Narcotics: Epidemiology and Pregnancy Risks," *International Journal of Technology Assessment in Health Care* 8 (Supp. 1), pp. 101–05, 1992; L. N. Robins et al., "Effects of In Utero Exposure to Street Drugs," *American Journal of Public Health* 83 (2), Supp., 1993.

9. Burkett et al., "Perinatal Implications of Cocaine Exposure," *Journal of Reproductive Medicine* 35, pp. 35, 1990; I. J. Chasnoff, "Perinatal Effects of Cocaine," *Contemporary Obstetrics and Gynecology*, 29, pp. 163–79, 1987; I. J. Chasnoff et al., "Prenatal Drug Exposure: Effects on Neonatal & Infant Growth & Development," *Neurobehavioral Toxicology and Teratology* 8, pp. 357–62, 1986; A. A. Flandermeyer, "A Comparison of the Effects of Heroin and Cocaine Abuse upon the Neonate," *Neonatal Network*, pp. 42–48, 1987; S. N. MacGregnor et al., "Cocaine Use During Pregnancy: Adverse Perinatal Outcome," *American Journal of Obstetrics and Gynecology* 1587, pp. 686–89, 1987; A. S. Oro and S. D. Dixon, "Perinatal Cocaine and Methamphetamine Exposure: Maternal and Neonatal Correlates," *Journal of Pediatrics* 222, pp. 571–78, 1987; C. S. Phibbs et al., "The Neonatal Costs of Maternal Cocaine Use," *Journal of the American Medical Association* 266(1), 1521–26, 1991; L. N. Robins et al., *op cit*; B. Zuckerman et al., "Effects of Maternal Marijuana and Cocaine Use on Fetal Growth," *New England Journal of Medicine* 320, pp. 762–68, 1989.

10. M. Aronson, M. Olegard, and R. Olegard, "Children of Alcoholic Mothers," *Pediatrician* 1, pp. 57–61, 1987; C. D. Cole et al., "Neonatal Ethanol Withdrawal: Characteristics in Clinically Normal, Nondysmorphic Neonates," *Journal of Pediatrics* 105, pp. 445–71, 1984; D. H. Ershoff et al., "Pregnancy and Medical Cost Outcome of a Self-Help Prenatal Smoking Cessation Program in a HMO," *Public Health Reports—Hyattsville* 105, pp. 340–47, 1990; R. E. Little et al., "Fetal Alcohol Effects in Humans and Animals," *Advances in Alcohol & Substance Abuse*, pp. 103–25, 1982; C. Orstead et al., "Efficacy of Prenatal Nutrition Counseling: Weight Gain, Infant Birth Weight, and Cost-Effectiveness," *Journal of the American Dietic Association* 85, pp. 40–45, 1985.

11. M. R. Harrison, "Unborn: Historical Perspective of the Fetus as Patient," *The Pharos* 45, pp. 19–24, 1982.

12. See also M. Mugford et al., "Cost Implications of Different Approaches to the Prevention of Respiratory Distress Syndrome," *Archives of Disease in Childhood* 66, pp. 757–64, 1991; I. R. Merkatz et al., "Ritodrine Hydrochloride: A Betamimetic Agent for Use in Preterm Labor. II. Evidence of Efficacy." *Obstetrics and Gynecology* 56, pp. 7–13, 1980; J. J. Fangman et al., "Prematurity Prevention Programs: An Analysis of Successes and Failures," *American Journal of Obstetrics and Gynecology* 170, pp. 744–50, 1994.

13. M. R. Harrison, "Fetal Surgery," *Western Journal of Medicine* 159, pp. 341–49, 1993; M. R. Harrison et al., "Fetal Treatment 1982," *The New England Journal of Medicine* 307, pp. 1651–52, 1982; International Surgery Registry, "Catheter Shunts for Fetal Hydronephrosis and Hydrocephalus," *New England Journal of Medicine* 315, pp. 336–40, 1986.

14. T. W. Clarkson et al., *Reproductive and Developmental Toxicity of Metals*, Plenum Press, N.Y.: 1983; M. Kirsch-Volders (ed.), *Mutagenicity, Carcinogenicity and Teratogenicity of Industrial Pollutants*, N.Y.: Plenum Press, 1984.

15. *Raleigh-Fitkin-Paul Morgan Memorial Hospital v. Anderson*, 42 N.J. 421, 201 A.2d 537 (per curiam), *cert. denied* 377 U.S. 985, 1964.

16. *Jefferson v. Griffin Spalding County Hospital Authority*, 247 Ga. 86, 274 S.E.2d 457, 1981.

17. W. A. Bowes and B. Salgestad, "Fetal Versus Maternal Rights: Medical and Legal Perspectives," *Obstetrics and Gynecology* 58, pp. 209–14, 1981.

18. "When the Courts Take Charge of the Unborn," *New York Times* April 27, 1983, p. A18.

19. "Pregnant Teen Held for Safety of Fetus," *St. Paul Pioneer Press and Dispatch*, Aug. 16, 1985, p. A3.

20. Becker, *Hastings Constitutional Law Quarterly*, 1991; V. Churchville, "D.C. Judge Jails Woman as Protection for Fetus," *Washington Post*, July 23, 1988, A1 and 8; M. Curriden, "Holding Mom Accountable," *ABA Journal*, 51–53, 1990.

21. Among the states in which criminal charges were brought against women who used illegal drugs while pregnant are: Alaska, Florida, Illinois, Indiana, Kentucky, Massachusetts, Minnesota, Michigan, Nevada, New York, North Carolina, Ohio, Oklahoma, and South Dakota.

22. M. Hansen, "Courts Side With Moms in Drug Cases," *ABA Journal* Nov. 1992, p. 18.

23. Johnson v. State of Florida, 578 So.2d 419 (1991).

24. *Jennifer Johnson v. State of Florida*, 602 So.2d 1288 (1992) at 1297.

25. *State v. Gray*, 584 N.E. 2d 710 (Ohio 1992); *State v. Bremer*, No 90–3227–FH (Mich. Ct. Ct. 1/31/91); *State v. Inzar*, Nos 90CRS6960 & 90CRS6961 (N.C. Super. Ct. 4/9/91); *People v. Morabite*, 580 NYS2d 843 (1992); K. Johnson, "Child Abuse Is Ruled Out in Birth Case," *New York Times*, 8/18/92, p. B1, B4.

26. Judge Jeffrey H. Gallet, quoted in B. Steinbock, *Life Before Birth*. N.Y.: Oxford University Press, p. 134, 1992. See also *Commonwealth v. Pellegrini*, No. 87970 (Mass. Sup. Ct. 1990).

27. D. Terry, "A Child is Born in Court Case Over Cesarean," *New York Times* 12/31/93, p. A12.

2

Fetus and Future Child

It might be helpful at this point to consider briefly the moral and legal status of the fetus, and the relevance of this dual status to the issues at hand. Certainly the position one adopts regarding the status of the fetus has a bearing on one's views of the permissibility of abortion (if one regards coherence as a virtue); but the connection between the status of the fetus and grounds for intervening in the life of a pregnant woman to prevent harm to the child she intends to bear is less clear. It is important to put the discussion in its proper context and to lay the groundwork for further analysis.

LEGAL STATUS OF THE FETUS IN THE UNITED STATES

Until very recently, the status of the fetus in Anglo-American law was fairly straightforward: A fetus had no legal rights. Indeed, with a few minor exceptions, none of the four areas of law which impact upon the fetus—abortion law, criminal law, tort law, and property law—recognized the fetus as having any legally protectable interests at all. But state legislators have been reconsidering this rule, and on occasion they have chosen to change it dramatically. Missouri legislators, for instance, amended existing state law to read that "unborn children have protectable interests in life, health, and well-being," and to require that all state laws be interpreted to provide fetuses with the same rights enjoyed by other persons. This issue, which is enormously controversial and engenders heated debate, will be on the political agenda for years to come.

Abortion Law

Laws pertaining to abortion have shifted as times and circumstances have changed. Until the midnineteenth century, the vast majority of states did not ban abortion before quickening (when the mother can

feel the fetus moving, at approximately the sixteenth week of pregnancy); yet by 1900 every state had outlawed abortions except for
those necessary to save the life of the mother (although the serious-
ness of the crime of abortion varied from state to state). The trend
began to be reversed again in the late 1960s, and by the time the
Supreme Court addressed the abortion issue in 1973, eighteen states
had adopted less stringent abortion laws. Four states allowed early
abortions to be performed on demand, while fourteen other states permitted abortions to be performed under certain circumstances (danger to the mother's life and physical or mental health, pregnancies
due to rape or incest, and serious fetal impairments).[1]

In its landmark 1973 ruling in *Roe v. Wade*, the U.S. Supreme
Court concluded that a woman has a constitutional right of privacy in
her decision whether or not to bear a child, giving her the legal right
to terminate her pregnancy (a right even her husband cannot override).[2]

But there are limitations on a woman's reproductive rights. The
Court determined that the right to seek an abortion does not include
the right to the means to have an abortion, so Congress may legitimately refuse to fund abortions for indigent women, and states may
legitimately prohibit the use of public facilities and public employees
in performing abortions.[3]

In addition, the Supreme Court has found a "compelling state
interest" in preserving the "potentiality of human life," so a woman's
legal right to seek an abortion is sharply curtailed in the final months
of pregnancy. Although the Court has consistently rejected the claim
that a fetus has any rights under the law, including the right to life, it
has determined that at a certain point in its development the fetus
ought to be protected:

> All this . . . persuades us that the word "person," as used in the
> Fourteenth Amendment, does not include the unborn. . . . We
> need not resolve the difficult question of when life begins. When
> those trained in the respective disciplines of medicine, philoso-
> phy, and theology are unable to arrive at any consensus, the judi-
> ciary, at this point in the development of man's knowledge, is not
> in a position to speculate on the answer. . . . We repeat, however,
> that the State does have an important and legitimate interest in
> preserving and protecting the health of the pregnant woman . . .
> and that it has still another important and legitimate interest in

protecting the potentiality of human life. These interests are separate and distinct. Each grows in substantiality as the woman approaches term and, at a point during pregnancy, each becomes "compelling."[4]

For sixteen years following the *Roe* decision, the Court consistently held that the state's interest in protecting potential life becomes compelling when the fetus becomes "viable"—that is, when the fetus "has the capacity of meaningful life outside the mother's womb."[5] Before fetal viability, abortion is allowed for almost any reason at all; after it, states may choose to permit abortion only when the life or health of the mother is at stake. The Supreme Court has not at any time designated viability as the point at which a fetus becomes a person in the eyes of the law; rather, fetal viability is simply the point at which the state's interest in protecting potential human life becomes compelling, although it is still not compelling enough to outweigh consideration for the life or health of the mother.

But with its ruling in *Webster v. Reproductive Health Services* in 1989, the Supreme Court began to allow more state regulation of abortion than had been permissible in the years following the *Roe* ruling and to shift emphasis away from viability as the critical demarcation point. Stating that, "We do not see why the State's interest in protecting human life should come into existence only at the point of viability, and that there should therefore be a rigid line allowing state regulation after viability but prohibiting it before viability," the Court signaled its willingness to reconsider and perhaps recast the *Roe* model.[6] The Court did not, however, couch any of its arguments or conclusions in terms of fetal rights, nor did it suggest that the fetus had any legal rights.

Criminal Law

In most states, the violent destruction of a fetus of any age without the consent of its mother is not an act of murder. An individual who hits a pregnant woman with a stick, intending to kill her viable fetus and succeeding, could be charged with assault and battery of the woman, but in the majority of states he will not be charged with murder for killing the fetus.[7] The legal response to this type of case does vary from state to state, however, because it depends on judicial interpretation of the particular state's legislation on the matter (as distinguished from judicial interpretation of the common law), and most state statutes do not address the question directly, leaving the courts free to interpret legislative intent. Most courts do so narrowly, claiming that if legislators had wanted to include fetuses within the meaning of the homicide law, they would have done so. Others apply a broader construction—utilizing notions of fairness or considerations of public policy—and in effect redefine the scope of the statutes. In response to the death of an eight-and-a-half-month-old fetus in an automobile accident, for example, the Massachusetts Supreme Court ruled in 1984 that a viable fetus is a person within the ambit of that state's motor vehicle homicide law.[8] The court did not find the defendant in that case to be guilty, however, recognizing that its decision "may have been unforeseeable."

A few state statutes specifically speak to the issue, making the court's job fairly straightforward. Unhappy with the outcome of a particular case—a man had savagely kneed his estranged and pregnant wife in the stomach, killing the fetus she was carrying; and the court had ruled that he was not guilty of murder because the fetus was not included under the California murder statute—California state legislators responded by designing a compromise of sorts between their belief that a fetus can be murdered and the widely accepted position that the fetus is not a person in the eyes of the law. Hence, rather than defining a fetus as a "person" (or a "human being," in the words of the statute), California legislators instead added a new category of murder victim. As amended, the California penal code now avers that "Murder is the unlawful killing of a human being, or a fetus, with malice aforethought." In 1994, the California Supreme Court affirmed that this includes all fetuses. And legislators in Minnesota voted in 1986 to impose criminal penalties for the "murder of an unborn child," which they defined as the "offspring of a human being conceived, but not yet born."

Tort Law

Most states accept the legal principle that a third party who negligently injures a fetus who is later born alive may be liable for damages; this is true of Canada and England as well.[9] Joel Feinberg explains how a court of law might think through a particular case involving prenatal harm:

> A negligent motorist who runs over a pregnant woman may cause damage to the fetus that causes it later to be born deformed

or chronically ill. Some time after birth that infant will have an active welfare interest in self-locomotion or health that may be harmed (doomed to defeat) right from the beginning. The child comes into existence in a harmed state caused by the earlier negligence of a motorist whose act initiated the causal sequence, at a point before actual personhood, that later resulted in the harm. The motorist's negligent driving made the actual person, who came into existence months later, worse off than she would otherwise have been. If the motorist had not been negligent, the child would have been undamaged.[10]

As Feinberg's example indicates, courts recognize the harm as befalling the child, not the fetus. In other words, the fetus as such need not be considered to have any legal standing at all in order for the courts to recognize a prenatal harm. Thus prenatal harm suits are not intended to vindicate the rights of the fetus. The courts recognize claims made for compensation on behalf of children who suffered prenatal injuries and were born alive.

The situation is a bit muddier when the tort involves recovery for a negligent prenatal act which results in death (i.e., a "wrongful death" suit). Some states are quite restrictive; the child must be born alive and then die of injuries wrongfully inflicted to it for a wrongful death action to be recognized. In other states, a wrongful death claim can be made on behalf of an unborn but viable fetus who died because of wrongfully inflicted injuries; while in still others, claims will be recognized for the wrongful death of any fetus regardless of its stage of development.[11] It should be noted, however, that in recognizing wrongful death suits, courts have not thereby conferred an important legal or moral status on the fetus, for the courts consider the harm as having befallen the parents, not the fetus. As the Supreme Court has explained, courts generally allow wrongful death suits in order "to vindicate the parents' interest and do not confer legal recognition of fetuses as 'persons' in the whole sense" of the term.[12]

Property Law

Many people mistakenly believe that a fetus may inherit property. But the Uniform Probate Code states that, "Relatives of the decedent [who are] conceived before his death but [who are] born thereafter inherit as if they had been born in the lifetime of the decedent." Thus

the right to property accrues to the individual who is alive and outside the mother, and the right attaches for inheritance purposes at conception—but only if the fetus survives birth. Hence the fetus itself
does not really have a right to property.

Discussion

The fetus is denied significant legal status because it is not considered
to be a *person* in the eyes of the law. As the Supreme Court explained
in *Roe v. Wade*:

> In areas other than criminal abortion the law has been reluctant to
> endorse any theory that life, as we recognize it, begins before live
> birth or to accord legal rights to the unborn except in narrowly
> defined situations and except when the rights are contingent
> upon live birth. . . . In short, the unborn have never been recog-
> nized in the law as persons in the whole sense.[13]

This finding has far-reaching implications. One of the most important
is that the Fourteenth Amendment to the U.S. Constitution, which
applies only to "persons," does not apply to the fetus. Hence the fetus
does not enjoy equal protection under the law, nor do considerations
of due process apply to it.

The U.S. Supreme Court could have decided to declare the fetus
to be a person in the eyes of the law. After all, the Court considers corporations to be persons for some purposes. They are persons under
the criminal law and the Internal Revenue Code, for instance, and
they are protected by the Fourteenth Amendment.[14] But corporations
are not persons for all purposes; the right against self-incrimination
guaranteed by the Fifth Amendment is not extended to corporations,
for example.[15]

The Court does not recognize corporations as persons because it
sees in corporations some sort of metaphysical being worthy of
respect. Instead, this notion of personhood is an artificial construct
based on utilitarian considerations: the benefits to society that would
accrue by recognizing corporations as persons for some purposes but
not for others, and the disbenefits of not doing so. One advantage of
recognizing corporations as persons is that significant limitations on
government activities are thereby set. If a corporation did not enjoy
the fundamental protections of the Fourteenth Amendment, then the
state could regulate any business, or even abolish it, for any reason
(or for no reason) and with only indirect regard for considerations of

fairness as they pertain to the persons who own the artificial entity. But by giving a corporation separate legal status, the Court ensures that the state abides by those minimum standards that society considers to be of fundamental importance, such as the provisions of the Fourteenth Amendment. This also serves to protect the individuals—owners, shareholders, and employees—who comprise the corporation and who are, in their own right, persons under the law.

In deciding whether to accord fetuses the status of persons, the Supreme Court also took social costs into account. Were the fetus considered to be a person, its "right to life would then be guaranteed specifically by the [Fourteenth] Amendment," noted the Supreme Court in *Roe v. Wade*.[16] This would mean that most abortions would be tantamount to murder. To be logically consistent and maintain any legal integrity, it would also mean that the mothers, physicians, and nurses involved in abortion would have to be prosecuted for murder.[17] Besides creating a new class of criminal, outlawing abortion would have other severely deleterious effects on women. In deciding *Roe*, the Court considered mental, physical, and financial harms that could befall women because of unwanted pregnancies:

> The detriment that the state would impose upon the pregnant woman by denying choice altogether is apparent. Specific and direct harm medically diagnosable even in early pregnancy may be involved. Maternity, or additional offspring, may force upon the woman a distressful life and future. Psychological harm may be imminent. Mental and physical health may be taxed by child care. There is also the distress, for all concerned, associated with the unwanted child, and there is the problem of bringing a child into a family already unable, psychologically and otherwise, to care for it. In other cases, as in this one, the additional difficulties and continuing stigma of unwed motherhood may be involved.[18]

In *Roe v. Wade*, therefore, the Court seems to have been persuaded that the advantages to society of maintaining the status quo—in which fetuses are not persons in the eyes of the law—outweigh the disadvantages, and it has not yet reversed itself. Bonnie Steinbock notes some other possible "ominous consequences" of recognizing the fetus as a legal "person:"

> The economic implications . . . are staggering. If fetuses were counted as dependents for purposes of federal income tax, a total

revenue loss of excess of $1 billion per year is possible. . . . [And
there could be] unforeseen effects on the legal system. Four weeks
after the Supreme Court's decision in *Webster*, Kansas City lawyer
Michael Box filed a lawsuit against the state's governor and attor-
ney general for jailing the fetus of a pregnant prison inmate without due process of law.[19]

Social costs are not, however, the main reason for denying the fetus
any significant rights. This position is also based on the reasonable
belief that the fetus is not the sort of being to whom rights naturally
accrue.

But this view has been under attack for years. Opponents claim
that a fetus should be recognized as having many of the same rights
as other human beings. It is time, they argue, to alter the law to reflect
the normative view of the fetus as a member of the moral community
and a bearer of rights. What these rights are, however, and when in its
development the fetus comes to possess them, remain matters of disagreement.

THE MORAL STATUS OF THE FETUS

A human fetus is a human being insofar as it is a member of the species *homo sapiens*, with the genetic structure typical of our species.
And since it is alive, it is a living human being. For many, this statement is factually true but morally irrelevant. For others it is an important moral claim indeed, because for them, the question "When does
human life begin?" is identical to the question "When does moral personhood begin?" Since a fetus is a living human being, some people
conclude that it is also a being with moral and legal rights to life.

It is crucial to note, however, that the question of whether a fetus
is a member of our species is not the same as the question of whether
it is a full-fledged member of our moral community (a "person"). The
former is a matter of fact, the latter is a normative judgment. Because
the concept of a "person" is a moral status concept, the issue of
whether the fetus is a person is not a scientific or medical question to
be settled simply by appeal to ontogeny or embryology. Indeed, two
people can agree on the scientific facts about fetal development and
still disagree fiercely on the moral status of the fetus. Identifying the
human fetus as a person in the moral sense, then, is a normative assertion, not a statement of fact. Moreover, the fact that the fetus is a

member of the species *homo sapiens* does not entail the conclusion that
it is a member of the moral community of persons, for the opposite
conclusion is equally plausible. Hence the fundamental question
remains: Is the fetus a person in the moral sense?[20]

To say that a being is a person is to recognize him or her as fully
a member of the moral community. More specifically, a person in the
moral sense is a being who has basic moral rights, including the right
to life. These moral rights are the basis for most legal rights. If we
reflect on the paradigm cases in ordinary life in which we most confi-
dently ascribe personhood to a being, we notice that we associate a
certain descriptive content (e.g., self-awareness, ability to choose and
to act on reasons, capacity to feel pleasure and pain) with the moral
concept of a person.[21] These qualities are given moral weight because
they are related to life within the moral community, to the reasons
behind the strictures of morality and the requirements of law.

But the concept of a person in the moral sense remains ill-defined
and controversial insofar as we cannot agree on its boundaries. While
most would agree that the concept refers to beings who are worthy of
respect and who enjoy certain fundamental moral rights, there is not
much consensus beyond these vague designations. Considerable disagreement, for example, still exists as to whether the term "person"
refers only to those beings who can be morally responsible for their
actions (the paradigm case), or if it also includes beings who have the
potential for being morally responsible for their actions, or if it
includes as well all beings (regardless of their capacities and potential-
ities) who are members of the same species as those who can be morally responsible for their actions, or if it includes all beings who meet
only some of the qualifications (such as the ability to experience pleasure and pain).

It has been suggested that the utilization of recently developed
techniques of fetal therapy would confer the status of personhood on
the fetus. As one commentator asks, "If the fetus can be treated, then
is it a patient? If it is a patient, then is it a person?"[22] And another
responds, "Treatment of the fetus . . . seems to confer on the fetus the
status of patient, someone with rights, interests, and claims upon us
which should be protected."[23] In other words, some people are suggesting that our ability to treat the fetus therapeutically may help
define its moral status and our obligations toward it.

This, however, is simply not the case. The ability to treat a fetus as
a patient has no bearing whatsoever on its status as a person, nor

does it reflect any light on what our obligations to the fetus should be. Not all patients are persons. A doctor may administer antibiotics to a cat, or operate on a mouse, but the ability to perform these procedures does not itself confer any moral status at all on the beings undergoing them. In addition, procedures to relieve fetal distress have existed for centuries, and the development of new and different therapies does not make the fetus any more of a person than it has been. The question of what we owe the fetus is not a technological one, but a moral one.

There are four basic ways of viewing the moral status of the human fetus: (1) The fetus is a person throughout its development; (2) the fetus gains the moral status of a person at some point in its development—e.g., the appearance of brain waves, the ability to feel pain, viability, and so on; (3) the fetus does not have the moral status of a person, and indeed has no moral status at all; or (4) the fetus does have some moral standing, although it is not a full-fledged person.[24]

All of the suggestions for the onset of personhood are somewhat arbitrary, and necessarily so. One reason for this is that the transition from a fertilized egg to a mentally competent adult (the paradigm case of a moral person) is a continuous development, not a series of discrete stages with abrupt transitions. The question, "When does personhood begin?" is similar to the question, "When does adulthood begin?" We decide that someone is adult enough to drive a car at the age of sixteen, adult enough to vote at eighteen, adult enough to drink liquor at twenty-one. But when is that individual really an adult?

We draw lines for social and/or legal purposes; but we must recognize that they are, in part, conventional stipulations—decisions of social policy. This is true also of any decision we may make regarding when in its development, if ever, a fetus becomes a person in the moral sense. But simply because the point at which we confer personhood on a being is in part arbitrary, it does not follow that it is inappropriate or wrong to do so. It simply means that, although the judgment is grounded in sound reasons, it is also partially subjective and thus it cannot satisfy everyone. Once we recognize this, perhaps, the question of the moral status of the fetus will cease being an occasion for sterile polemic and will open to reasoned resolution.

However, no public consensus seems forthcoming, or even likely, concerning the controversy over the moral status of the fetus. This contentious debate will not be furthered here, either, for I shall not

argue for or against the moral status of the fetus. It simply is not necessary to posit that the human fetus is a person in order to be able to
argue that it should be treated in certain ways if it is being carried to
term. Indeed, although the moral status of the fetus plays a significant
role in the controversy over abortion, it is largely irrelevant to the
issue of the prevention of prenatal harm.

THE FETUS AND THE FUTURE CHILD

Most commentators have analyzed the problem of preventable prenatal harm in terms of a conflict between a pregnant woman and her
fetus. One conclusion is that a physician sometimes has "an obligation to the fetus that could not be waived by the mother."[25] An
equally plausible alternative is that, "It is wrong to allow obstetrics or
the state to subsume the interests and the civil rights of pregnant
women to those of the products of conception within them."[26]

These views of the dilemma are clearly colored by different views
of the moral status of the fetus. In one instance, the fetus is given significant moral status; in the other, it has the value of a mere body part.
But any attempt to present the debate over preventable prenatal harm
in this manner—that is, to view it in terms of a maternal–fetal conflict—is doomed to failure. The problem is that the issue on which the
debate thereby rests—the moral status of the fetus—is a matter of
great controversy, and one that is far from being resolved.

Assuming Something About the Moral Status of the Fetus

One problem with analyzing the debate over preventable prenatal
harm in terms of a maternal–fetal conflict, then, is that it will inevitably bog down in preliminary arguments over the moral status of the
fetus, making any resolution of the problem at hand highly unlikely.
Yet it is not just the controversial nature of the moral status of the
fetus that stands in the way of a resolution of the dilemma at hand. A
social consensus on the moral status of the fetus would do little to
help.

Assume, for a moment, that a general agreement has emerged
that a fetus is a "person" in the moral sense. Since a fetus is now considered to possess many of the same moral and legal rights as other
persons, it seems to follow that the state should act to protect its
rights (especially the fundamental and universal right not to be
harmed). But this argument simply will not stand up to scrutiny. For

even if the fetus were a person and possessed a right not to be harmed, it would not necessarily follow that the state should act to protect that right, since the state must balance this right against the rights and interests of the pregnant woman, including her right to decide what happens to her own body. At most, conferring moral and/or legal personhood on the fetus would ground a *prima facie* case for arguing that the state should act in its behalf; but this conclusion needs to be buttressed by other arguments, and these arguments must be strong enough to outweigh the power of the various countervailing considerations based on the pregnant woman's rights.

Now let us assume that there is general agreement that the fetus is not a person, indeed, that its moral status is quite low. Would it follow that a pregnant woman has *carte blanche* to act any way she wishes while she is pregnant? No. One may consistently hold that a fetus has no moral or legal rights, and still argue that a pregnant woman should not be allowed to cause severe and avoidable prenatal harm.

The basis of this position is the belief that the effects of her actions on the health of her *future child*, not on the health of her fetus, are what matter (at least to those for whom the fetus is of little moral concern). If a woman continues her pregnancy to term, then a child will be born who will bear the consequences of whatever happened to it *in utero*. In those cases in which a child is born, another person is involved, a person who has the same moral and many of the same legal rights that the mother has, including the right not to be harmed. Thus even if a fetus is not considered a person in the moral or legal sense, there still are important interests of a person which must be weighed against those of the pregnant woman: the interests of her future child. A pregnant woman should act for the sake of the child that the fetus will become. Her obligations, in other words, are to her future child, not to her fetus.

Moral Obligations

The argument that a woman is not free to behave in any way she wishes while she is pregnant is based on the conviction that she is—at least sometimes—morally responsible for the condition of the child to whom she gives birth. This position is simply an extrapolation from the widely accepted general moral obligations to refrain from harming others (the duty of nonmaleficence) and to contribute to the welfare of others (the duty of beneficence).

There is a chance that every pregnancy will go to term. For this reason, a pregnant woman incurs some moral responsibility for the condition of the future child from the beginning of the pregnancy. This does not mean that she is morally obligated to act always in the best interests of her future child, for her responsibilities are necessarily limited. They must be weighed against her other responsibilities (to herself and perhaps to her other children, her spouse, her employer). Concern for these other responsibilities may even lead a woman to decide to terminate her pregnancy. But if the pregnant woman is free to have an abortion and does not do so, then she has chosen not to avoid a situation in which she will affect the well-being of another person (the child she will bear), and in so choosing she can be deemed to have assumed moral responsibility for at least some aspects of the well-being of that future person.[27]

The pregnant woman's duties are to the postfetal person the fetus will become IF it is carried to term; she has no obligations to the fetus *qua* fetus. Consequently, even though a pregnant woman has a moral duty to refrain from causing harm to her future child, she has no duty to bring that child into being. In other words, there is no suggestion here that the fetus has any rights, including the right to receive medical treatment or the right to be born.

I am not arguing that a pregnant woman should or should not be compelled to act in certain ways, nor am I suggesting that a public policy setting out limitations on a pregnant woman's freedom of choice would be appropriate. Such conclusions would be premature. There is a notable divergence between acts which are morally required and acts which should be legally required. Indeed, acts which may be regarded as ethically proper in particular instances may at the same time be considered as inappropriate when expanded to the level of social policy. Actions which may prevent harm on an individual level may produce even greater harm if that type of action became a general practice, for instance, or some other arrangement might be more effective in reducing the harm. In other words, it makes perfect sense to hold on the one hand that an action is morally right, and to hold on the other hand that it should not be instituted as social (legal) policy. Thus further reasons are needed to justify state involvement in these cases.

So far I have simply noted some general and fairly vague conclusions about a woman's *moral* duties; I believe she is morally obligated to act in the interests of her future child throughout her pregnancy.

But I have not said anything at all about her *legal* duties. This complex subject will be addressed at length in the following chapters.

A Woman's Legal Right to Seek an Abortion

A common objection to even considering state intervention in these cases is that the Supreme Court's ruling in *Roe v. Wade*, which gives a woman the legal right to seek an abortion, makes otiose any discussion of state intervention to prevent prenatal harm. According to some commentators, it is unreasonable to posit that the state could legitimately prevent prenatal harm by overriding a pregnant woman's freedom of choice, since the state's recognition of a pregnant woman's legal right to have an abortion is inconsistent with a policy of encouraging or requiring her to act in certain ways.[28] As long as a woman may legally abort her fetus, it is contended, she cannot be compelled to undergo medical treatment or lifestyle changes on its behalf.

Given that a pregnant woman may legally have an abortion, it does seem to make sense to allow her also to act in any way she wishes with regard to her fetus. After all, since a pregnant woman is permitted to sever her relationship with the fetus entirely, it seems inconsistent to constrain her activities so that she does not harm it in other ways. Since abortion is allowed, would it not make more sense (and be more consistent) also to allow other sorts of harm to the fetus?

If we ask the questions in this manner, then of course the answer is that the state may not interfere. But these are not the right questions. Recall that our concern is not with the condition of the fetus, but with the condition of the born child, a person whose interests the state should protect.

It would be a mistake to assume that a woman's legal right to seek an abortion determines all of her reproductive rights and responsibilities. A woman's right to have an abortion does not imply the right to refuse to provide medical treatment to a child she intends to bear; and an obligation to refrain from causing prenatal harm does not imply an obligation to forgo having an abortion. Instead, a pregnant woman's obligation to change her lifestyle or to undergo medical treatment for the sake of the child she intends to bear is logically independent of her right to have an abortion. Thus it is reasonable to conclude that, although a woman has the right to abort her fetus, she does not have the liberty to cause serious harm to the child she intends to bear.

A significant advantage of this position is that it is consistent with current Anglo-American law in two important respects: (1) The law does not recognize the fetus as a person; and (2) it does recognize the wrongfulness of prenatal negligent acts or omissions which show up later as injuries to a child. This is not something that is appropriately included within that notorious class of "legal fictions," but instead is a logical and principled position based on the consideration that, although the harm was caused while the person was *in utero*, the person now born is the one who suffers it.

PRELIMINARY CONCLUSIONS

I have not argued that the status quo—where most pregnant women are free to act in any way they wish regardless of the harm they cause to the children they bear—should be changed in any particular direction, or even that it should be changed at all. My point has been, rather, that these are open questions; and my objective in this chapter has been to explore some of the basic concepts, values, and issues at stake in this complex discussion.

The conclusions so far are that (1) a pregnant woman has some moral obligations to act in the interests of her future child; (2) it is not inconsistent to allow abortion yet disallow certain activities during pregnancy that would harm future children; (3) the moral status of the fetus is largely irrelevant to the prevention of prenatal harms; and therefore (4) we need not assume anything about the moral status of the human fetus, or argue the moral and legal merits of a woman's right to seek an abortion, in order to determine her other reproductive responsibilities (if any). For our purposes, therefore, the controversy over the fetus's moral status will remain unaddressed. Indeed, harm to the fetus *per se* is not at issue here; our concern, instead, is with those prenatal negligent acts or omissions which show up later as injuries to the child. Surely we can all agree that the born child is a being of significant moral worth who deserves our concern and perhaps even our protection. The question for us is: Ought the state intervene in the lives of pregnant women in order to prevent serious prenatal harm? The next chapter will continue the debate by exploring reasons in favor of state intervention.

NOTES

1. K. Luker, *Abortion and the Politics of Motherhood*, Berkeley: University of California Press, 1984.

2. *Roe v. Wade*, 410 U.S. 113, 1973; *Planned Parenthood of Central Missouri v. Danforth*, 438 U.S. 52, 1976.

3. *Beal v. Doe*, 432 U.S. 438, 1977; *Harris v. McRae*, 448 U.S. 297, 1980; *Maher v. Roe*, 432 U.S. 464, 1977; *Webster v. Reproductive Health Services*, 492 U.S. 490, 1989.

4. *Roe v. Wade, op. cit.*, p. 158–63.

5. *Roe v. Wade*, p. 163.

6. *Webster v. Reproductive Health Services*.

7. M. Starozewski, "Wrongful Death of a Fetus: Does a Cause of Action Arise When There is No Live Birth?" *Villanova Law Review* 31, pp. 659–95, 1986.

8. *Commonwealth v. Daniel I. Cass*, 392 Mass. 799, 467 N.E. Rptr 1324, 1984.

9. R. Beal, "Can I Sue Mommy? An Analysis of a Woman's Tort Liability for Prenatal Injuries to her Child Born Alive," *San Diego Law Review* 21, pp. 325–70, 1984; L. D. P. Fleisher, "Wrongful Births: When Is There Liability for Prenatal Injury?" *American Journal of the Diseases of Children* 141, pp. 1260–65, 1987.

10. J. Feinberg, *The Moral Limits of the Criminal Law, Volume One, Harm to Others*, p. 96.

11. T. A. Borowski, Jr., "No Liability for the Wrongful Death of Unborn Children—the Florida Legislature Refuses to Protect the Unborn," *Florida State University Law Review* 16, pp. 835–61, 1988; M. Starozewski, "Wrongful Death of a Fetus: Does a Cause of Action Arise When There is No Live Birth?" *Villanova Law Review* 31, pp. 659–95, 1986.

12. *Roe v. Wade*, p. 162.

13. *Roe v. Wade*, pp. 161–62.

14. *First National Bank v. Bellotti*, 435 U.S. 765, 1978; *NAACP v. Button*, 371 U.S. 415, 1963; *Smyth v. Ames*, 169 U.S. 466, 1898.

15. *Bellis v. U.S.*, 417 U.S. 85, 1974.

16. *Roe v. Wade*, pp. 156–57.

17. And what would happen to the hapless assistant in an *in vitro* fertilization clinic who drops a petri dish of human zygotes? Would she be prosecuted for manslaughter? See D. Mathieu, "Crime and Punishment: Abortion as Murder?" *Journal of Social Philosophy*, 23, pp. 5–22, 1992.

18. *Roe v. Wade*, p. 153

19. B. Steinbock, *Life Before Birth*, N.Y.: Oxford University Press), p. 103, 1992.

20. Analysis of this controversial question is necessarily brief; for further discussion see J. Garfield and P. Hennessey, eds., *Abortion: Moral and Legal Perspectives*, Amherst, Mass.: University of Massachusetts Press, 1984; M.W. Shaw, and A. E. Doudera, eds., *Defining Human Life: Medical, Legal & Ethical Implications*, AUPHA press, Ann Arbor, Mich.: 1983; B. Steinbock, *op cit.*; L. W.

Sumner, *Abortion and Moral Theory*, Princeton: Princeton University Press, 1981.

21. Joel Feinberg suggests that, "In the commonsense way of thinking, persons are those beings who, among other things, are conscious, have a concept and awareness of themselves, are capable of experiencing emotions, can reason and acquire understanding, can plan ahead, can act on their plans, and can feel pleasure and pain." J. Feinberg, "Abortion," in T. Regan (ed.), *Matters of Life and Death*, 2nd ed., Random House, N.Y.: p. 262, 1986.

And Mary Anne Warren proposes the following criteria for personhood:

> 1. consciousness (of objects and events external and/or internal to the being), and in particular the capacity to feel pain; 2. reasoning (the developed capacity to solve new and relatively complex problems); 3. self-motivated activity (activity which is relatively independent of either genetic or direct external control); 4. the capacity to communicate by whatever means, messages of an indefinite variety of types, that is, not just with an indefinite number of possible contents, but on indefinitely many topics; 5. the presence of self-concepts, and self-awareness, either individual or social, or both.

M. A. Warren, "On the Moral and Legal Status of the Fetus," *The Monist*, pp. 43–61, 1973.

Although these suggestions for the descriptive content of the concept of personhood differ in detail, they are unanimous in relying on cognitive ability—as opposed to membership in a species—as the morally relevant criterion.

22. R. M. Henig, "Saving Babies Before Birth," *New York Times Magazine*, Feb. 28, 1982.

23. D. J. Roy, "Fetal Therapy: Ethical Considerations," in C. Nimrod and G. Griener (eds.), *Biomedical Ethics and Fetal Therapy*, Ontario, Canada: Wilfrid Laurier University Press, pp. 59–66, 1988.

24. It is important to note at this juncture that, while persons are the only beings who enjoy a full complement of rights, they are not the only beings who count morally. Some beings who are not usually considered to be persons—such as cows and pigs—may have moral status, though of a different kind. Simply because they are capable of pleasure and pain they deserve moral consideration, even though they may lack many of the rights that persons have.

25. T. M. Mackenzie and T. C. Nagel, "Commentary: When a Pregnant Woman Endangers Her Fetus," *Hastings Center Report* 16, pp. 24–25, 1986.

26. B. K. Rothman, "When a Pregnant Woman Endangers Her Fetus: Commentary," *Hastings Center Report* 16, p. 25, 1986.

27. So H. T. Engelhardt, Jr., suggests that, "The very availability of abortion, perhaps paradoxically for some, has increased the plausibility of maternal duties to fetuses in that a woman's continuing with a pregnancy is more of an expression of free choice than was the case in the past." H. T. Engelhardt, Jr., "Current Controversies in Obstetrics: Wrongful Life and Forced Fetal Surgical Procedures," *American Journal of Obstetrics and Gynecology* 151, pp. 313–18, 1985.

28. John Fletcher, for example, worries about the "inconsistency of encouraging fetal therapy on the one hand and respecting parental choice on the other," while Marc Lappé suggests that, "Whatever social, medical, or legal sanctions existed for protecting the fetus against potential abuse during pregnancy in the past now may have been seriously compromised by the Supreme Court's abortion decision." And Robert Blank cautions that, "In the not-so-remote future, the Court must resolve the logical inconsistency of holding a woman responsible for harming her fetus but not for terminating its existence." J. Fletcher, "The Fetus as Patient: Ethical Issues," *Journal of the American Medical Association* 246, pp. 772–73, 1981; M. Lappé, "The Moral Claims of the Wanted Fetus," *The Hastings Center Report* 5, pp. 11–13, 1975; R. Blank, *Life, Death and Public Policy,* DeKalb, Ill.: Northern Illinois University Press, 1988.

3

Arguments in Favor of Coercing a Pregnant Woman to Act in the Interests of Her Future Child

INTRODUCTION

When a pregnant woman acts or fails to act (including refusing medical care) in a way that will harm the child she intends to bear, her physician has five courses of action available: (1) accept her decision and treat her accordingly; (2) transfer her to another physician who will accede to her wishes; (3) try to persuade her to behave differently; (4) negotiate a compromise plan of action; or (5) ask a court of law to order her to comply with the recommended treatment. Overriding a mentally competent woman's right to refuse treatment without prior court approval is not a viable alternative; not only would this course of action violate her rights, but it would expose the physician to civil and criminal liability. As Justice Cardozo stated in a now-famous decision, "Every human being of adult years and sound mind has a right to determine what shall be done with his own body; and a surgeon who performs an operation without his patient's consent commits an assault, for which he is liable in damages."[1]

A physician has at present no legal obligation to pursue court involvement in what ordinarily is a private treatment decision, but many physicians feel morally obligated to do so. Should the courts be used to coerce pregnant women into undergoing medical treatment? Or are the women free to make their own choices?

Chapter One argued that a pregnant woman is morally obligated to act in the interests of the child she will bear (whether her moral obligations involve undergoing invasive medical procedures will be discussed later). Now, however, our concern is with the grounds for believing that at least some of a pregnant woman's *moral* obligations should also be regarded as *legal* obligations. In other words, the question this chapter explores is: Are there good reasons for holding that the state may interfere in the life of a pregnant woman in order to prevent prenatal harm?

STATE INTERVENTION

There are two sources of state power to interfere with a pregnant woman's autonomy in order to prevent prenatal harm: police power, which the state uses to prevent people from harming each other, and *parens patriae* power, which is the state's limited paternalistic power to promote the well-being of certain especially vulnerable individuals, such as young children and the mentally incompetent. That the state *can* interfere to prevent harm or promote well-being in certain instances is obvious. The important question is: Under what circumstances is it legitimate for the state to do so? Is it legitimate, for instance, for the state to interfere with a pregnant woman's activities in order to prevent harm to or promote the well-being of her future child? Is it legitimate to make criminal certain activities of pregnant women because they cause prenatal harm?

The fact that the state has the power to limit the choices of pregnant women plus the contention that pregnant women have moral obligations to take reasonable care of the fetuses they intend to carry to term are not enough to justify coercive state intervention to prevent prenatal harm. The belief that a particular action is morally proper is not a conclusive basis for constructing social policy, and additional reasons are needed to justify state involvement in these cases.

Three types of supporting arguments are available. The first is a consequentialist argument: Preventing certain types of prenatal damage creates more good than harm overall. The second type of argument involves the rights of the future child: One could argue, for instance, that a child has a right to begin life with a sound mind and body, or one could base an argument on the more general right not to be harmed, a right that is enforceable as to conduct occurring before birth. For those who remain unconvinced by assertions of the rights of future persons, a different type of stance is available. This argument is based on the premise that a pregnant woman is obligated to meet certain standards of care for the sake of her future child—even if the child has no corresponding rights to such care—and that these obligations should be enforced by the state. We shall deal, in turn, with each of these types of arguments.

AN APPEAL TO CONSEQUENCES

Picture a low-birthweight infant in the neonatal intensive care unit suffering from heroin withdrawal. She is feverish, hypertonic, and respiring rapidly; she trembles constantly and vomits intermittently; her high-pitched cry is incessant, as is her frantic fist-sucking. Now picture the infant in the crib beside her. He is severely brain-damaged because his oxygen supply was cut off during delivery and his mother refused to undergo a cesarean section. And picture the child born with fetal alcohol syndrome [FAS]. She is tiny, even her head and brain are smaller than normal; she is irritable and restless; she may have serious visual and auditory problems; and her face resembles the faces of other FAS children more than it does her parents.[2]

The basic consequentialist argument is simply that if we permit pregnant women to do as they please—to ingest alcohol or cocaine, to refuse medical care, to work with chemicals known to cause reproductive damage—then we at the same time permit grave harm to befall tens of thousands of innocent beings each year: the children to whom the women give birth. Much of this harm could be prevented and, because it causes so much suffering, many people conclude that it *should* be prevented.

Consider, for example, the case of a pregnant woman who pays insufficient attention to controlling her diabetes. Not only is her own health at risk, but she greatly increases the chances that her child will be born prematurely and with severe malformations. Since both the woman and her child reap the benefits of her adherence to a strict treatment regimen, and since the serious harm to both can easily be avoided, it makes sense, according to a utilitarian calculation, to require the woman in this instance to take her medications and keep to her diet.

This type of utilitarian reckoning, which is concerned with the benefits to individuals in particular, is buttressed by considerations of the benefits to society in general. The high costs of treatment in neonatal intensive care units would be reduced, mitigating the financial burden on private insurance companies, the hospitals that often must absorb much of the cost, and the taxpayers who fund Medicaid programs (which cover the hospital costs for many indigent children). In addition, the expense and difficulties of institutionalizing mentally and physically handicapped individuals would also decrease—as would the demands for special education programs—as the numbers of severely handicapped individuals dwindle. At the same time the numbers of productive, self-supporting, tax-paying citizens would increase. Thus, it could be argued, society would benefit more were the state to intervene in the activities of pregnant women than were it to allow pregnant women the freedom of choice they have enjoyed in the past.

On these grounds, then, one could argue both that a pregnant woman has a moral obligation to refrain from causing prenatal harm (because the benefits to the child outweigh the disbenefits to her) and that the state may enforce this obligation (because the benefits to society at large outweigh the disbenefits to pregnant women). So there are good utilitarian arguments for permitting state intervention in order to prevent at least some cases of serious prenatal harm.

But how much weight should we give these arguments? The answer, of course, is a matter of great controversy. One set of countervailing considerations involves the rights of the pregnant woman. Many people in our society believe that an individual's fundamental rights may not be abridged for utilitarian purposes, since these rights outweigh considerations of social benefit. State intervention into the lives of pregnant women, according to this line of thought, would be permitted only insofar as it does not interfere with the women's constitutional rights. But it should be noted that the debate does not end here, for we first must determine which rights a pregnant woman enjoys, and whether these rights indeed outweigh the social benefits of preventing prenatal harm. In addition, the rights of the pregnant woman are not the only rights at stake. If children have rights that accrue during the fetal stage, and if pregnant women have corresponding obligations to honor those rights, then the consequentialist arguments in favor of limiting the mother's choices will be strengthened considerably.

The designation of the scope and limits of these rights thus plays an important role in our discussion, and it is fair to say that the consequentialist arguments can be assessed accurately only in light of them. In the following chapter, we shall explore the rights of the pregnant woman; this chapter examines the alleged rights of future persons.

ARGUMENTS BASED ON THE RIGHTS OF FUTURE PERSONS

Increased awareness of the causes of prenatal harm plus the development of new techniques for preventing the maturation of serious defects while the child is *in utero* have led some commentators to assert two rights of the future person: the right to begin life with a sound mind and body, and the right not to be harmed. Either (or both) of these rights might be invoked to justify state intervention into the lives of pregnant women without their consent.[3]

In *Smith v. Brennan*, a 1960 case involving a child who was born with deformed feet and legs caused by the effects of an automobile accident which occurred while he was still *in utero*, the New Jersey Supreme Court ruled that,

> Justice requires that the principle be recognized that a child has a legal right to begin life with a sound mind and body. If the wrongful conduct of another interferes with that right, and it can be established by competent proof that there is a causal connection between the wrongful interference and the harm suffered by the child when born, damages for such harm should be recoverable by the child.[4]

In this ruling, the court appeared to go beyond the usual finding of prenatal harm to posit a "legal right to begin life with a sound mind and body." Similarly, the New York Supreme Court in *Park v. Chessin* held that there is a "fundamental right of a child to be born as a whole, functional human being."[5]

One important question, of course, is whether or not a person does indeed have an inalienable and primary right to begin life with a sound mind and body. Although the *Smith* court announced the right, the actual holding states that damages were recoverable because the automobile accident caused harm to the child while he was still *in utero*. In other words, the court recognized a fairly straightforward tort and probably did not mean to create a new category of right separate and apart from traditional tortious acts that cause identifiable harm.

It has been proposed, however, that the right to begin life with a sound mind and body should be interpreted more broadly and more dramatically. One commentator, for instance, suggests that the court's ruling "would seem to establish the principle that the child's right to a healthy life takes precedence over the parents' right to reproduce."[6] Understood in this manner, the right to begin life with a sound mind and body would potentially be a powerful means of championing the welfare of children and limiting the freedom of parents (especially pregnant women).

How should the parameters of such a right be set? It seems reasonable to suggest that recognizing a right to begin life with a sound mind and body would require that a child be made better off than he otherwise would be. A fetus with a treatable genetic anomaly, for example, would receive the appropriate medical care so that he could be born unimpaired.[7]

If the right to be born with a sound mind and body is construed to imply a right to be made better off than one otherwise would be, then this right is necessarily a limited one. I can think of no sound reason for recognizing a right to be made beautiful, or a genius, or a star athlete—or even pretty, smart, or strong. The right to be born with a sound mind and body should not be interpreted in terms of perfection (however that is construed) or as implying that the goal of childbearing is similar to the U.S. Army's promise to help each recruit to "be all that you can be." Instead, the right should be more modestly regarded as a right to be as free as possible from significant pain and dysfunction, and this in turn is plausibly interpreted as a right to receive adequate medical care.

The Right to Receive Adequate Medical Care

Although most industrialized nations provide their citizens with universal access to beneficial health care, the United States does not. Indeed, in the United States there is no general legal right to receive medical care and no requirement that medical benefits be offered to everyone regardless of ability of pay. Further, the U.S. Supreme Court has ruled that although Congress subsidizes many medically necessary services through various programs, it has no legal obligation to subsidize all medically necessary services.[8] In addition, while federal and state governments support a variety of programs providing health care, they regularly slash their funding—including their funding of those programs aimed at caring for children—with often disastrous results for the ailing individuals.[9]

But this may change. President Clinton has vowed to institute a national health insurance program which would substantially increase access to health care. Although his proposals have been defeated so far, they are not dead. Given that traditional proponents of the status quo—such as business corporations and medical associations—now support reform, some significant changes in the American health care system will no doubt be made.

One impetus for change is the widespread belief that health care is not merely another commodity like washing machines and carpets, that instead it has a special importance in our lives that mere commodities do not. The President's Commission for the Study of Ethical Problems in Medicine and Biomedical and Behavioral Research, which documented the persistence and prevalence of this view in America, has argued that the special moral importance of health care creates societal obligations to make it available to everyone:

> Most Americans believe that because health care is special, access to it raises special ethical concerns. In part, this is because good health is by definition important to well-being. . . . In a society concerned not only with fairness and equality of opportunity but also with the redemptive powers of science, there is a felt obligation to ensure that some level of health services is available to all.[10]

And many people believe that this moral stance should be reinterpreted in the form of a legal right to health care. Although the scope of a general legal right to health care is a matter of great dispute—whether it should include all desired care or all "needed" care or be limited to some primary set of health services—there seems to be general agreement that it should in any event include basic prenatal care, which is effective in saving lives and substantially improving health.[11]

But it would be unwise to base an analysis of the dilemma at hand on this right, since it is more hypothetical than real. And although access to health care benefits may widen in time, it is not clear that individuals will be considered to have a legal right to this care. Indeed, whether the arguments for a moral right to health care provide adequate justification for a legal right to health care is a matter of debate.[12] This is not to say that ill health should not be prevented when possible, or that claims for a general right to health care should be discounted entirely. Rather, the point is that the controversy concerning proper state interventions with a pregnant woman's activities for the sake of her future child cannot be resolved by appeal to an alleged general right to health care that is itself almost as controversial.

Another interpretation of the right to medical care, however, has more force. According to this interpretation, although there may be no general legal right to medical care enjoyed by everyone, there is a distinctive right to medical care enjoyed by children because of their special vulnerability. In other words, one could argue that children have a moral and legal right to receive basic medical care, and their parents and other caregivers have the corresponding duty to provide that care.

A Child's Right to Medical Care

While parents have a broad moral and legal authority to consent to or refuse medical treatments for their children, this authority is not absolute. Even many supporters of strong parental autonomy recognize that this authority is not the only value, and that human lives should not be sacrificed to it. Thus, although parental authority creates a strong case for noninterference, it is generally agreed that it can justifiably be overridden by considerations of important interests of children. Indeed, all states recognize as child neglect a parent's refusal to provide adequate medical treatment (although, as we shall see, this rule is open to varying interpretations and exceptions).

It could be argued that, in addition, fetuses who will be brought to term should be provided with adequate medical care. Michael Bayles, for instance, suggests that it should be legally impermissible for a pregnant woman to fail to provide a particular medical benefit to a fetus who will be carried to term if failure to provide a similar medical benefit to a born child would be regarded as child neglect or abuse.[13]

While initially plausible, this approach has several serious shortcomings. First, there is no legal consensus on the grounds for legitimate state interference with parents' failure to provide medical treatment to their children, even in life-and-death cases. While all states recognize as culpable a parent's refusal to allow the administration of life-saving medical treatments to her child, this rule is sometimes breached. One court, for instance, permitted the parents of an institutionalized twelve-year-old boy with Down's syndrome to refuse permission for cardiac surgery needed to correct a congenital ventricular septic defect, while another permitted the parents of an infant with Down's syndrome to refuse permission for relatively simple corrective surgery needed to join the child's esophagus and stomach.[14] And sometimes the strength of a parent's religious beliefs is determinative. Parents who substitute religious treatment for medical care are protected from criminal liability by exemptions in most state child protection codes (even though failure to seek medical care for other reasons would constitute child neglect), and parents have escaped criminal sanction even when their children died from curable diseases.[15] The courts granted these exemptions based on the First Amendment's guarantee of free exercise of religion.

Yet this exemption has been rejected by some courts. For instance, several courts have overruled parents' strong religious beliefs by ordering children whose lives were at stake to undergo blood transfusions over the objections of their Jehovah's Witness parents.[16] And some parents who denied their children life-saving medical care for religious reasons have faced criminal prosecution even in those states with religious exemptions. In Indiana, two couples who were members of the Faith Assembly sect were convicted of reckless homicide and child neglect for the deaths of their infants, and a jury in Florida convicted a Christian Science couple of third-degree murder and child abuse for rejecting medical treatment for their daughter in favor of prayer.[17]

Courts have sometimes ordered medical treatment over the parent's objections even when the child's condition was not life-threatening:

> Although not commonly, some courts, for example, have prosecuted parents for neglect when their refusal to consent was for treatment that was characterized as 'highly desirable,' though not necessary to save the life of a child. Once declaring the child neglected, courts have, against the religious objections of parents, ordered removal of tonsils, ordered plastic surgery for a massive facial deformity, ordered treatment for emotional ailments, and ordered surgery for a foot deformity.[18]

In sum, there is no consensus in the law with regard to the circumstances under which parents must provide medical care for their children or face criminal penalties. There are some rules of thumb, however: When a child's life is at stake, the state usually (but not always) requires the parents to seek medical treatment for her; when the child's health is compromised—but her life is not at stake—then the state usually (but not always) allows the parents the discretion to decide.

But even if there were general agreement about when parents must provide medical treatment to their children, we would still be far from resolving the question of what to do with a pregnant woman

who refuses medical treatment (and this is the second problem with
Bayles' proposal). He is correct to a certain extent; were there a consensus that the state may *not* intervene in a parent's decision regarding appropriate care of his or her child in certain circumstances, then
it would follow that the state would not be justified in intervening in
a comparable decision of a pregnant woman regarding her future
child as well. But it is important to note that the opposite is not true.
Even if there were a consensus that the state may legitimately intervene in a parent's decision regarding her child's medical treatment in
certain circumstances, it would not necessarily follow that the state
may interfere with the decision of a pregnant woman.

For instance, most people would no doubt agree with the assertion
by Joseph Goldstein, one of the most ardent supporters of parental
authority, that state interference with parental decisions is justifiable
when necessary to provide "any proven, nonexperimental medical
procedure when its denial would mean death for a child who would
otherwise have an opportunity for either a life worth living or a life of
relatively normal healthy growth toward adulthood."[19] Indeed, state
intervention to prevent the death of a child who might go on to live a
full and healthy life seems uncontroversial, at least to those of us who
reject the proposition that, if one believes in the power of God, then
one must avoid all secular life-saving interventions.

But we cannot apply this standard directly to the case of a fetus
because (unlike the child) the fetus exists within someone's body.
Although the reason for state intervention—saving a life—would be
the same in both cases, the justifications for intervention are different.
Acting on behalf of an unborn child is more invasive and intrusive to
the pregnant woman—insofar as the treatment invades her body—
than acting on behalf of the born child would be to a typical parent. In
other words, all of the arguments in favor of allowing parents to
decide whether and how their children will receive medical treatment
are available to pregnant women *plus* one argument that is not usually available to parents in general: the argument that she has a right
to decide what will happen to her own body. Hence, standards for a
reasonably prudent *pregnant* parent must be devised, distinct from
standards for reasonably prudent parents in general.

There is another shortcoming to resting state intervention to prevent prenatal harm on the future child's alleged right to receive adequate medical care. Because this argument simply holds that (at least)
some forms of medical care must be provided, it permits other sorts

of harms to go unchallenged. Arguably then, pregnant cigarette smokers who receive periodic medical checkups and take their prescribed medications would be exempt from interference with their addictions, despite the evidence that smoking during pregnancy may impede fetal growth. For those who wish to be able to protect future persons from all varieties of serious harm, this basis may be too limiting. Thus the alleged right to receive adequate medical care must be buttressed by another right—the general right not to be harmed—in order to include a wide range of prenatal harm.

The Right Not to Be Harmed

The right not to be harmed is a widely accepted and fundamentally important right which serves as a foundation for our moral and legal codes. Indeed, it is generally accepted in our society that one of the most important goals of state action is to prevent harm to persons, and that this goal may legitimately involve interfering with individual liberty. As the philosopher Joel Feinberg states,

> In short, state interference with a citizen's behavior tends to be morally justified when it is reasonably necessary (that is, when there are reasonable grounds for taking it to be necessary as well as effective) to prevent harm or the unreasonable risk of harm to parties other than the person interfered with. More concisely, the need to prevent harm (private or public) to parties other than the actor is always an appropriate *reason* for legal coercion.[20]

Some theorists argue that the sole legitimate reason for the state's limiting a person's liberty is to prevent him or her from harming another person. It is significant to note, however, that even if you do not agree that an individual's liberty may be limited only to prevent harm to a third party, you may still believe that the need to prevent harm provides a stronger reason for limiting liberty than any other value.

The right not to be unjustly harmed is even regarded as being enforceable by the state against conduct occurring before birth. The argument for this is one that the tort law recognizes as legitimate; the harm with which we are concerned is suffered by the child after birth, not by the fetus *in utero*.

As Chapter One noted, practically all aspects of a pregnant woman's life take on moral significance because of the potential to harm another person, her future child. There is considerable evidence, for instance, that consuming alcohol, using narcotics, and eating improperly may cause fetal damage; even everyday activities such as drinking coffee and smoking cigarettes may be harmful. A woman who abstains from these activities during pregnancy, however, greatly improves her fetus's health and chances for survival, as does one who alters her lifestyle during pregnancy.[21] Therefore, it makes sense to offer pregnant women information about the effects of lifestyle choices on the outcome of a pregnancy and to encourage—even try to persuade—them to behave differently.

The difficult question is whether more should be done. Those who are disturbed by the plight of seriously impaired, disadvantaged infants—infants who would have been born healthy had their mothers behaved differently—argue that a pregnant woman should be required to change her lifestyle for the sake of the child she is carrying. The argument is fairly straightforward: By indulging in substance abuse, for instance, the pregnant woman who intends to carry her pregnancy to term is harming another and is thereby violating one of the most fundamental rights of a person, the right not to be harmed; the harm to a woman occasioned by her abstinence would be minor compared with the great benefit to the future child; thus, coercing a pregnant woman to alter her lifestyle may be justifiable under some circumstances.

This argument is buttressed by the contention that the state has certain obligations to protect the well-being of individuals, obligations which should be applied equally to all, including newborns. Indeed, one primary obligation of the state is to provide equal protection to all persons. This obligation may be regarded as being grounded in utilitarian concerns (society will benefit most this way) or as being grounded in the principle of equality; the foundational arguments are not really germane here. What is important is that most people would agree that the state does have, and should have, a commitment to the equal protection of all persons.

ARGUMENTS BASED ON A PREGNANT WOMAN'S OBLIGATIONS

Our society is characterized by a high regard for individual rights, and persons on every side of an issue can be expected to couch their arguments in terms of one or more rights. But what are they really talking about? What is a *right*? What types of beings possess rights? Which rights do they have? Are there rights that outweigh considerations of utility? If so, what are these rights? How should we argue for them? What does it mean to say that a right carries a correlative obligation? How should we resolve conflicts among rights? In sum, the issue of rights is an enormously complex and controversial one, and a host of fundamental questions remain controversial.

Because so many issues regarding the scope and power of rights are matters of continuing debate, and some people are thereby unpersuaded by appeals to rights, we need also to consider arguments that avoid references to rights altogether. We have explored one of these so far: the argument based on consequences. Another type of argument is available which also refrains from appealing to the alleged rights of the future child; this one is based on the claim that a pregnant woman has certain obligations to her future child—obligations which may or may not carry correlative rights—and that these obligations are similar to her obligations to other people. While these obligations are not grounded on the rights of the future person, they are related to its interests.

A Pregnant Woman's Moral Obligations to Her Future Child

In the previous chapter it was argued that one's position on the moral status of the fetus has little impact on the issue at hand because there are good arguments for preventing prenatal harm regardless of the moral status of the fetus. These arguments are based on the important interests of the future person (the person the fetus will become if it is brought to term). In essence, the argument is that even if a fetus is not considered to be a person, there still are important interests of a person—the interests of the future child—that must be taken into account. Once a pregnant woman forgoes her right to have an abortion, then, it could be argued that her actions should be constrained by considerations of the welfare of the child that the fetus will become. Her obligations, in other words, would be to the future child, not to the fetus. So even if a pregnant woman has the legal right to have an abortion, it does not follow that she has the freedom to behave in any way she wishes while she is pregnant, for her choices may be limited by considerations of the well-being of the future child.

It follows that a pregnant woman incurs these moral obligations to her future child only if she intends to carry the fetus to term. If a woman is free to terminate her pregnancy but does not do so, then she has chosen not to avoid a situation in which she and she alone can affect the well-being of another person (the child she will bear), and in so choosing she can be deemed to have assumed responsibility for the condition of that future person. And, it could be argued, society should recognize these moral obligations to be legal obligations as well, backed by the coercive power of the state.[22]

Although it is not always desirable to recognize moral duties as legal duties, one area in which moral responsibility and legal responsibility coincide pertains to what the noted legal scholar H. L. A. Hart calls a person's "role-responsibility:"

> A sea captain is responsible for the safety of his ship, and that is his responsibility, or one of his responsibilities. A husband is responsible for the maintenance of his wife; perhaps for the upbringing of their children; a sentry for alerting the guard at the enemy's approach. . . . These examples of a person's responsibilities suggest the generalization that, whenever a person occupies a distinctive place or office in a social organization, to which specific duties are attached to provide for the welfare of others or to advance in some specific way the aims or purposes of the organization, he is properly said to be responsible for the performance of these duties, or for doing what is necessary to fulfill them."[23]

It could be argued that part of the "role-responsibility" of a pregnant woman is to provide for the welfare of the child she will bear. Consider the following case. Arthur is the public health director for the state of Arizona. It has come to his attention that a certain underground well is contaminated, but he neglects to publicize the fact or to inform the authorities in the area. So people continue to drink the poisoned water, and many become very ill. Here Arthur has had nothing to do with the poisoning of the well, nor does he influence people to drink from it. He simply sits at his desk and works on other matters. Thus we could give an adequate causal explanation of the poisonings without mentioning Arthur. Yet although he did not cause the harm, he still is to a certain degree responsible for it—both morally and legally—since, as part of his position as public health director, he had a duty to prevent people from drinking the contaminated water. In the same way, a pregnant woman may be responsible—both morally and legally—for the impaired health of the child she bears.

Discussion

So far I have argued that there are sound reasons—reasons based on utilitarian considerations, the rights of future persons, and the moral obligations of pregnant women—for holding that a woman should not be free to do whatever she wishes with her body while she is pregnant. This implies that there are some circumstances under which it would be legitimate to coerce a pregnant woman to act in the interests of her child-to-be.

But what are these circumstances? And what sorts of coercion would be appropriate?

At this stage of our investigation, any answer to these questions would be premature. Before we can come to any conclusions we must first analyze the nature of a woman's (proposed) legal obligations as well as the counterarguments to recognizing any legal duty on a woman's part to her future child.

REMARKS ON THE NATURE OF A PREGNANT WOMAN'S LEGAL OBLIGATIONS TO ACT IN THE INTERESTS OF HER CHILD-TO-BE

A parent's legal duties toward his or her child are based in large part on the interests of the child, but they are limited by the interests and rights of others (including those of the parent herself). Thus a parent is not obligated to do what is in the child's best interest, but rather the parent must act within some acceptable range of these interests, a "range of reasonableness."[24] This range is necessarily flexible, given the economic and social variances (and inequities) across society, the range of values and beliefs within society, and the broad scope of a typical parent's responsibilities: to her other children, her spouse, her employer, herself.

In application, then, this standard may be very similar to a "minimum needs" standard, which holds that a parent must satisfy at least certain minimum needs of his or her child. Should a parent fall below this range, creating significant risk of serious and long-lasting harm to his or her child, then the state may step in to protect the child. The California Supreme Court has proposed that the fundamental question to be asked in these cases is: "What would an ordinarily reasonable and prudent parent have done in similar circumstances?"[25]

Society could also recognize a flexible standard of due care on the part of a pregnant woman with regard to the child she will bear. This legal standard of care would involve refraining from acts which a reasonably prudent pregnant person would avoid when that person knows or, in the exercise of reasonable care, should know that such acts cause prenatal harm. The pregnant woman's duty would also extend to the provision of those benefits (such as some forms of medical treatment) that a reasonably careful pregnant person would provide. Using such standards would allow a woman to engage in risky conduct which the reasonably prudent pregnant person would pursue, and would allow her to act in ways that cause relatively minor prenatal harm.

One objection to this formula is that "reasonableness" is simply not a reliable standard when it comes to a woman's actions during pregnancy. Dawn Johnsen, for instance, worries that,

> Given common stereotypical public concepts of the 'proper' role of women, particularly pregnant women, there is very little behavior that might not be found by a jury to be 'unreasonable.' This is particularly a risk when juries are confronted with injuries that will otherwise go unremedied, as is likely often to be true in such cases. It would not, in fact, be 'unreasonable' for a pregnant woman, faced with the prospect of post-natal civil liability according to community standards of propriety, to assume that the only safe course of behavior is to lie prone for nine months.[26]

But this assumption is unwarranted. The reasonableness standard is not an ideal of perfection to which pregnant women should aspire; it does not require that a woman give up her whole life, or even a large part of her life, to her pregnancy. Indeed, the point of setting a flexible standard of reasonableness—a standard that varies according to community mores, access to medical care, the level of medical technology available, the stage of the pregnancy, and so on—is to posit a minimum standard below which one cannot fall without being viewed as culpably negligent. Thus, although a pregnant woman is not expected to do everything in her power to ensure a healthy baby (such as staying in bed for nine months), she is expected to show at least a modicum of due care for the well-being of her future child.

It seems plausible to contend that the standard of care would involve two distinct levels of obligation. The woman assumes the first one by becoming pregnant, regardless of whether she does so voluntarily or not. While she is pregnant, the possibility remains that a child will come into being who will be affected by her actions, so she has at least some level of obligation of due care to this future person. She may end this obligation, of course, by having an abortion.

The pregnant woman assumes the second level of obligation by forgoing her right to have an abortion for any reason other than jeopardy to her life and/or health, and hence at least tacitly committing herself to carry the fetus to term. Once she makes this decision, or at least allows the fetus to reach the point at which abortions are permitted only to mitigate risks to maternal life and/or health, she puts herself in a special relationship to her future child. This relationship can be seen as carrying more demanding obligations, obligations which are similar to those of any parent to his or her child.

It is generally held that the parent-child relationship involves positive duties of aid as well as negative duties not to cause harm, and that parents are expected to sacrifice more for their children than they would for strangers. At this later stage of pregnancy, then, a woman may be required to undergo more than minimally invasive therapies in order to prevent serious harm to her child-to-be, and she may be required to accept significant limitations on her freedom of action in order not to cause harm. But there are good reasons for positing that a pregnant woman's obligations at the earlier stage, the first level of obligation, should be substantially less burdensome.

First Level of Legal Obligation

Women become pregnant for a variety of reasons that have nothing to do with the desire to have a child: They are raped, their method of contraception fails, they take inadequate precautions against getting pregnant, and so on. But whatever the circumstances of conception, it is often true that a pregnancy is unintended and unwelcome. Thus we should be hesitant about presuming that all pregnant women regard themselves as parents; and we should be hesitant about adding too many extra burdens—in the form of legal obligations to undergo invasive medical treatments or difficult lifestyle changes—on a woman whose pregnancy may already be burdensome to her and who retains the option of having an abortion.

Given these considerations, it would make sense to understand a woman's legal obligations during the early stage of pregnancy as similar to the duty of due care she owes to any other person (e.g., any stranger), which is relatively undemanding. According to common-sense morality and most ethical theories, one has a general, though limited, duty of care toward strangers, independent of any voluntary assumption of responsibility for their welfare.

One strong case for a discretionless duty to aid a stranger is offered by James Childress (drawing on Eric D'Arcy's work):

> A has a duty of beneficence to do X for P: 1) when P is at risk of significant loss or damage (such as severe injury or death), 2) when A's action is necessary to prevent this loss or damage, 3) when A's action would probably prevent it, 4) when the likely harms to A are minimal, and 5) when the benefit that P will probably gain outweighs the likely harm to A.[27]

If we substitute "future person" for "P" and "pregnant woman" for "A" in Childress's example, we can see that all of his conditions may pertain to the cases at hand. The pregnant woman may choose to end her obligations at this early stage by having an abortion.

Legal Obligations to Strangers

The backbone of our legal system is the conviction that one person should not harm another. There is, in other words, a generally recognized legal duty to refrain from harming another person, a duty whose strength is not diminished when strangers are involved. Hence the law extracts monetary damages and in some situations imposes criminal penalties upon those who cause harm to others through negligent, reckless, or willful conduct.

It could be argued that many activities of pregnant women fall under this rubric. A pregnant woman who ingests crack, for instance, could be said to show reckless disregard for the risk of harm which her conduct poses for the child she intends to bear. And a pregnant woman who negligently causes an automobile accident which injures her fetus could reasonably be accused of misconduct with regard to her future child. It would be a fairly straightforward task, then, to apply the principles of some legal prohibitions against harming others to pregnant women who cause prenatal damage.

But we are also interested in those instances in which the pregnant woman does not directly cause harm to her future child but instead refuses to prevent a harm from occurring; in other words, she fails to take action to avoid the harm. One example of this would be a pregnant woman who refuses to take a prescribed medicine which would ameliorate a genetic anomaly in her fetus; another would be a woman who refuses the cesarean section needed to save her distressed fetus. The issue here is whether a pregnant woman should ever be legally obligated to come to the aid of her future child, in addition to being legally obligated to refrain from harming him or her.

The proposal that the courts should recognize that a pregnant woman has a limited obligation to prevent serious harm to her future child even in the early stages of pregnancy is consonant with many legal systems: for instance, Czechoslovakia, France, Germany, Holland, Hungary, Italy, Norway, Poland, Portugal, Rumania and Turkey have statutes that create a general duty to rescue (so long as the risk to the rescuer is minimal). But it seems to founder when we confront the reality of Anglo-American law, which generally assumes and imports that there is no legal duty to aid a stranger.[28] I may notice that a stranger is about to walk into a deep pit because he is completely absorbed in looking at a rainbow, and at very little inconvenience to me, simply by giving a shout, I could save him from serious harm. But I do not. I simply watch him continue to walk while he admires the rainbow, until, with a shriek, he falls into the pit. Does the law hold me liable for his harm? No. Does the law claim that I should have aided him? No. Does the law pay any attention to me at all? No.

Indeed, Anglo-American law has not deigned to notice a horrifying list of one person's failure to aid another:

> The common-law tradition has left unpunished even harmful omissions of an immoral kind—malicious failures to warn a blind man of an open manhole, to lift the head of a sleeping drunk out of a puddle of water, to throw a rope from a bridge to a drowning swimmer, to rescue or even report the discovery of a small child wandering lost in a wood, and so on. Not only negligent but wicked samaritans have escaped answerability to the law, which in English-speaking countries has not only declined to punish them, but has not even made them liable for damages to those they have failed to aid.[29]

If according to our legal tradition a person need not take the smallest trouble to prevent serious harm to a stranger, is there any basis for claiming that a pregnant woman should be held accountable for failing to aid the child she may (or may not) bear?

Were this the whole story, it would seem unfair to hold pregnant women to standards that are applied to no one else.[30] But the situation is a bit more complicated. The first point to be noted is that the strength of the assumption that there is no legal duty to aid a stranger seems to be waning: Several states (Alaska, Minnesota, Vermont, Rhode Island, and Massachusetts), for instance, have passed statutes delineating those (limited) circumstances in which people are required to aid strangers in distress, and courts are increasingly recognizing exceptions to the rule.[31] Even more significantly, the objections usually raised against positing a legally enforceable duty to aid are irrelevant to the cases at hand.

The most common challenge to establishing a legal duty to aid strangers in peril is that it would interfere too much with an individual's liberty and welfare, either because the sacrifice in a particular instance would be too great or because the small sacrifices required to aid the large numbers of people who require assistance would inevitably become overwhelming. However, both of these objections fail when applied to pregnant women.

First, only minimal sacrifices on the pregnant woman's part would be required at this stage—undergoing relatively risk-free and proven forms of therapy, such as inoculations or doses of safe medications—and these need not be any more onerous than state regulations of other activities. As John Robertson points out, "Compelling certain diagnostic tests or even medications is not materially different from fluoridation or compulsory vaccinations."[32] The second reason the typical objections to an enforceable duty to aid a stranger fail in these cases is that compelling a pregnant woman to prevent harm to her future child is not at all likely to result in further impositions on her to aid a large number of other strangers. It is easy to distinguish precisely whom she is expected to aid (the being inside her) from all other persons in need of assistance of some sort.

A different type of objection to imposing a general legal duty to aid a stranger is based on the idea that it is difficult, if not impossible, to determine which individual is required to come to the aid of a particular stranger. Since strangers are in no special relationship to one another, in principle there are many potential benefactors for anyone in need. And in any given instance there will most likely be several people who could come to the aid of a particular person, yet each of them might refrain from acting on the reasonable assumption that one of the others, perhaps one who is more able, would assist the stranger. Given this, the argument continues, it is unfair to single out one person and charge him or her with failing to aid a particular stranger in peril.

This objection, however, simply has no force in the situations under discussion here. Since the harm to be prevented is harm to a future person—who now exists within the woman's body—there is no one else who could act instead of the pregnant woman. Thus it would not do to say that it is unfair to single her out among an indefinitely large number of possible benefactors, since she is the only possible benefactor.

We may conclude, then, that the usual arguments against holding one stranger legally responsible for helping another have very little force when applied to pregnant women.[33] Hence we are well on our way to being able to contend with confidence that a pregnant woman may have legal obligations to refrain from causing harm and also to take steps to prevent harm to her future child—even at the beginning of a pregnancy—so long as these obligations impose no significant burdens on her. But we are not yet there, for the countervailing considerations have yet to be addressed.

Determining When a Pregnant Woman's Legal Obligations to Her Future Child Become More Stringent

The second level of obligation—the more demanding duties owed to one's own child—does not come into force until it is clear that the pregnant woman will go to term. This may or may not be a matter of choice on her part; a pregnant woman need not voluntarily accept a special relationship with her future child in order to be treated as having assumed responsibility for its well-being. The rationale for this position begins with a brief examination of the power of the state to limit a woman's right to seek an abortion.

In 1973, the Supreme Court ruled in *Roe v. Wade* that a pregnant woman has a legal right to seek an abortion, but that her freedom to do so changed throughout her pregnancy. The Court held that, as a woman's pregnancy advanced, so did the state's power to regulate abortions, and the Court delineated three stages at which the level of state control may change. During the first stage of pregnancy—roughly the first trimester—the Court ruled that a woman may seek an abortion for any reason, free from all state intervention other than the requirement that the procedure be performed by a licensed physician. After the first trimester, the state may choose to regulate the abortion procedure in ways that are "reasonably related to maternal health." During the third stage—when the fetus is viable—the state's interest in protecting potential human life is strengthened considerably, and the

Court ruled that the state may go so far as to proscribe abortion "except where it is necessary, in appropriate medical judgment, for the preservation of the life or health of the mother."[34]

Since that time abortion procedures have become considerably safer, and in 1983 the Supreme Court ruled that many of the second-trimester restrictions placed on abortion procedures ten years earlier were no longer necessary.[35] In effect, then, the Court collapsed the original three stages of pregnancy into two. During the first stage—which begins at conception and proceeds until the fetus is able to survive outside its mother's body (the point of "fetal viability")—the state has little power to limit abortions. After the fetus is viable, however, the state's power to intervene is strong, and it can go so far as to prohibit all abortions except for those needed to save the life or health of the mother.

Consequently, there is now one major point—fetal viability—which designates when the state may intrude into a woman's decision to seek an abortion. It is important to note, however, that viability may not continue to be that point, since it is an arbitrary and shifting criterion, posing an enormous number of legal and ethical problems. One major difficulty is that the point of viability may be different for each fetus, since it depends upon, among other factors, maternal health, fetal weight, gestational age, genetic composition, and available medical care.[36] Hence the notion of fetal viability is rarely used in areas of the law not pertaining to abortion. The Rhode Island Supreme Court, for instance, concluded that, "If we profess allegiance to reason, it would be seditious to adopt so arbitrary and uncertain a concept as viability as a dividing line between those persons who shall enjoy the protection of our remedial laws and those who shall become, for most intents and purposes, nonentities."[37]

In its 1989 decision in *Webster v. Reproductive Health Services*, the Supreme Court indicated its willingness to abandon the trimester analysis in general and the emphasis on fetal viability in particular. It will be years before the issues are resolved in all states, but a good guess is that viability as a major criterion will be discarded and a more secure line of demarcation will be drawn between a woman's unqualified right to seek an abortion and the state's authority to curtail that right.

But no doubt there will continue to be some line of demarcation between the stage at which a pregnant woman may seek an abortion for any reason and the stage at which the state may limit her choices. The relevance of this to our discussion is that, before any line of demarcation has been reached, a pregnant woman cannot be said to have committed herself to carrying the pregnancy to term, since she may seek an abortion for any reason. After that time has passed, however—and the state permits her to seek an abortion only for certain critical reasons (such as danger to her life or health)—we may reasonably assume that she will continue the pregnancy to term.

In sum, it makes sense to conclude that a pregnant woman does not incur the second, more stringent, level of obligation to her future child until it is uncontroversially the case that she intends to carry the pregnancy to term, and this would not be until she has forgone her legal right to seek an abortion for reasons other than risk to her life or health. Thus she would have no legal obligation to undergo any significant burdens for the sake of her future child before that time.

RESTRICTIONS ON STATE POWER

So far we have explored arguments in favor of recognizing that a woman has some legal obligations to act in the interests of her future child. But other factors must be considered to determine whether or not legal coercion may be allowed. Among the most important of these are the Fourteenth Amendment's requirements of due process of law and equal protection under the law.

Requirements of Due Process

Due process of law is a constitutional guarantee of fundamental fairness, an affirmation of respect for those liberties which, as the Supreme Court stated, are "so rooted in the traditions and conscience of our people as to be ranked as fundamental."[38] Due process requirements are designed to assure that the rights and interests at stake are respected, and to avoid abuses and errors in the state's decision to intervene. Before pregnant women could be held to particular standards of behavior, these standards would have to be authorized by statute or developed through court-created common law and widely promulgated. To prevent the woman who is the party in a precedent-setting case from being subjected to the newly created common law (about which she could have had no warning), the judge should have the discretion to make his or her decision completely nonretroactive. Thus, only future parties would be subjected to the new common law's coercion. In addition, judicial review of the decision to intervene must be available.

Unfortunately, physicians have not always acted in accordance with even the most minimal requirements of due process. A case was reported in 1984, for instance, in which physicians performed a cesarean section on a pregnant woman in order to save an acutely distressed term fetus, even though the woman continually and "adamantly" refused to give consent to the surgery and even though a court order had not been secured.[39] This is tantamount to assault and battery. A physician is not justified in interfering with a pregnant woman's decision simply because it is detrimental to the welfare of her child-to-be. Instead, the physician must go through regular institutional channels such as the courts. It is important to note, however, that seeking judicial review is not always sufficient to meet the requirements of due process, as Chapter Four will demonstrate.

The Fourteenth Amendment also guarantees that states afford equal protection under the law to all persons who are "similarly situated." Some commentators have interpreted this to mean that it is wrong to place legal constraints on pregnant women that are not also placed on men and nonpregnant women. But this conclusion is too strong. There may be circumstances in which a class of pregnant women, with their unique needs and responsibilities, can be rationalized as appropriately separate from women generally. In these cases, state regulation of pregnant women may be necessary without having to regulate all women or all persons. At least in principle, then, some state intervention into the activities of pregnant women may be constitutional.

Proportionality

Although the factor motivating state intervention in the lives of pregnant women is the prevention of serious harm to future persons, it does not follow that the appropriate social policy would be to interfere in every instance in which a pregnant women is risking significant harm to her future child. Administering such a program would no doubt prove unworkable, inefficient, awkward, and unreasonably intrusive. Imagine the state monitoring each parent to ensure that all children are provided with nutritious diets and sufficient levels of affection; the thought makes me shudder.

In short, other factors must also be considered, especially proportionality: The intervention should not create more harm than it is aimed to alleviate. Allowing legal interference in every instance in which a future child is or could be harmed might create more harm than good, and thereby would defeat the whole point of intervening. This stands as a powerful reason for limiting state intervention. It also leads to the conclusion that state interference would be justifiable only if four conditions can be met: (1) The harm to be prevented to the future person greatly exceeds the degree of invasion to the pregnant woman, (2) the intervention is expected to be successful; (3) the intervention involves the least intrusive means available; and (4) a policy permitting such interventions will be, on the whole, beneficial to society in general. A few words on the first two conditions are in order here; the others will be discussed in later chapters.

Weighing Particular Harms and Benefits

Determining whether the harms to be prevented to the future person in fact greatly exceed the degree of invasion to the pregnant woman is not an easy task. It involves weighing three interrelated factors: (1) magnitude of harm; (2) probability that the harm will occur; and (3) probability that the harm can be prevented or removed. No simple formula for the application of these factors in all situations exists; at best, one can give a general outline of their scope and relevance.

The question of the magnitude of the harm involved has two parts: (1) To what extent will the future child be harmed by his mother's actions? and (2) to what extent will the pregnant woman be harmed if her decision is overruled and her body is invaded? Answering these questions requires determining which interests are at stake (e.g., a woman's interest in making her own decisions, a child's interest in not being disabled), and the degree to which each interest will be invaded (a matter of duration times severity). One interest at stake, for instance, would be the woman's interest in bodily integrity, and different actions would invade it to different degrees. The extent of harm to this interest caused by a mandatory inoculation is substantially less than that caused by a forced cesarean section. Since it makes a difference how important the interest is and whether it is being only slightly thwarted or downright defeated, these two actions would require different types of justification.[40]

Determining the probability that the pregnant woman's actions will in fact cause grave harm to her future child is also an important and troublesome factor. There should be ample evidence to indicate that there is a high probability of serious harm to the future child if steps are not taken to intervene on its behalf, but this certainty is often lacking. For instance, the probability of the risk of harm is especially difficult to determine in instances of environmental or workplace hazards because many of the harms in question have a multitude of contributing causes and often are the result of cumulative or synergistic influences. And although we have significant evidence that drinking alcohol and ingesting crack during pregnancy may cause serious prenatal harm, there is no evidence that this is always the case. Hence it is often difficult in any particular instance to determine with certainty whether or not the future child is at grave risk of serious harm.

The third factor to be considered is the probability that the harm to the future child can be avoided or removed. Intervention makes sense only when there is a significant or high probability that a harm can be prevented or at least ameliorated. One is obligated neither to make futile efforts to prevent harm, nor to suffer especially risky or experimental measures. The central question is easily discerned: What constitutes a "significant" probability that intervention will be successful?

With respect to fetal therapies, the answer involves three factors: (1) The general reliability of this type of therapy as determined by prevailing standards of the medical profession; (2) its estimated efficacy in this instance; and (3) the value of the expected results (for example, the value of a generally healthy life or of a brief life filled with great pain).

It is appropriate to allow the pregnant woman the discretion to choose from various treatment options when the proposed medical care is a matter of debate within the medical community and there is no medical consensus regarding the appropriate treatment for the child. The difficult questions regarding the scope of her discretion do not concern a choice among ordinary therapies but rather involve a decision to reject them entirely, or to forgo a less-than-satisfactory conventional therapy in favor of a promising but unorthodox one. This issue cannot be decided in isolation from the other interests mentioned, but it does point to the importance of one factor: the value of the expected results. It makes a difference whether the treatment can be expected to cure the child, to mitigate the symptoms without curing, or to save the child's life but leave her in a permanently coma-tose state. The general principle is intuitive: The obligation of a parent to utilize a particular therapy decreases in direct proportion with the tentativeness of the desired results of that therapy.

The problem of determining the scope and limits of the obligation to provide effective therapy is not unique to fetal therapy; it is present throughout medicine. Reflection on this factor, however, does lead to the conclusion that social and legal policy must be selective. To assert that no fetal therapy should be mandated, or that all should be, would be unreasonable. Different therapies promise different out-comes, and only those that are likely to be effective in avoiding or ameliorating severely deleterious conditions may be required. The final decision, of course, cannot be made without balancing the sever-ity of the harm to the future child against the cost to the pregnant woman of interfering with her life.

PRELIMINARY CONCLUSIONS

So far, this chapter has argued that there are good moral and pruden-tial reasons for trying to prevent prenatal harm, reasons based on three types of considerations: (1) utility (i.e., more good than harm will result); (2) the future person's positive right to receive adequate medical care and her negative right not to be harmed; and (3) the pregnant woman's general moral obligations to refrain from harming another and to aid another, as well as her special obligation to care for her future child. In other words, it makes good moral sense to argue that a pregnant woman does not have *carte blanche* to act any way she wishes, at least if her actions will cause harm to her future child. In addition, this chapter has contended that it may be justifiable for the state to intervene to prevent some prenatal harm, but that two impor-tant factors ought to be taken into account before doing so: due pro-cess and proportionality.

While there may be good arguments in favor of limiting the lib-erty of pregnant women in order to protect their offspring, these argu-ments are far from justifying any and all types of state intervention. Two considerations are especially germane here. First is the practical matter of proportionality. Allowing the state to interfere in every instance in which a future child is or could be harmed would no doubt create more harm than good, and this stands as a powerful reason for limiting state intervention. And second are the profound policy implications of the varying degrees of a pregnant woman's duties to her future child. I have argued that there are two distinct levels of obligation to which pregnant women may be held—the first involves minor duties of due care, while the second level involves more stringent duties similar to those in a parent-child relationship—and that the burdens a pregnant woman may be expected to bear grow as the pregnancy advances. For those whose primary concern is preventing prenatal harm, the conclusion is a sad one: The state is not justified in intervening to prevent even serious prenatal harm if the problems are caused during the early stage of pregnancy and dealing with them would place an unwarranted burden on the mother.

The discussion so far has been fairly abstract, and necessarily so. We cannot make reasonable conclusions about concrete cases until all of the relevant moral, legal, and public policy issues have been addressed. And so far we have considered only a small subset of those arguments that bear on the issue at hand; only the arguments in favor of coercing a pregnant woman to behave in certain ways have been advanced. We have been looking, in other words, at the rights of the future child, the duties of the pregnant woman to her future child, and possible benefits—to the children and to society in general—of preventing prenatal harm. But there are many other arguments to examine before a final determination can be made. We must, for instance, consider a pregnant woman's duties in conjunction with her rights and liberties, and we must examine other sorts of factors that militate against state intervention in these cases, such as the disbenefits that might result.

Thus although the thrust of the discussion so far has been that it is reasonable to impose some legal limitations on the choices open to pregnant women, these conclusions are only preliminary because other important relevant ingredients have yet to be taken into account. The arguments against state intervention into the lives of pregnant women, which will be examined in the next chapter, are at least as strong as the arguments in favor of state intervention.

NOTES

1. *Schloendorff v. Society of N.Y. Hospitals*, 211 N.Y. 125, 105 N.E. 92, 1911. For more on this subject, see R. R. Faden and T. L. Beauchamp, *A History and Theory of Informed Consent*, N.Y.: Oxford University Press, 1986.

2. A typical FAS child is born with a complex of facial abnormalities which include small eye openings, a small upturned nose, and thin upper lips.

3. It should be noted, however, that these rights do not necessarily imply that there is also a right to be born. For example, the duty to provide medical treatment to the fetus who will be carried to term is a duty to the postfetal person she will become IF she is carried to term, and it need not entail a duty on the part of her mother to carry her to term.

4. *Smith v. Brennan*, 31 N.J. 353, 157 A.2d 497, 1960.

5. Park v Chessin 400 N.Y.S. 110, 1977 The "right to begin life with a sound mind and body" has been adopted by other courts (e.g., *In re Baby X*, 97 Mich. App. 111, 293 N.W.2d 736, 1980 and *Womack v. Buckhorn*, 384 Mich. 718, 187 N.W.2d 218, 1976); but the right of a child to be born as a "whole, functional human being" has held little sway, and indeed was rejected almost immediately by the New York Court of Appeals (*Becker v. Schwartz*, 46 N.Y.2d 401, 386 N.E.2d 807, 413 N.Y.S.2d 895, 1978).

6. M. W. Shaw, "Conditional Prospective Rights of the Fetus," *The Journal of Legal Medicine* 5, pp. 63–116, 1984, at p. 95.

7. There is another possible interpretation of this right: that a child who cannot be born healthy may have the right not to be born at all.

Consider the following hypothetical case. Diagnostic procedures performed on Mrs. D. reveal that the fetus she is carrying is severely impaired: the fetus has spina bifida (an open spinal column), hydrocephalus (excess fluid on the brain), microcephaly (an abnormally small head and brain), and an improperly formed brain stem. Although it is anticipated that the child will survive past infancy, it is clear that he cannot be born with, and will never enjoy, "a sound mind and body," nor will he ever be a "whole, functioning human being." If the child has a right to be born sound and whole, and this right cannot be met, does it follow that he has a right not to be born at all?

The existence of such a right would have profound effects. If a child has a right to begin life with a sound mind and body, then any action which interferes with that right would be *prima facie* wrongful, even if the action does not worsen the condition of the child. This means that bringing an impaired child into the world—even if it is not possible under the circumstances to produce a healthy child—would be wrong, since it violates his right to be born healthy. Margery Shaw, for instance, argues for such a position, and suggests that legislators at least consider prohibiting certain acts by pregnant women: exposing a fetus to "the mother's defective intrauterine environment caused by her genotype," for instance, and carrying a seriously defective child to term (see "Genetically Defective Children: Emerging Legal Considerations," *American Journal of Law & Medicine* 3, pp. 333–40, 1977 and "The Potential Plaintiff: Preconception & Prenatal Torts," in A. Milunsky & A. J. Annas (eds.), *Genetics and the Law, II*, N.Y.: Plenum Press, 1980.

There are several ways for the state to recognize this right. One method of protecting a right not to be born unhealthy is to monitor all potential parents and refuse to permit those individuals who are likely to pass on severely deleterious genes to reproduce. We could, in other words, create a legal duty to refrain from passing on certain genes. The state could screen all men and women of child-bearing age; those who are fertile and who are at high risk of having seriously impaired children could be sterilized.

A second method of protecting the right not to be born would be to monitor all pregnant women and to require those who are carrying severely impaired fetuses to obtain abortions. This would mean compelling some pregnant women to get abortions against their wills and against their most fundamental beliefs.

Another alternative is to utilize the tort law: The child could be allowed to sue for compensation for have being born severely impaired, or someone could sue on the child's behalf. Courts have been confronted with the difficult task of addressing these suits—usually referred to as "wrongful life" cases—since the early 1960s (see Chapter Six). In a wrongful life suit, the child argues that her being born with serious impairments (even though there was no possibility that she could be born without the impairments) was a harm that calls for compensation, and she claims damages for having to live with her permanent and severe handicaps. In a way, the child claims that her suffering is so great that it would have been better had she not been born.

And finally, infanticide could be legalized. Infanticide is an option insofar as the desire to prevent prenatal harm is motivated by the desire to reduce human suffering, and one way to reduce human suffering is to eliminate the people who suffer the most. Infanticide for any reason at all is not the issue here; we are considering infanticide as a means of mitigating human suffering in the same way we are considering state intervention into the lives of pregnant women to prevent prenatal harm as a means of mitigating human suffering. In other words, infanticide may be considered to be an alternative means of dealing with devastatingly severe prenatal harm, and it offers the potential for reducing the suffering occasioned by some prenatal harm without intruding on the autonomy of pregnant women.

While theoretically plausible, none of these alternatives offers a viable solution to the dilemma at hand. Most courts continue to reject wrongful life suits, for instance, and states are increasingly moving to prohibit them by statute. And given the serious shortcomings of the other proposals—the invasions of privacy, the overtones of prejudice, the negation of individual liberty, the assault on self-determination, the lack of respect for human life, the unacceptable increase of state control, and the inevitable abuse of such discretionary power—these options are likely to be anathema to most people. They are not being recommended here.

8. *Harris v. McRae*, 448 U.S. 297, 1980; *DeShaney v. Winnebago County Department of Social Services* 851 U.S. 1071, 1989.

9. D. Chang and J. Holahan, *Medicaid Spending in the 1980s: The Access–Cost Containment Trade-Off Revisited*, University Press of America, 1990; S. Rosenbaum et al., "Incantations in the Dark: Medicaid, Managed Care, and Maternity Care," *Milbank Quarterly* 4, pp. 661–93, 1988; B. Starfield, "Motherhood and Apple Pie: The Effectiveness of Medical Care for Children," *Milbank Memorial Fund Quarterly* 63, pp. 523–46, 1985.

For a comparison of maternal and infant care policies of the United States and ten Western European countries, see C. A. Miller, "Maternal and Infant Care: Comparisons Between Western Europe and the United States," *International Journal of Health Services* 23, pp. 655–64, 1993. See also M. Sulvetta et al., *International Infant Mortality Rankings: A Reflection of Public Policies*, Washington, D.C.: Urban Institute Press, 1993.

10. President's Commission for the Study of Ethical Problems in Medicine and Biomedical and Behavioral Research. *Securing Access to Health Care, Volume One: Report*, Washington, D.C.: Government Printing Office, pp. 11–12, 1983.

11. Committee to Study the Prevention of Low Birthweight, Institute of Medicine. *Preventing Low Birthweight*, Washington, D.C.: National Academy Press, 1985; E. S. Fisher et al., "Prenatal Care and Pregnancy Outcomes During the Recession: The Washington State Experience," *American Journal of Public Health* 75, pp. 866–69, 1985; S. L. Gortmaker, "The Effects of Prenatal Care Upon the Health of the Newborn," *American Journal of Public Health* 69, pp. 653–60, 1979; T. R. Moore et al., "The Perinatal and Economic Impact of Prenatal Care in a Low-Socioeconomic Population," *American Journal of Obstetrics and Gynecology* 154, pp. 29–33, 1986; J. L. Murray and M. Bernfield, "The Differential Effect of Prenatal Care on the Incidence of Low Birth Weight Among Blacks and Whites in a Prepaid Health Plan," *New England Journal of Medicine* 319, pp. 1385–91, 1988; F. Rahbar et al., "Prenatal Care and Perinatal Mortality in a Black Population," *Obstetrics and Gynecology* 65, pp. 327–29, 1985; J. J. Fangman et al., "Prematurity Prevention Programs: An Analysis of Success and Failures," *American Journal of Obstetrics and Gynecology* 170, pp. 744–50, 1994.

12. Although this is not the place to give a comprehensive survey of the complex debate over the existence of a right to health care, a few comments on two basic methods for arguing for the general right are in order. We can reject immediately the method that relies upon any naturalistic assertions, such as the claim that one has a right to receive health care because one has a need for health care. Ever since the eighteenth century, when David Hume argued that value judgments cannot be deduced from a statement of fact without an intervening nonfactual value premise, such inferences have been discredited. Moreover, needing something—even needing it desperately—is not the same as having a right to it. And recognizing a personal moral obligation to respond to a need is not the same as recognizing a legal duty of the state to respond to that need.

A different, more plausible, method is to derive the right to health care from the existence of other rights. The argument would be as follows: One has a certain set of political rights (e.g., the right to free speech and the right to vote); In order to exercise these rights, one needs a certain set of basic goods (such as decent health); since everyone has these political rights, everyone should also have the means of exercising them, and the means should be provided to them as a matter of right; since one needs medical care in order to have good health, one also should have the right to medical care. This argument, however, does not really work. The recognition of a political right does not require the state to correct any natural condition that prevents the exercise of that right.

13. M. D. Bayles, *Reproductive Ethics*, Englewood Cliffs, N.J.: Prentice-Hall, Inc., 1984.

14. *In re Philip B.*, 92 Cal. App. 3d 796, *cert. denied* 445 U.S. 949, 1980; *In re Infant Doe*, No. GU 8204–004A (Monroe County Circuit Court), 1982.

15. "Faith Healing Exemptions to Child Protection Laws: Keeping the Faith Versus Medical Care for Children," *Journal of Legislation* 12, pp. 243–63, 1985; K. Rothenberg, "Medical Decision Making for Children," *BioLaw, Volume I*, Frederick, Md.: University Publications of America, pp. 149–76, 1988.

16. "Faith Healing Exemptions to Child Protection Laws: Keeping the Faith Versus Medical Care for Children," *Journal of Legislation* 12, pp. 243–63, 1985; K. Rothenberg, "Medical Decision Making for Children," *BioLaw, Volume I*, Frederick, Md.: University Publications of America, pp. 149–76, 1988.

17. C. E. Anderson, "When Faith Healing Fails," *ABA Journal*, pp. 22–23, 1989; "Faith Healing Exemptions to Child Protection Laws: Keeping the Faith Versus Medical Care for Children," *Journal of Legislation* 12, pp. 243–63, 1985.

18. K. Rothenberg, "Medical Decision Making for Children," *BioLaw, Volume I*, Frederick, Md.: University Publications of America, pp. 153–54, 1988.

19. J. Goldstein, "Medical Care for the Child at Risk: On State Supervision of Parental Autonomy," in W. Gaylin and R. Macklin (eds.) *Who Speaks for the Child? The Problem of Proxy Consent*, N.Y.: Plenum Press, 1982, p. 162.

Although most people might agree with this statement, not all would. Members of religious sects who believe in faith healing rather than secular methods of medical care would find this conclusion highly objectionable. Their concerns will be addressed in Chapter Four.

20. J. Feinberg, *The Moral Limits of the Criminal Law, Volume One, Harm to Others*, N.Y.: Oxford University Press, p. 11, 1984.

21. M. Aronson and R. Olegard, "Children of Alcoholic Mothers," *Pediatrician* 14, pp. 57–61, 1987; C. D. Cole et al., "Neonatal Ethanol Withdrawal: Characteristics in Clinically Normal, Nondysmorphic Neonates,"

Journal of Pediatrics 105, pp. 445–71, 1984; R. E. Little et al., "Fetal Alcohol Effects in Humans and Animals," *Advances in Alcohol & Substance Abuse*, pp. 103–25, 1982; C. Orstead et al., "Efficacy of Prenatal Nutrition Counseling: Weight Gain, Infant Birth Weight, and Cost-Effectiveness," *Journal of the American Dietic Association* 85, pp. 40–45, 1985; I. J. Chasnoff et al., "Temporal patterns of cocaine use in pregnancy," *Journal of the American Medical Association* 261, pp. 1741–44, 1989; D. H. Ershoff et al., "Pregnancy and Medical Cost Outcomes of a Self-Help Prenatal Smoking Cessation Program in a HMO," *Public Health Reports—Hyattsville* 105, pp. 340–47, 1990.

22. See, e.g., J. Robertson, "Procreative Liberty and the Control of Conception, Pregnancy and Childbirth," *Virginia Law Review* 69, pp. 405–64, 1983.

23. H. L. A. Hart, *Punishment and Responsibility*, N.Y.: Oxford University Press, p. 242, 1976.

24. R. Veatch, "Limits of Guardian Treatment Refusal: A Reasonableness Standard," *American Journal of Law and Medicine* 9, 427–70, 1984.

25. *Gibson v. Gibson*, 3 Cal.3d 914, 479 P.2d 648, 92 Cal. Rptr. 288, 1971.

26. D. Johnsen, "The Creation of Fetal Rights: Conflicts with Women's Constitutional Rights to Liberty, Privacy, and Equal Protection," *Yale Law Journal* 95, 599–625, p. 616, n. 68, 1986.

27. J. F. Childress, *Who Should Decide? Paternalism in Health Care*, N.Y.: Oxford University Press, p. 31, 1982; E. D'Arcy, *Human Acts: An Essay in Their Moral Evaluation*, Oxford: Clarendon Press, 1963.

28. S. Levmore, "Waiting for Rescue: An Essay on the Evolution and Incentive Structure of the Law of Affirmative Obligations," *Virginia Law Review* 72, pp. 879–941, 1986; R. A. Prentice, "Expanding the Duty to Rescue," *Suffolk University Law Review* 19, pp. 15–54, 1985.

29. J. Feinberg, *The Moral Limits of the Criminal Law, Volume One, Harm to Others*, N.Y.: Oxford University Press, p. 127, 1984.

30. And this is precisely what some commentators conclude. See, e.g., N. K. Rhoden, "Judges in the Delivery Room," *California Law Review* 74, pp. 1951–2030, 1986.

31. Laws requiring one stranger to aid another who is in distress are generally known as "Bad Samaritan" laws. They are to be distinguished from the more widely adopted "Good Samaritan" laws, which do not impose a duty to rescue but instead shield the rescuer (usually a health care professional) from legal liability should he harm the accident victim he is attempting to help.

Courts have recognized a variety of relationships between strangers—carrier and passenger, uninjured automobile accident victim and injured victim—that warrant one to aid the other. See, for instance, *Farwell V. Keaton*, 396 Mich. 281, 210 N.W.2d 217, 1976 and *Tarasoff v. Board of Regents of the University of California*, 17 Cal.3d 425, 551 P.2d 334, 131 Cal. Rptr. 14, 1976.

The U.S. Congress decided to establish a different sort of obligation to aid. The 1986 Consolidated Omnibus Budget Reconciliation Act (42 U.S.C.

1395dd) requires hospitals with emergency services that participate in the Medicare program to stabilize all emergency cases and all women in active labor before transferring or discharging them.

32. J. A. Robertson, "The Right to Procreate and *in Utero* Fetal Therapy," *Journal of Legal Medicine* 3, pp. 333–66, 1982, at pp. 359–60.

While fluoridation may not be an apt example, since in most places nonfluoridated water and water filters are available for purchase by people who wish to reduce their intake of fluoridated water, Robertson's general point is nonetheless sound.

33. It is important to note as well that there are many cogent arguments in favor of a general legal duty to aid a stranger in distress. See J. Feinberg, *The Moral Limits of the Criminal Law, Volume One, Harm to Others*, N.Y.: Oxford University Press, 1984; A. M. Honoré, "Law, Morals, and Rescue," in J. M. Ratcliffe (ed.), *The Good Samaritan and the Law*, N.Y.: Doubleday and Co., Inc., pp. 225–42, 1966; S. Levmore, "Waiting for Rescue: An Essay on the Evolution and Incentive Structure of the Law of Affirmative Obligations," *Virginia Law Review* 72, pp. 879–941, 1986; E. J. Weinrib, "The Case for a Duty to Rescue," *Yale Law Journal* 90, pp. 247–93, 1980.

34. *Roe v. Wade*, 410 U.S. 113, 1973.

35. *City of Akron v. Center for Reproductive Health*, 462 U.S. 416, 1983.

36. Since the Court's ruling in *Roe v. Wade*, there has been considerable discussion about what "fetal viability" really means: When precisely is a fetus viable? The Supreme Court decided not to decide this question. In *Planned Parenthood of Central Missouri V. Danforth*, 438 U.S. 52, 1976 for instance, the Court stated that it is not the "proper function of the legislature or the courts to place viability, which essentially is a medical concept, at a specific point in the gestation period . . . the determination of whether a particular fetus is viable is, and must be, a matter for the judgment of the responsible attending physician." In a later case, the Court reiterated its position, noting that there is no general community standard of viability and that it must be decided on a case-by-case basis [*Colautti v. Franklin*] 439 U.S. 379, 1979. The Court thus gave broad discretion to physicians in making their decisions.

In one sense, this was a very reasonable stance for the Court to take. If viability as a criterion is inexact and shifting, then so be it. It is much better for physicians, who keep pace with new medical developments, to decide when a particular fetus is viable than for courts of law or legislative bodies to attempt this onerous task. Yet in a way this discretion is burdensome for physicians and their patients, who seek assurance through legal guidelines. In fact, health care providers often set their own straightforward and arbitrary limits on performing abortions. Even before the Supreme Court's 1989 ruling in *Webster v. Reproductive Health Services*, many physicians would not abort a fetus who had gestated for twenty weeks or more unless it was necessary to save the life or health of the mother.

For more detailed discussions of the viability issue, see N. Fost et al., "The Limited Moral Significance of 'Fetal Viability,'" *Hastings Center Report* 10, pp. 10–13, 1980; N. K. Rhoden, "Judges in the Delivery Room," *California Law Review* 74, pp. 1951–2030, 1986.

37. *Presley v. Newport Hospital*, 117 R.I. 177, 365 A.2d 748, 1976.

38. *Snyder v. Massachusetts*, 291 U.S. 97, 1934.

39. R. Jurow and R. H. Paul, "Cesarean Delivery for Fetal Distress Without Maternal Consent," *Obstetrics and Gynecology* 63, pp. 596–98, 1984.

40. For more on this general topic, see J. Feinberg, *The Moral Limits of the Criminal Law, Volume One, Harm to Others*, N.Y.: Oxford University Press, 1984.

4

Arguments Against Legally Requiring a Pregnant Woman to Act in the Interests of Her Future Child

The previous chapter argued that there are good reasons for claiming that a pregnant woman has both moral and legal duties to act in the interests of her future child, and it argued further that these obligations fall into two stages. During the first stage, she would be expected to assume only minimal burdens, while during the second stage the burdens may be greater. To understand and assess this proposed hierarchy of obligations more fully, we need to contrast a woman's obligations at three different phases: (1) when she is not pregnant; (2) when she is pregnant but it is not clear that she will carry the pregnancy to term (and she may legally obtain an abortion for any reason); and (3) when it is clear that she will carry the pregnancy to term (i.e., the pregnancy is so advanced that she may legally get an abortion only to save her own life and/or health). The first part of this chapter examines issues peculiar to phases one and two; the second and longer part analyzes more general arguments against permitting state intervention into the lives of pregnant women that take all three phases into account.

ARGUMENTS AGAINST PERMITTING STATE INTERFERENCE WITH A PREGNANT WOMAN DURING THE FIRST STAGE OF PREGNANCY

Let us begin with two simple but troublesome truths. The first is a matter of logic: To hold women to different standards of behavior depending on whether or not they are pregnant requires that the women know that they are pregnant. The second is a matter of fact: Many women are pregnant for months before they are aware of their condition (this is especially true for drug addicts, many of whom have irregular menstrual cycles and/or pay little attention to the timing of their menses).[1] Thus, if we want pregnant women to act in the interests of their future children even during the first few months of gestation, we confront a set of three equally unappealing choices: (1) We require a woman to fulfill an obligation (e.g., reduce alcohol and tobacco intake) she does not know she has (because she does not know she is pregnant); or (2) we require all women (pregnant or not) to uphold standards that are applied to *no* men (that is, we require all women to act as though they were pregnant, in order to ensure compliance during the early months of pregnancy); or (3) we require only those pregnant women who are conscientious enough to seek medical care—and who thus have provided proof of their pregnancies—to abide by these standards, and permit other pregnant women to act however they wish. (Before her condition is apparent to anyone else, a woman who knows she is pregnant yet does not wish to adapt her lifestyle for the sake of her future child could always deny that she was aware of her condition.) Our choices, then, are as follows: We either (1) demand the impossible, (2) discriminate against all women, or (3) provide a strong incentive for women to avoid prenatal care.

In addition, a woman's legal right to seek an abortion at this stage creates a variety of dilemmas. The previous chapter argued that, although a pregnant woman may not have *carte blanche* to behave however she wishes, she may circumvent the imposition of unwanted medical treatments or lifestyle changes by having an abortion (at least during the early stage of pregnancy). This position carries two disquieting ramifications.

First, some women would choose to have abortions simply in order to avoid having to accede to someone else's notion of reasonable due care, and hence the number of abortions may increase. A woman in the grip of an addiction, for instance, may choose to have an abortion rather than enter a treatment program. Anyone who is against abortion in principle would find this prospect alarming; indeed, advocates of a fetus's "right to life" may want to prohibit coercive measures aimed at preventing prenatal harm for fear that more women would choose to have abortions rather than alter their behavior. And it is a problem for state policy as well. It is one thing for the state to allow abortions; it is quite another for the state to adopt policies which are likely to prompt additional abortions.

The other troubling feature of the argument so far is based on exactly the opposite concern. Although women have the legal right to seek an abortion, many are unable to exercise that right. Part of the problem is that abortions cost money, and not all women who wish to have an abortion can afford the procedure. Although some state Medicaid programs pay for abortions, many of them do not, and the U.S. Supreme Court has upheld this denial of benefits.[2] In addition, even before the Supreme Court's decision in *Webster*, and certainly since, physicians have been reluctant to perform abortions after about twenty weeks' gestation (even though no fetus is viable at that point). So those women who fail to realize in time that they are pregnant, and those who realize it but cannot decide how to deal with it in time, may be unable to find a physician willing to perform the procedure. The harsh reality, then, is that many women who desperately want an abortion do not have access to the procedure. Were society to impose upon pregnant women the legal obligation to conform to a standard of due care during all stages of pregnancy, a good number of women would find themselves obligated to accept further burdens on pregnancies they already regard as oppressive but which they are unable to terminate.

These are realistic concerns, and they provide additional reasons for keeping the legal requirements of due care at a minimum and imposing no significant burdens. Indeed, I would argue that the combination of all of these factors outweighs the arguments in favor of recognizing a legal duty on a pregnant woman's part to act in the interests of her child-to-be at this early stage of pregnancy (although her moral duty remains).

GENERAL ARGUMENTS AGAINST PERMITTING STATE INTERVENTION INTO THE LIVES OF PREGNANT WOMEN

Three recent California cases illustrate the concerns of both those who are in favor of and those who oppose state intervention to prevent prenatal harm. In the first two cases, criminal charges were brought against women because they caused prenatal harm to their children; in the third case, the state actively intervened to extend physical confinement of a pregnant woman in order to prevent prenatal harm.

Heroin Addiction

Margaret Reyes was a heroin addict and pregnant with twins when, near term, she was told by a public health nurse that her continued use of heroin and refusal to seek prenatal care would jeopardize the health and perhaps even the life of her children. Ms. Reyes ignored the warning, and her children were born addicted to heroin and suffering from withdrawal symptoms. Ms. Reyes was arrested and charged with felony child endangerment under Section 273a of the California Penal Code. This statute reads, in part,

> Any person who, under circumstances or conditions likely to produce great bodily harm or death, . . . having the care or custody of any child, . . . willfully causes or permits such child to be placed in such situation that its person or health is endangered, is punishable by imprisonment.

There are two ways the statute could have been applied in this case. The first would be to extend it to include the protection of fetuses. That is, one could interpret the reference to "any child" in the statute as pertaining to the unborn as well as the born. The court, however, firmly rejected this interpretation. The statute includes no mention of a fetus, the court noted, and if state legislators had intended this statute to apply to fetuses, they would have said so explicitly. Indeed, the court determined that the fetus is not included in any of California's criminal statutes:

> [A]n unborn child has been held not to be a 'human being' within contemplation of the murder statute . . . or the manslaughter statute . . . an unborn child has been said not to be included in the designation 'minor child' in the failure to provide statute . . . an unborn child has been held not to be a 'person' as that word is used in the Fourteenth Amendment to the United States Constitution . . . the United States Supreme Court has held an unborn child is not a 'dependent child' within the meaning of the Aid to Families with Dependent Children provisions.[3]

Hence the court rejected the contention that the felony child endangerment statute applied to fetuses. Although the court invited lawmakers to amend the statute to include fetuses, state legislators have not done so.

The prosecution also presented an alternative interpretation of the case: This was not a case of harm to two fetuses, but rather the case concerned harm to living children. Although the harmful *acts* were committed before the children were born, the prosecution argued, the *effects* of the acts were not realized until after birth, when the children were separate from their mother and recognized as persons under the law. But the court rejected this interpretation as well, basing its conclusion on the fact that Ms. Reyes did nothing to harm her children after they were born, when the law recognizes them as persons worthy of protection:

> It is not contended that petitioner did anything to endanger the persons or health of the children after their birth, and if petitioner placed the children in such a situation that their persons or health were endangered, she did so when she used heroin and failed to seek prenatal medical care during the last two months of her pregnancy, that is, when the children were yet unborn.[4]

The court concluded therefore that Ms. Reyes's actions while she was pregnant were not proscribed by the child endangerment statute.

This second move by the court is interesting in the light of the treatment of prenatal harm in tort law. Recall that, as explained in Chapter Two, every state recognizes a prenatal negligent act or omission which shows up as injury after birth as a legitimate cause for bringing forward a civil suit. That is, all states recognize claims made for compensation on behalf of children who incurred injuries prenatally and were born alive.

Had this been a civil suit, then, the outcome of the case might have been quite different, for there was no disagreement as to the deleterious effects of Ms. Reyes's actions on her children. However, because this was a criminal case, not a civil one, the court was limited to appealing to relevant state criminal statutes, since fetal endangerment is not a common-law crime in California.

It is not surprising that the court rejected the prosecution's interpretation of this case, since criminal statutes are ordinarily applied strictly in order to respond to the requirements of due process. The question now is: Should the criminal law reflect the same concerns as the tort law? In other words, given that Ms. Reyes's drug use (which harmed her children) would be recognized as actionable in a civil court, should it be made a criminal offense as well?

Negligence

In November 1985, when Pamela Rae Stewart was approximately thirty-three weeks pregnant, she sought medical care for vaginal bleeding. Her physician diagnosed a condition of placenta previa and prescribed a standard course of treatment: She should stay off her feet as much as possible, refrain from sexual intercourse, take regular doses of a certain medication designed to suppress early labor, and seek medical care immediately if she begins to bleed again.

Less than two weeks later, Ms. Stewart gave birth to a severely brain-damaged child who survived for only about five weeks. In September 1986—almost ten months after the infant's death—Ms. Stewart was arrested and charged with fetal abuse.

Exactly what happened prior to the child's birth is a matter of dispute. The prosecution claimed that Ms. Stewart had not taken her medication as instructed, that she had intercourse with her husband against doctor's orders, that the bleeding was a result of having had intercourse, and that she had been bleeding for twelve hours before she reached the hospital. In addition, the prosecution contended, amphetamines were found in the infant's system. The prosecution concluded that these actions caused the death of the child, and decided to bring criminal charges against Ms. Stewart.

Rather than using the child endangerment statute, however, since it had been rejected by the court in the *Reyes* case, the prosecution this time used a different part of the California penal code, Section 270, which reads in part:

> Every parent of any child who willfully omits, without lawful excuse, to perform any duty imposed upon him by law, to furnish necessary food, clothing, shelter, or medical attendance for such child, is guilty of a misdemeanor. . . . A child conceived but not yet born is an existing person so far as this section is concerned.

Ms. Stewart's description of what happened differed considerably from that of the prosecution. Although Ms. Stewart admitted that she had had sexual relations with her husband, and that she had begun to bleed soon afterward, she contended that she had rushed immediately to the hospital. She also claimed that she had continued to take the prescribed medication, and that the drugs in the child's system were antihistamines, not amphetamines. Her main defense, however, was not based on the facts of the case, but on the argument that Penal Code Section 270 was not applicable to her situation.

One of the defense's arguments was that employing Penal Code Section 270 in this manner fatally conflicted with legislative intent.

The purpose of this section of the penal code was to enforce financial obligations, the defense claimed, not to ensure proper medical care or to punish neglectful parents. In addition, the defense argued, since this statute had never before been employed in the manner in which the prosecution now wished to use it, the defendant could not have known that it would be applied to her actions. Ms. Stewart had no warning—nor did anyone else—that the California penal code would be applied to prenatal harms. Thus, the defense concluded, the prosecution was guilty of applying *ex post facto* laws and of violating the defendant's right to due process.

The court agreed with the defense, and ruled that Section 270 "does not impose the duty upon pregnant women to seek prenatal care."[5] The ruling seems based on an appropriate interpretation of this particular statute. The California Supreme Court had ruled earlier that the primary purpose of the statute was to obtain financial support for children, and the statute had been used solely for that purpose since its enactment in 1872.

Our concern, however, is not only with the proper application of a particular statute in a particular case, but also with the more general issue of whether or not prenatal harm is appropriately and justifiably included in the range of criminal statutes and, if so, how such criminal treatment could best be structured to meet fairness standards and also fulfill the purposes of the criminal law. As the judge in the *Stewart* case noted, "It would appear to the court that since the state has an interest in the health of an unborn child [in] the third trimester, the state Legislature could pass a statute protecting the health of an unborn child under narrow conditions."[6] Many bills to that effect have been proposed in California, but none have passed into law.

Inability to Provide Basic Care

Kay Smith was homeless, mentally impaired, and pregnant. She previously had given birth to two children, both of whom had been taken by the state on the ground that she was unable to care for them. She now was institutionalized—she had been certified to be institutionalized for fourteen days—but was due to be released. When the Department of Public Social Services (DPSS) learned that Ms. Smith was going to be released before the birth of her child, it sought a court order to detain her in secure custody. DPSS argued that both Ms. Smith and her future child would be at jeopardy were she released before she gave birth.

The case was heard in juvenile court on May 6, 1980, the day Ms. Smith was due to be released from the mental institution. The court found that the fetus was a "child" under the provisions of the state child welfare code, and ordered that the fetus be kept under detention until its birth; thus Ms. Smith, too, was ordered to be kept institutionalized. She was maintained in the mental ward of a hospital for over six weeks, until she delivered on June 23, 1980.

The case was appealed. Although the California State Court of Appeals dismissed the appeal as moot because Ms. Smith could not be found and because the child had been born, it did rule on the actions of the lower court. Among its most important findings, the Court of Appeals determined that a fetus is not a child within the meaning of the California child welfare statute, and so the order of the juvenile court had no statutory authority.[7]

Discussion

Proponents of state intervention look to cases like these to support their arguments. In the Pamela Rae Stewart case, for example, her physician's list of instructions does not seem unduly burdensome. She was told to take a certain medication for a couple of weeks, refrain from having sexual intercourse, refrain from ingesting illegal drugs, and get as much rest as possible. Advocates of state intervention question which is likely to cause more harm: requiring her by law to follow these instructions or not requiring her to do so. We must weigh the relatively minor inconvenience and discomfort to Ms. Stewart, it is contended, against the death of a child who, had his mother behaved differently, would presumably be alive and healthy today. This is a utilitarian calculation. We weigh the possible harms and benefits, and choose the alternative that would produce the least harm and/or the greatest benefit.

A legitimate goal of state intervention with pregnant women is the prevention of harm to their future children. And the guiding concern behind the intervention is in principle the welfare of these children. But as we shall see from a closer examination of the cases described, efforts to act on these laudable intentions must be scrutinized carefully. State intervention may cause more harm than it prevents; it may discriminate unfairly against pregnant women; and a professed interest in the welfare of children may mask a more controversial attitude toward the place of women in society.

Of those who argue against state intervention to prevent prenatal harm, most hold that no interventions should be allowed. They would probably agree with Martha Field's contention that, "No maternal action, not even drug abuse, should justify pre- or post-birth sanctions for pregnant women's behavior."[8] As with arguments in favor of state intervention to prevent prenatal harms, there are a variety of arguments available against state intervention. We shall analyze four of the strongest: (1) appealing to the rights of pregnant women, (2) employing consequentialist calculations, (3) claiming unfair discrimination against pregnant women, and (4) invoking the problems of drafting and implementing fair, workable laws.

RIGHTS OF PREGNANT WOMEN

The Rights of Liberty and Privacy

Arguments against state interference with the lives of pregnant women in order to prevent prenatal harm are often couched in terms of the women's rights of liberty and/or privacy. Dawn E. Johnsen, for instance, avers that, "The magnitude of the intrusion on women's rights threatened by the current expansion of fetal rights implicates basic constitutional liberty and privacy interests that have been recognized by the Court in *Roe* and in other cases;" while Lawrence J. Nelson and Nancy Milliken state that, "The philosophical question confronting society is whether it wishes to enforce a policy that would entail on an unprecedented scale serious invasions of a woman's privacy, restriction of her civil liberties, and interference with her religious and personal beliefs;" and Janet Gallagher points out that, "Court intervention may mean drastic invasion, not only of women's bodies but of their liberty." [9]

Government invasion of individual liberty and privacy is nothing new, of course, and it occurs every minute of every day in America. We need a license from the state to drive our cars, a blood test before we can get married in many states, and a passport in order to travel abroad. Indeed, a large proportion of state rules infringe in some measure on the liberty and privacy of competent adults. We are not allowed to drive our vehicles faster than the posted speed limit, we are not allowed to walk naked down the corridors of high schools, we are not allowed to withhold intimate details of our financial interactions from the Internal Revenue Service, and our luggage and briefcases and purses are X-rayed by strangers every time we board a commercial aircraft. To claim, then, that state actions to prevent prenatal harm would infringe on the liberty and privacy of pregnant women is not to assert anything very alarming or even surprising.

But this is not the claim. The assertion is, rather, that the sort of state intervention we are considering would interfere *too much* with pregnant women's liberty and privacy, that it would infringe *unfairly* on these important rights. But what does this really mean? How, in other words, do we characterize the rights of liberty and privacy? And which infringements with them would be inappropriate and unfair?

Clearly the rights of liberty and privacy are not without limits. Nor are they distinctly and uncontroversially delineated. The term *privacy*, for instance, does not appear anywhere in the U.S. Constitution or its amendments. And Ronald Dworkin argues persuasively that it is "absurd to suppose that men and women have any general right to liberty at all, at least as liberty has traditionally been conceived by its champions . . . as the absence of constraints placed by a government upon what a man might do if he wants to."[10]

The scope and power of the "rights" of liberty and privacy, in other words, are open to interpretation. One requirement of this interpretation is to distill which aspects of the terms are germane to the debate at hand. Without going into exegetical detail, I will simply assert that the notion of liberty relevant here is the freedom from unwanted touching (or the right to bodily integrity); and the relevant aspect of privacy involves private decision making (or the freedom from unwanted intrusion by the state into one's intimate affairs). These rights can be derived from the Fourth Amendment's prohibition against unreasonable searches and seizures, the Fourteenth Amendment's requirements of due process of law, the Ninth Amendment's recognition that the Constitution does not enumerate all rights "retained by the people," as well as from various aspects of the common law.

The right to bodily integrity is taken very seriously in our society, and as we shall see, it frequently is judged to outweigh important state interests. The Supreme Court has recognized a right to private decision making in a number of cases, employing it as the foundation for ruling against a variety of laws: those forbidding parents to send their children to private schools, laws prohibiting married couples from using contraceptives, laws forbidding interracial marriages, and laws forbidding abortion.[11]

The right of bodily integrity and the right of private decision making meet where medical treatments are involved, as evidenced by the widespread acceptance of the doctrine of informed consent within the medical community. The use of this doctrine in the therapeutic setting gradually emerged from malpractice suits involving nonconsensual touching of a patient's body. In a famous 1914 case, for instance, the New York Supreme Court ruled that, "Every human being of adult years and sound mind has a right to determine what shall be done with his own body; and a surgeon who performs an operation without his patient's consent commits an assault, for which he is liable in damages."[12] Courts have consistently ruled that physicians may not treat competent patients without their consent, irrespective of considerations of the quality of care. And in recent years all medical and research codes of ethics have held that physicians must obtain the informed consent of patients before undertaking invasive therapeutic or research procedures. Even the U.S. Congress has endorsed this position with the Patient Self-Determination Act.[13]

Although the presumption always should be in favor of respecting a person's right of bodily integrity and right of private decision making, it must be remembered that the courts have not regarded these as unqualified rights. Indeed, the U.S. Supreme Court has recognized as legitimate several instances of forced bodily intrusion without consent. The Court has upheld vaccinating and sterilizing people against their wills, for instance, as well as having blood samples taken.[14] Lower courts have even allowed bullets to be removed from suspects in order to obtain evidence in criminal cases.[15] This is not to say, of course, that the right of bodily integrity and the right of private decision making may easily be overridden, or even to suggest that all of these intrusions were justified; rather, the point is that, although these rights are very important indeed, courts have not recognized them as automatically outweighing all other considerations.

In making their determinations, courts generally weigh the individual's interests against the state's interests at stake in the particular case. Included also in the calculation are other relevant factors, such as whether there are less invasive alternatives to the proposed intrusion by which the state could achieve its goals, whether the intrusion will successfully yield the desired results, and whether the intrusion would have a major or minor impact on the individual.

Interestingly, courts generally have ruled that, even if there is no other way to meet the state's goal and the method proposed will be successful, bodily intrusions would not be permitted if they put the individual at substantial risk of harm. In allowing a blood sample to be taken from an individual, for instance, the Supreme Court noted that,

> The integrity of an individual's person is a cherished value of our society. That we today hold that the Constitution does not forbid the State's minor intrusions into an individual's body under stringently limited conditions in no way indicates that it permits more substantial intrusions, or intrusions under other conditions.[16]

In another case, the Supreme Court deemed the forced removal of a bullet from the left side of a felony suspect to be one of these unwarranted intrusions. The Court stated that a crucial factor in its determination was the severity of the proposed medical procedure, which would require the administration of a general anesthetic, and the extent to which the procedure might threaten the health of the individual.[17] And when asked to permit the forcible pumping of a criminal suspect's stomach, the Court responded in horror that the suggestion was "conduct that shocks the conscience."[18]

The courts do not always look to the well-being of the individual, however. Some lower courts have ordered the administration of intrusive measures on one person for the sake of another, including requiring one individual to undergo medical treatment in order to benefit another. These range widely in degree of intrusion, from vaccinations to blood transfusions to cesarean sections to the removal of an internal organ.[19] It would be instructive at this juncture to examine a case of a court-ordered removal of a body organ—a kidney—without the donor's consent.

Court-Ordered Removal of a Body Part

Twenty-eight-year-old Tommy Strunk needed a kidney transplant, and his physicians discovered that the most compatible donor was his brother Jerry, aged twenty-seven. Jerry, however, had an IQ of 35 (a mental age of about six) and was institutionalized. Their parents agreed that Jerry should donate one of his kidneys to his brother, but the case was taken to county court as a precautionary measure. In court, a consulting psychiatrist and a representative of the Department of Mental Health concurred with Mr. and Mrs. Strunk, and so eventually did the judge. The court explained that Jerry was being ordered to donate a kidney because his "well-being would be jeopardized more severely by the loss of his brother than by the removal of a kidney." The circuit court—to which the case was appealed—concurred, and the operations were performed.[20]

A careful reading of the court's opinion reveals that the best interests of the donor were not of primary concern. As one of the judges noted in his dissent,

> The majority opinion is predicated upon the finding of the circuit court that there will be psychological benefits to the ward but points out that the incompetent has the mentality of a six-year-old child. It is common knowledge beyond dispute that the loss of a close relative or a friend to a six-year-old child is not of major impact.[21]

Although the judge's psychological generalization may not be accurate, it does point out that there is a very strong burden of proof to be borne by those who say that the loss of a brother would cause more harm than the risks and pains of major surgery (especially to someone who cannot understand what is happening to him) and the permanent loss of a kidney. And it suggests that the risks to the donor were not given much weight. The court found the risks to Jerry's life of living with only one kidney to be equal to commuting sixteen miles a day by car. But the court did not seem to take seriously the other costs involved: the risks associated with undergoing major surgery and general anesthesia, and the pain involved in recovery. There was another serious risk to Jerry as well: If he lost normal functioning of his remaining kidney, dialysis would not have been available to him, for mentally retarded people in Kentucky were not offered dialysis treatment when this case occurred.[22]

The reason the court gave for permitting the organ transfer from Jerry to Tommy is also notable. The court argued that it was employing the doctrine of substituted judgment, that it was acting as Jerry Strunk would have acted were he competent to choose. As John Robertson explains,

> For over 150 years, the substituted judgment doctrine has regulated the judicial response to claims of needy relatives upon incompetents, and has permitted depletion of incompetent estates with no direct benefit to them solely to help others. The rationale

for this practice—that respect for persons requires courts to follow the putative wishes of the incompetent were he otherwise, even if such a course provides no direct benefit to the incompetent—is *prima facie* relevant in determining whether tissue and organs may be taken from incompetents to benefit close relatives in need. If property can be invaded because of minimal risk to the incompetent's interest, then presumably the body could also be invaded if the risks are commensurate.[23]

But this presumption is unsound. There is no justification for lumping property and body together, and there is no justification for maintaining that if it is legitimate to invade someone's property, it also is legitimate to invade his body.

So another way of understanding this case is that Jerry Strunk was simply used for the sake of his brother. This may have been true in another case as well, in which the court allowed a fourteen-year-old girl with Down's syndrome to donate a kidney to her brother.[24] While these cases provide legal precedents for compelling one family member to undergo extremely invasive medical procedures for the sake of another family member, we should be very cautious about applying them to the question of whether pregnant women should be compelled to undergo treatment for the sake of their future children. In one very significant sense, the kidney donor cases and the forced treatment of pregnant women cases are incommensurate: The donors in the kidney cases were incompetent to decide for themselves, while in the typical case with which we are concerned, the pregnant women are competent to make their own decisions—and this competence stands as a strong reason against asking for the court's intervention (just as incompetence may be a good reason to seek a court ruling).

But this is not the only basis for caution in using the *Strunk* and *Little* cases to justify compelling a pregnant woman to undergo treatment for the sake of her future child. The kidney donor cases raise the very real concern that individuals, including pregnant women, may be used as mere means in order to benefit others. While using one person to benefit another is not uncommon—most of us are regularly used as means to benefit others insofar as we are taxed to pay for social service programs from which we receive no direct assistance—the cases at issue here involve considerably greater intrusion: intrusion into the very bodies of the individuals, not merely their wallets. Many people find this prospect offensive, especially in a country

founded on the right of each individual to "life, liberty, and the pursuit of happiness." As John Fletcher asks, "Could anything be as morally repugnant as physically restraining and tying down a pregnant
woman who refused surgery?"[25]

The case of Robert McFall and David Shimp illustrates this stance
(in contrast to the kidney donor cases). In 1978, thirty-nine-year-old
Robert McFall was diagnosed as having aplastic anemia, a condition
which usually is fatal. McFall's physician predicted that with a bone
marrow transplant, McFall's chances of surviving a year would
increase from 25 percent to between 40 and 60 percent. The doctor
searched for a genetically compatible donor, and eventually came
close to finding one in McFall's cousin, David Shimp. Shimp underwent the first series of tests, in which he was found to have tissue
compatibility with McFall; but then Shimp refused to be tested further for genetic compatibility. So McFall sued Shimp, to try to compel
him to donate some of his bone marrow. The court ruled against
McFall, stating that,

> For a society which respects the rights of *one* individual, to sink
> its teeth into the jugular vein or neck of one of its members and
> suck from it sustenance for *another* member, is revolting to our
> hard-wrought concepts of jurisprudence. Forcible extraction of liv-
> ing body tissue causes revulsion to the judicial mind.[26]

McFall died of intracranial bleeding two weeks later.

Discussion

This section began by asking which infringements on a pregnant
woman's rights of liberty and privacy would be inappropriate and
unfair, and reviewed a series of legal cases as a first step toward an
answer; but there are many other considerations which also must be
taken into account before a conclusion can be drawn. As Chapter
Three demonstrated, for instance, there are good reasons to assert that
a woman does not have *carte blanche* to do whatever she wants while
pregnant and that she may have certain moral and legal obligations
toward her future child, obligations which do not play a part in any
of the legal cases described here. In other words, because the proper
response to the issue at hand—overriding a pregnant woman's prefer-
ences in order to protect the interests of her future child—calls for a
balancing of interests, consequences, rights, and obligations, it is pre-

mature to conclude that a pregnant woman's rights of bodily integrity and private decision making may never be overridden. Yet because these rights are fundamentally important in our society, they may be abridged only in order to uphold something else that is of even greater importance. Thus the•question for us—whether the protection of the interests of a woman's future child is ever reason enough to override her rights of self-determination and privacy—remains open.

CONSEQUENTIALIST ARGUMENTS

It was argued earlier that the state has a legitimate interest in the prevention of prenatal harm, and that this interest may be important enough to outweigh the pregnant woman's right to be left alone. This would be so, of course, only when state intervention could be expected to be successful; that is, only when state intervention would indeed prevent harm to the future child. The previous chapter noted the potential benefits to children of attempts to prevent prenatal harm; but there is also a plethora of potential negative effects on them and on their mothers.

Critics of state intervention claim that, instead of reducing suffering, state intervention in these cases will only increase it. A pregnant woman who fears that her physician will report her to state authorities might be unwilling to divulge the details of her life, for instance, to avoid unwanted limitations on her choices. She may even refrain from seeking medical care altogether.[27] Many of these women have what are considered to be high-risk pregnancies, and they are precisely the women who need medical care the most.

It is conceivable, then, that coercive measures designed to help a child could result instead in discouraging his drug-abusing mother from obtaining prenatal care, or encouraging her to refrain from telling the truth about her condition to the physician. Other negative possibilities abound. Janet Gallagher surmises that, "Coercive measures may lead to concealed pregnancies, nonassisted births, an upsurge in abandonment, and even infanticide."[28] Were this the case, the big losers would be the children. In response to these and other "potentially regrettable consequences of forced medical or surgical procedures," the Committee on Bioethics of the American Academy of Pediatrics recommends that court intervention should be sought only "in rare cases" and "should be seen as a last resort to be undertaken with great caution."[29]

Although opponents of state interference take the possibility of these negative consequences as conclusive, it is important to note that instituting state involvement in prenatal matters may not have these effects. All fifty states require by law that many professionals—pediatricians, emergency room physicians, teachers, social workers—report suspected cases of child abuse to state authorities and thus initiate mechanisms designed to remove children from the custody of their parents, yet the efficacy of these professionals has not been destroyed. However, because there is a real possibility that something could go drastically wrong were pregnant women required by law to behave in certain ways, careful exploration of the social consequences is warranted before action is taken on a public policy level.

Methods of dealing with prenatal damage after it has occurred may also cause more harm than good. Bringing criminal charges against a woman for fetal abuse, for instance, may not have much deterrent effect, for the choices of many pregnant women—such as the three described at the beginning of this chapter—are often not amenable to rational incentives. Criminal sanctions may be counterproductive. The newborn of a woman in jail would be without his mother during crucial bonding stages, and a mother who is imprisoned after the birth of her son because of harm she caused him while pregnant may thereby resent him and may mistreat him should she regain custody.

These consequentialist arguments against incarceration will not appeal to everyone, of course. Someone who believes that punishment is justified because the guilty deserve to be punished (who holds, in other words, a retributivist theory of punishment) would most likely be indifferent to the potential negative effects of punishing a mother for having caused prenatal harm, and would instead argue that, if she wrongfully caused harm, then she should be punished, regardless of the consequences.

There are two telling criticisms of this type of retributivist stance. One could argue that, even though the woman may deserve punishment, it does not follow that she should be punished, since countervailing considerations—such as the disbenefits to her child—may be more important. Thus one may reasonably conclude that it is better not to punish her at all, but to deal with the problem in some other way. Alternatively, one could claim that punishment is never morally good (since it is an infliction of harm), and it is justified only if its "good" consequences (e.g., deterrence of undesirable activity) outweigh its "bad" consequences (e.g., the punished women are harmed and their infants are left without their mothers). I am suggesting here that punishing women for having caused prenatal harm is likely to have more disbenefits than benefits, and therefore is not justified.

It is also important to note that other methods exist for reducing the incidence of prenatal harm, methods which are likely to be more successful than the coercive measures already discussed. Many prenatal injuries are not caused intentionally, but instead are the result of the mother's ignorance about the special circumstances of pregnancy: the nutritional requirements, the effects of certain drugs, the consequences of maternal infections, and so on. Health education, then, is an important element in the prevention of prenatal harm. It should be required of all school children and made available to everyone else, and it should include information about the special needs of pregnant women.

Education will not solve the problem of preventable prenatal harm, of course, for some pregnant women will continue to pay insufficient attention to the welfare of the children they will bear even though they are aware of the consequences of their acts. One likely explanation for this behavior is that the women do not wish to be pregnant. And the proper response to this is obvious: Improve methods of contraception, make them more easily affordable and more widely available, and reduce the barriers to abortion during the first trimester of pregnancy. A consequentialist calculation of the net benefits of these measures in relation to more coercive measures (such as threatening to imprison a mother after the birth of an impaired child) would no doubt rank the former as preferable. Improved social services will reduce the incidence of prenatal harm with few negative repercussions.

The "Slippery Slope" Arguments

A different sort of consequentialist argument is called the "slippery slope" argument. There are two parts to this argument: the *logical* version and the *practical* version.

The logical version of the slippery slope argument says, in effect, that it is not possible to formulate a principle which will permit just the actions we want to permit while also excluding all those we want to exclude. Thus, unless we wish to allow the state to interfere in every aspect of a pregnant woman's life, we must not take the first step—we must not permit any intrusion at all into a pregnant woman's liberty—

for that would also logically commit us to permitting the most severe and most unjust interferences with her liberty as well.

The strength of this argument lies in the accuracy of the statement that there are no good reasons for accepting some intrusions on a pregnant woman's liberty while rejecting others. But is this true? Are there really no rational grounds for distinguishing one type of state interference from another in these cases? The answer lies in an examination of a set of related factors which must be considered before the conclusion can be drawn that any intervention is truly justified. These include two types of requirements: (1) due process of law and (2) proportionality (which weighs the nature and extent of the harm to be prevented, the probability that it will occur, the probability that it can be avoided, and the degree of the intrusion).

Limits have been set in other types of cases. The Supreme Court makes a distinction, for instance, between the minor invasion of taking a blood sample from a suspect and the major invasion of pumping his stomach, and legislators of every state in the nation believe that a line can be drawn between the legitimate exercise of parental discretion and the illegitimate infliction of child abuse. The previous chapter argued that rational limits can be set in pregnancy cases as well, but no doubt these limits would not satisfy those who oppose all state interventions into the activities of pregnant women.

The other version of the slippery slope argument—which is characterized as the practical version—is based on predictions of outcomes, not logic. The basic contention of this argument is that once we allow any intrusion at all into the lives of pregnant women, even intrusions of the most minor sort, then more morally questionable intrusions will in fact follow; we will continue to change and loosen our principles as we become psychologically accustomed to what previously seemed extraordinary and unacceptable. First a pregnant woman might be forbidden to take certain illegal drugs known to cause fetal damage, then she might be forbidden to use other, otherwise legal, teratogenic substances such as alcohol and tobacco. Then the state might require her to take certain vitamins and eat certain foods because the importance of maternal nutrition during pregnancy is well-known. Eventually the state would prohibit her from taking some over-the-counter drugs (such as cough medicines and antacids), require her to get a certain number of hours of bed rest, monitor her sexual activity, and so on. Indeed, the argument goes, potentially almost everything a pregnant woman does will be open to state control (since almost everything a pregnant woman does may cause prenatal harm).

How could conformity to these strictures be ensured? George Annas suggests that, "Effectively monitoring compliance would require confining pregnant women to an environment in which eating, exercise, drug use, and sexual intercourse could be controlled. This could, of course, be a maximum security country club."[30] After all, could we trust a pregnant woman who is addicted to nicotine to cease smoking simply because a judge ordered her to do so? And would not a drug addict be more likely to hide than to submit to weekly urine tests? The only way we can be certain that pregnant women are not doing anything that will harm their future children is to monitor their every activity.

But, as Annas points out, "such massive invasions of privacy can only be justified by treating pregnant women during their pregnancy as nonpersons."[31] This is not paranoia speaking. The history of women is fraught with domination and subjugation and denial of basic rights. In the past, women in this country could not hold public office, serve on juries, or bring suit in their own names; women could not practice law, or bartend, or work extended hours; women could not even vote. All of these restrictions have since been lifted in the United States, but the worry remains that the attitude behind them—which views men and women as fundamentally dissimilar, with distinct social roles to play—still persists.

The view that men and women are intrinsically different is an old and familiar one. And the implications drawn from it—that men belong in the public world of work while women belong in the home caring for their families—is one many people find appealing. But while this view of the distinctive spheres of men and women reflects a very common world view, it is not a world view that is universally accepted or appreciated. And it is certainly not a world view that should be imposed on those who do not share it, at least in our pluralistic society, where many people believe that, with regard to social roles, there are no significant differences between men and women. It would be unfair, then, to impose a set of values on people who do not share them, to treat all women as though their primary function were to propagate the species and thereby to deny them access to alternative lifestyles.

THE CLAIM OF UNFAIR DISCRIMINATION

This brings us to a related concern: that laws requiring pregnant women to behave in certain ways are unfairly discriminatory. The protest here is that requiring a pregnant woman to act on behalf of her future child imposes restraints on her freedom that are materially different from other socially accepted limitations on people's activities, and even materially different from other accepted limitations on her own activities when she is not pregnant.

One basic contention is that it is unjust to demand things of pregnant women that are demanded of no one else in society. No man, for instance, is required to undergo any kind of bodily invasion at all for the sake of someone else. The advent of organ and tissue transplantation techniques highlights this situation: No competent adult is legally required to give a kidney or bone marrow or blood to any other person, be it stranger or close family member, even if denial of help means the death of that individual.[32]

A person may even refuse to donate a life-saving organ after death. Dead bodies are not considered legitimate sources of transplantable organs if the deceased had refused while alive to be a donor or if the family of the deceased declines to allow the organs to be removed. Although we may question the validity of this rule, it is unlikely that it will be altered in the near future. The argument for it—and it is one that has found strong political support—is based on the importance of individual liberty. People should be free to refuse to donate their organs after death and free to refuse to donate the organs of a deceased relative.

One result of this policy is a severe shortage of transplantable organs in this country. It has been estimated that at any one time approximately 24,000 people are waiting for a donor organ to become available.[33] Many of these people will never receive the organs upon which their lives depend; in 1990, for instance, 2,206 people died while waiting for a transplant.[34] If cadavers are not routinely used to benefit others, and people die as a result, then pregnant women should not be used to benefit others either. Indeed, there is "no good reason why pregnant women should be treated with less respect than corpses."[35]

The argument grounded on the claim of unfair discrimination, then, is straightforward: If no individual, alive or dead, need undergo any sort of bodily intrusion against his or her will for the sake of another person, including a relative, then it is unjust to insist that a pregnant woman undertake a comparable form of medical treatment against her will for the sake of another person, including a future person.[36]

The claim of unfair discrimination against pregnant women is strengthened by the fact that men also cause prenatal harm through their lifestyle choices. A father's excessive use of alcohol, for instance, may deleteriously affect his offspring's IQ and may impair the fetus's ability to gain weight.[37] A variety of prenatal harms—low birth-weight, cleft palate and cleft lip, even some cancers—have been linked to nicotine use by fathers.[38] And there is evidence that cocaine can bind to human spermatozoa, which can transport it to the egg and so create problems in the resulting embryo.[39] Even a father's workplace may be hazardous to his child's health.[40]

Given that a man's lifestyle may have disastrous consequences for his offspring, it is clearly unfair to pass laws constraining the choices of mothers while allowing fathers to behave as they wish. Men should be held accountable as well.[41] Thus the state has two alternatives. It may either (1) place a burden of restraint on all sexually active heterosexuals who do not use birth control or (2) allow women to make the same imprudent choices as men. In either case, it is essential to educate everyone about the dangers of their lifestyle choices to their children.

DIFFICULTY OF DRAFTING AND IMPLEMENTING LEGISLATION

Legitimate state intervention into the lives of pregnant women presupposes that the women have been put on notice that society expects them to meet a reasonable standard of due care and will not tolerate certain activities. One effective way to do this is through legislation. Certain behaviors of pregnant women could be legally proscribed through a body of "crimes against the fetus" statutes.[42] Indeed, such laws are necessary if criminal penalties are to be imposed, since crimes in this country are set by statute, not through the common law (as are torts).

Statutorily prohibiting prenatal harm in general would not work, in part because some prenatal harm simply cannot be avoided. The air in most large cities in the United States is so polluted, for example, that the carbon monoxide a pregnant woman inhales is tantamount to her smoking a pack of cigarettes a day.[43] In addition, there are certain deleterious conditions for which no medical treatment exists, or that cannot be detected in time to permit intervention. The law, then, should speak only to that set of prenatal harm that can be prevented. Ideally, the law would include all and only those whose behavior we wish to change and exclude those whom we believe it is improper to coerce.

As a point of departure, consider the actions of Pamela Rae Stewart, as described by the prosecutor:

> Defendant's concealed argument is that a mother, with impunity, may ignore the warnings of her doctor despite the knowledge that she is experiencing a problem pregnancy. She may ply her body with dangerous, illegal and harmful drugs with no thought to its effect on the helpless human being growing in her womb. She may subject herself to the rigors of sexual intercourse without concern for the effect on the baby. And even though specifically warned, she may lay bleeding for hours without seeking available medical attention as her baby is deprived of its only source of nourishment. Such extreme disregard for any other human life, not to mention one whose only chance of survival depends upon the mother who carries him, approaches the level of maliciousness and conscious disregard for human life, which would properly support a second-degree murder conviction, not to mention one for a violation of Penal Code section 270.[44]

Let us assume for the sake of argument that the prosecutor has accurately described the facts. What precisely did Ms. Stewart do that was so terribly wrong? She stopped taking her prescribed medication, she had intercourse with her husband, she took some sort of drug (the prosecutor claims amphetamines, Ms. Stewart claims antihistamines), and she postponed seeking medical care. Except for taking amphetamines (which she denies), Ms. Stewart's actions were not especially troublesome, yet the combination of factors resulted in the birth of a severely brain-damaged child who died in infancy.

Could we devise a law (or set of laws) that would speak to analogous cases yet exclude women who have good reasons to engage in similar activities? Surely we do not want to prohibit by statute sexual relations between consenting adults (especially married couples); nor can we reasonably put limits on how much time may lapse between the realization that medical care may be needed and the seeking of such care. There are, after all, a large number of quite acceptable reasons for postponing medical care, one of which is the sensible judgment that whatever is wrong is not wrong enough to warrant the bother and expense of professional treatment.

So the proposal for dealing with cases such as Ms. Stewart's through a set of laws dealing with particular activities—sexual relations between consenting adults, judgments about the need for medical care, and so on—is untenable. Such laws would intrude too much on the privacy and autonomy of all of us. Instead, it might make sense to address these cases in light of her one overarching failure: She failed to follow her physician's instructions. The proposal, then, is to require pregnant women to conform to their physicians' recommendations.

But would we really want to make criminal all failures to follow a physician's advice? After all, physicians are not invariably correct. In the past, they routinely prescribed X-rays and diuretics for pregnant women, for instance, practices that are discouraged today. And medical interventions accepted today are fraught with uncertainties as well, as the American College of Obstetrics and Gynecologists points out:

> Medical knowledge and judgment have limitations and fallibility, which the obstetrician must recognize when assigning clinical risks and benefits in order to advise patients. Methods for detecting fetal distress or deterioration are not always reliable indicators of poor outcome; therefore, assigning a degree of risk to the fetus is difficult. In addition, expected benefits for the fetus cannot always be achieved.[45]

The prevalence of uncertainties in medicine stands as a strong disincentive for requiring by law that a pregnant woman follow her physician's advice.

Perhaps, though, it should be illegal for a pregnant woman to ignore a physician's recommendation when doing so causes prenatal harm. The woman, in other words, could be punished after the fact. But even when a physician's diagnosis is accurate and his or her recommended treatment course is the standard one, a policy of punishing a woman for having failed to conform has serious problems. The first is that, unless medical care is provided free-of-charge, we must expect that there will be legitimate financial reasons for not following some physicians' instructions. We could hardly fault a pregnant woman for not purchasing a prescription drug she believed she could not afford, or for not quitting the job she needs to support her family in order to obtain the recommended number of hours of bed rest. In addition, if we permit physicians to make decisions for pregnant women, we give them unprecedented power over one group of people, power that they do not have over any other. Physicians have the legal and moral duty to obtain the informed consent of all competent patients, including pregnant women. To make an exception to the informed consent rule in the case of pregnant women would be to discriminate unfairly against them.

The type of law we have been considering is too dangerously vague to be taken seriously. It would also probably be unconstitutional. As the Supreme Court has noted, "A vague law impermissibly delegates basic policy matters to policemen, judges and juries for resolution on an *ad hoc* and subjective basis with discriminatory application."[46] The worry that such laws would be open to discriminatory implementation and abuse is not an idle one. The case of Kay Smith, described at the beginning of this chapter, is instructive. First, her rights of due process were violated when her case was heard in a juvenile court—which is not constituted to handle cases of the mental competence of adults—and so she was not judged according to the specific statutes which determine the state's right to restrict her liberty due to her mental illness. Second, although lawyers for the state argued in court that Ms. Smith's pregnancy was very near term and that her detention would therefore last approximately only a fortnight, she in fact remained institutionalized for more than six weeks. One has to wonder if the stage of her pregnancy was misrepresented so that the state's proposal would appear less onerous to her.

I am not arguing that Ms. Smith should have been released before the birth of her child. A homeless, mentally impaired, near-term pregnant woman who cannot care for herself should be a legitimate exception to a rule forbidding state intervention. The point is, rather, that the procedure for deciding her fate was seriously flawed, and so her rights of due process were violated. Even though the presence of due process very likely would have produced the identical outcome in Ms. Smith's case, the state should have adhered to the requirements of due process, under the theory that following the correct procedure will produce the desired (i.e., fair) outcome considerably more often than will ignoring the requirements of due process.

Another important concern is relevant here: It is probably not coincidental that all three of the cases described at the beginning of this chapter involved women who were poor. Most of the pregnant women who have been subject to state intervention have been indigent or disadvantaged in some way. A national study conducted in 1987 showed that, of the twenty-one cases in which court orders were sought to intervene in the decisions of pregnant women, all of them involved women who were receiving public assistance or who were treated in a teaching-hospital clinic. In addition, 81 percent of the women were minorities (African, Asian, or Hispanic), and 24 percent spoke English as a second language.[47]

Another study—this one conducted on women who enrolled for prenatal care in one Florida county in 1989—raises the question of discriminatory implementation of the law even more pointedly. The researchers concluded that, although white women are just as likely to use drugs and alcohol during pregnancy as black women, blacks are much more likely to be reported to state authorities for drug use than whites:

> The proportion of white women reported for any drug use (48 of 4290 who delivered live-born infants) was 1.1 percent, whereas the proportion of black women reported for any drug use (85 of 793) was 10.7 percent. Thus, a black woman was 9.6 times more likely than a white woman to be reported for substance abuse during pregnancy. The difference was evident despite the fact that in the population we surveyed the frequency of positive results on toxicologic testing of urine samples obtained at the first prenatal visit was similar for white women (15.4 percent) and black women (14.1 percent).[48]

The authors of the study were unable to explain their results, but unfair discrimination would not be a bad guess.

One alternative to instituting vague laws that are open to discriminatory implementation and abuse is to spell out precisely what activities are prohibited and/or required. To accomplish this, however, we must abandon the goal of developing laws which would include a wide variety of prenatal harm—since, as already pointed out, the state's power to interfere with individuals' lives would be too great—and instead adopt the less onerous task of developing laws that cover a few specific forms of prenatal harm. The case of Margaret Reyes is relevant here. Ms. Reyes ingested heroin during her pregnancy, and her twin children were born with heroin addictions. Since heroin is already considered to be an illegal substance, and since ingesting an illegal substance while pregnant is a straightforward action easy to describe, designing a statute prohibiting it seems relatively unproblematic.

The trouble with this proposal, however, is that we again run the risk of being arbitrary. Only those activities which we are able to describe satisfactorily in a statute will be prohibited or required, while equally harmful behavior goes unchallenged simply because it cannot be codified adequately.

Finally, before we decide to invoke the criminal law as a social response to prenatal harm—before we decide to create a new class of criminal—we should be certain that there is a strong preponderance of reasons in favor of doing so, for to be given a criminal status in our society is to be given a condemnation; indeed, we often refer to it as being "branded" a criminal. Joel Feinberg calls this the "expressive function [of punishment]: punishment is a conventional device for the expression of attitudes of resentment and indignation, and of judgments of disapproval and reprobation."[49] This chapter has argued that there is no such preponderance of reasons in favor of criminal legislation; indeed, this chapter has argued that the balance falls against regarding pregnant women as potential criminals. But even if the arguments fail to persuade that the balance of reasons lies against criminalizing certain activities of pregnant women, at least it should go far in showing that a clear preponderance of reasons in support of criminal legislation does not exist.

CONCLUSION

This chapter has argued that there are compelling reasons against allowing the state to intervene with the activities of pregnant women even when it is clear that their children will be carried to term. The state should not monitor a pregnant woman's activities in order to prevent harm to or promote the well-being of her future child, nor should it criminalize certain activities of pregnant women because they cause prenatal harms.[50] These conclusions are based on a variety of arguments: (1) A woman's fundamental rights of bodily integrity and private decision making should not be subordinated to the welfare of someone else; (2) requiring pregnant women to behave in certain ways will have seriously negative consequences: pregnant women will be unwilling to be candid with their physicians or they will not seek prenatal care at all, the number of abortions will increase, or grave hardships will be imposed on already burdened pregnant women; (3) a few reasonable limitations on the activities of pregnant women will lead inevitably to many unjust and onerous limitations (the "slippery slope" arguments); (4) it is not fair to demand things of pregnant women that are demanded of no one else in society, so requiring pregnant women to behave in certain ways or risk legal penalties is unfairly discriminatory; and (5) the obstacles to drafting and implementing fair, workable laws seem insurmountable.

Of course, not all of the arguments presented here are compelling. One could argue, for instance, that it is not impossible to draft responsible laws which would make at least some of a pregnant woman's obligations to her future child clear and not unduly burdensome. After all, other laws considered by many people to be necessary—including child abuse and neglect laws—require equal subtlety and raise similar concerns. And the fact that all prenatal harm cannot be prevented is not reason enough to forgo preventing any of it.

In addition, we should be cautious about concluding that laws limiting the liberty of pregnant women are bound to be abused. It is not clear that imposing some minimal legal requirements of due care on pregnant women would inevitably lead to the imposition of unfair burdens. Chapter Three argued for the opposite position, that a legal duty of due care on the part of a pregnant woman with regard to the child she will bear should be recognized and that this duty—which is based on a standard of reasonableness—would not be unduly onerous. Indeed, while "slippery slope" arguments should be taken seriously, since the potential for abuse in these cases is real, they should not be taken too seriously. It is possible to conjure up potentially terrible consequences for every public policy initiative, even the most benign.

So some of the arguments in this chapter are stronger and more reliable than others. An important question at this juncture is whether any combination of them is strong enough to justify the position that state interference into the activities of pregnant women is always wrong (because such interference would violate important rights of pregnant women), unfair (because the rules cannot be enforced impartially), or useless (because more harm than good would be produced in the process). Should this be the case, it would be reasonable to

advocate as a public policy position that the state may never intervene into the lives of pregnant women in order to prevent prenatal
harm.

The arguments in this chapter, however, may not have shown
that all types of state intervention to prevent prenatal harm are
improper, but only that many of them are. Indeed, I believe that this
chapter has presented a strong array of reasons to conclude that, even
though a pregnant woman has moral obligations to act in the interests
of her future child throughout her pregnancy, there are compelling
reasons against legally requiring her to meet certain standards of due
care before it is uncontroversially clear that she intends to bring the
pregnancy to term. This conclusion has far-reaching implications for
state intervention. The state would not be justified in acting to prevent some very serious prenatal harm during the early stage of a
woman's pregnancy.

The issue now, then, is the strength of the arguments against state
intervention during the later stage of pregnancy (the stage at which
her moral duties are most strong because she clearly will be carrying
the pregnancy to term). Perhaps some state interventions to prevent
prenatal harm at this stage are warranted. It is the object of the following two chapters to synthesize the arguments presented so far and to
relate them to concrete cases.

NOTES

1. I. J. Chasnoff, "Perinatal Effects of Cocaine," *Contemporary Obstetrics
and Gynecology*, 29, pp. 163–79, 1987.

2. The U.S. Supreme Court has ruled that individual states may limit
state Medicaid funding to medically necessary abortions [*Maher v. Roe*, 432
U.S. 464, 1977] or to abortions necessary to save the mother's life [*Williams v.
Zbaraz*, 448 U.S. 358, 1980]; states are not required to make public hospitals
available for elective abortions and may bar public employees from participat-
ing in elective abortions [*Webster v. Reproductive Health Services* 492 U.S. 490,
1989]; and Congress may ban the use of federal Medicaid funds for abortions
except when necessary to save the mother's life [*Harris v. McRae*, 448 U.S. 297,
1980].

3. *Reyes v. Superior Court of the State of California*, 141 Cal. Rptr. 912, 1977.

4. *Reyes v. Superior Court of the State of California, op. cit.* p. 913.

5. M. Himaka, "Judge Drops Prenatal Care Case Against Mother," *The
San Diego Union*, 1987, p. A1.

6. Himaka, *op cit.*

7. *In re Steven S.*, 126 Cal.App.3d 23, 178 Cal. Rptr. 525, 1981.

8. M. A. Field, "Controlling the Woman to Protect the Fetus," *Law, Medicine, and Health Care* 17, pp. 114–29, 1989.

9. J. Gallagher, "Position Paper: Fetus as Patient," in S. Cohen and N. Taub (eds.), *Reproductive Laws for the 1990s*, p. 187; D. Johnsen, "The Creation of Fetal Rights: Conflicts with Women's Constitutional Rights to Liberty, Privacy, and Equal Protection," *Yale Law Journal* 95, 599–625, p. 614, 1987; L. J. Nelson and N. Milliken, "Compelled Medical Treatment of Pregnant Women: Life, Liberty and Law in Conflict," *Journal of the American Medical Association* 259, 1060–66, p. 1065, 1988.

10. R. Dworkin, *Taking Rights Seriously*, Cambridge, MA: Harvard University Press, 1977, and "We Do Not Have a Right to Liberty," in R. Cunningham (ed.), *Liberty and the Rule of Law*, College Station: Texas A & M University Press, 1979.

11. *Pierce v. Society of Sisters*, 268 U.S. 510, 1925; *Griswold v. Connecticut*, 381 U.S. 479, 1965; *Loving v. Virginia*, 388 U.S. 1, 1967; *Roe v. Wade*, 410 U.S. 113, 1973.

12. *Schloendorff v. Society of N.Y. Hospitals*, 211 N.Y. 125, 105 N.E. 92, 1914. In a more recent case, a Kansas court stated that, "Anglo-American law starts with the premise of thoroughgoing self-determination. It follows that each man is considered to be master of his own body, and he may, if he be of sound mind, expressly prohibit the performance of lifesaving surgery, or other medical treatment." *Natanson v. Kline*, 186 Kan. 393, 350 P.2d 670, 1960.

13. The Patient Self-Determination Act was signed into law as part of the Omnibus Budget Reconciliation Act of 1990 and went into effect November 1991.

14. *Breithaupt v. Abram*, 352 U.S. 432, 1957; *Buck v. Bell*, 274 U.S. 200, 1927; *Jacobson v. Massachusetts*, 197 U.S. 11, 1905; *Schmerber v. California*, 384 U.S. 757, 1966.

15. *Bowden v. State*, 256 Ark. 820, 510 S.W.2d 879, 1974; *State v. Allen*, 291 S.E.2d 459, 1982; *State v. Richards*, 585 S.W.2d 505, 1979; *U.S. v. Crowder*, 543 F.2d 312, 1972.

16. *Schmerber v. California*, 384 U.S. 757, 1966, p. 772.

17. *Winston v. Lee*, 470 U.S. 753, 1985.

18. *Rochin v. California*, 342 U.S. 165, 1952.

19. *Application of the President and Directors of Georgetown College, Inc.* 7331 F.2d 1000 (D.C. Cir.), *cort denied* 337 U.S. 978, 1964, *Jefferson v. Griffin Spalding County Hospital Authority* 247 Ga. 86, 274 S.E. 2d 457, 1981, *Little v. Little*, *Raleigh Fitkin-Paul Morgan Memorial Hospital v. Anderson* 42 N.J. 421, 201 A.2d 537 (per curiam), *cert denied* 377 U.S. 985, 1964.

20. *Strunk v. Strunk*, 445 S.E.2d 145, 35 A.L.R.3d 683, 1969.

21. *Strunk v. Strunk, op cit.* p. 150.

22. Dialysis machines—artificial kidneys—were very strictly rationed in the days before Medicare assumed responsibility for the cost of that treatment. For more on this case, see W. Cook, "Incompetent Donors: Was the First Step or the Last Taken in Strunk v. Strunk?" *California Law Review* 58, pp. 754–74, 1970.

23. J. A. Robertson, "Organ Donations by Incompetents and the Substituted Judgment Doctrine," *Columbia Law Review* 76, pp. 48–78, 1976.

24. *Little v. Little*, 576 S.E.2d 493, 1979.

25. J. Fletcher, "Drawing Moral Lines in Fetal Therapy," *Clinical Obstetrics and Gynecology* 29, pp. 595–602, 1986.

26. *McFall v. Shimp*, No. 78–17711 In Equity (C.P. Allegheny County, PA), 1978, p. 92.

27. There is some evidence that this is the case. See M. L. Poland et al., "Punishing Pregnant Drug Users: Enhancing the Flight from Care," *Drug and Alcohol Dependence* 31, pp. 199–203, 1993; Rubenstein, *Yale Law and Policy Review* 1991.

28. J. Gallagher, "Position Paper: Fetus as Patient," *op cit.*, p. 214.

29. American Academy of Pediatrics, Committee on Bioethics, "Fetal Therapy: Ethical Considerations," *Pediatrics* 81, pp. 898–99, 1988.

30. G. J. Annas, "Pregnant Women as Fetal Containers," *Hastings Center Report*, 16, pp. 13–14, 1986.

31. Ibid.

32. In the cases previously mentioned, where a kidney was taken from one family member (without his consent) to give to another, the donors were incompetent to decide for themselves.

33. Aaron Spital, "The Shortage of Organs for Transplantation," *New England Journal of Medicine* 325, pp. 1243–46, 1991.

34. Glenn Ruffenach, "Trying to Cure Shortage of Organ Donors," *Wall Street Journal* 3/13/91, p. B1.

35. L. J. Nelson and N. Milliken, "Compelled Medical Treatment of Pregnant Women: Life, Liberty and Law in Conflict," p. 1065.

36. Several types of bodily invasion required by the state against the will of the individual were mentioned. The issue, though, is not what has been done, but what should be done. Chapter Five will explore the matter further.

37. R. E. Little and C. F. Sing, "Father's Drinking and Infant Birth Weight: Report of an Association," *Teratology* 36, pp. 59–65, 1987; C. Ervin et al., "Alcoholic Fathering and Its Relation to Child's Intellectual Development," *Alcoholism: Clinical and Experimental Research* 8, pp. 362–65, 1984.

38. E. M. John et al., "Prenatal Exposure to Parents: Smoking and Childhood Cancer," *American Journal of Epidemiology* 133, pp. 123–32, 1991.

39. R. A. Yazigi et al., "Demonstration of Specific Binding of Cocaine to Human Spermatozoa," *Journal of the American Medical Association* 266, pp. 1956–59, 1991.

40. J. R. Wilkins and R. A. Koutras, "Paternal Occupation and Brain Cancer in Offspring," *American Journal of Industrial Medicine* 14, pp. 299–318, 1988; D. A. Savitz et al., "Effects of Parents' Occupational Exposures on Risk of Stillbirth, Preterm Delivery, and Small-for-Gestational-Age Infants," *American Journal of Epidemiology* 129, pp. 1201–18, 1989.

41. Joseph Losco and Mark Shublak argue that males may even face a greater legal liability for causing prenatal harm than females because, while a pregnant woman can get an abortion, there is no similar "late stage remedy available to males to render them blameless." J. Losco and M. Shublak, "Paternal–Fetal Conflict," *Politics and the Life Sciences* 13, pp. 63–75, 1994.

42. "Comment: Criminal Liability of a Prospective Mother for Prenatal Neglect of a Viable Fetus." *Whittier Law Review* 9, pp. 363–96, 1987; J. Parness, "Crimes Against the Unborn," *Harvard Journal on Legislation* 22, pp. 97–172, 1985.

43. L. M. Longo, "Environmental Pollution and Pregnancy," *American Journal of Obstetrics and Gynecology* 137, p. 162, 1980.

44. E. L. Miller, Jr. and R. C. Phillips, "Points and Authorities in Opposition to Defendant's Demurrer and Motion to Dismiss," *People v. Stewart*, No. M508197 (San Diego Municipal Court) 1987.

45. American College of Obstetricians and Gynecologists Committee on Ethics, "Statement of the Committee on Ethics," Washington, D.C.: American College of Obstetricians and Gynecologists, 1987.

46. (*Grayned v. City of Rockford*, 408 U.S. 104, 1971, p. 109)

47. V. E. B. Kolder et al., "Court-Ordered Obstetrical Interventions," *The New England Journal of Medicine* 316, 1192–96, 1987.

48. I. J. Chasnoff et al., "The Prevalence of Illicit-drug or Alcohol Use During Pregnancy and Discrepancies in Mandatory Reporting in Pinellas County, Florida," *New England Journal of Medicine* 322, pp. 1202–06, 1990.

49. J. Feinberg, "The Expressive Function of Punishment," in his *Doing and Deserving*, Princeton: Princeton University Press, p. 98, 1970.

50. This conclusion is advocated by a number of commentators, e.g., J. C. Merrick, "Maternal Substance Abuse During Pregnancy," *Journal of Legal Medicine* 14, pp. 57–71, 1993; L. Rubenstein, "Prosecuting Maternal Substance Abusers," *Yale Law and Policy Review* 9, pp. 130–60, 1991; B. L. Becker, "Order in the Court," *Hastings Constitutional Law Quarterly* 19, pp. 235–59, 1991; B. Steinbock, *Life Before Birth*, N.Y.: Oxford University Press, 1992; N. K. Schiff, "Legislation Punishing Drug Use During Pregnancy," *Hastings Constitutional Law Quarterly* 19, pp. 197–234, 1991; M. A. Field, "Controlling the Woman to Protect the Fetus," *Law, Medicine and Health Care* 17, pp. 114–29, 1989; G. J. Annas, "Pregnant Women as Fetal Containers," *Hastings Center Report*, 16, pp. 13–14, 1986; D. Johnsen, "Promoting Healthy Births Without Sacrificing Women's Liberty," *Hastings Law Journal* 43, pp. 569–614, 1992.

5

Practical Applications: Intervening During Pregnancy

In order to prevent serious prenatal harm, the state could employ any number of interventions into the lives of pregnant women. The previous chapters have explored many of these in an abstract way, concentrating on general moral and legal principles and public policy concerns. This chapter, however, will delve into the practical implications of the arguments presented so far and will analyze some concrete cases. Because all of the options for interfering with a woman's liberty in order to prevent prenatal harm cannot be explored here—these are too numerous and diverse to permit comprehensive consideration—a sampling of cases will be analyzed.

There are four stages during which the state can act to prevent prenatal harm: during pregnancy, during delivery, before conception, and after birth. This chapter explores some options available to the state during a woman's pregnancy and delivery. The next chapter will examine interventions to prevent prenatal harm before a woman even becomes pregnant and after she gives birth.

MANDATING MEDICAL TREATMENT

The cesarean section is a surgical technique that is widely available and generally accepted as warranted in a variety of circumstances.[1] The issue here is not, however, whether the procedure should ever be recommended but rather: should it ever be required? That is, would a court of law be justified in compelling a pregnant woman to undergo a cesarean section against her will?

Chapter Three contended that a pregnant woman has moral obligations to accept certain burdens in order to prevent and/or avoid causing serious prenatal harm, and that there are sound reasons for holding that some of these moral obligations should be legal obligations as well. But these obligations are not without limits. Mandating

the administration of surgical intervention would be justified only if
the following conditions are met:

(1) The woman is in the final stage of pregnancy (and so her
    duty of care is at its most stringent);

(2) The harm to the child is a harm of great magnitude to a very
    important interest (i.e., it is either life-threatening or would
    result in a life of grave affliction);

(3) The probability that the harm will occur without the interven-
    tion is very high, as is the level of certainty of the diagnosis;

(4) A very high probability exists that the intervention will pre-
    vent the harm (i.e., there is a very good chance that the fetus
    will survive the operation and that the operation will be a suc-
    cess);

(5) The risks that the intervention will harm the woman are rela-
    tively minor;

(6) All requirements of due process are met.

On the other hand, Chapter Four offered a variety of arguments
against adopting any policies that require pregnant women to act in
the interests of their future children. Of these, one of the strongest
asserts that coercing a pregnant woman to accept medical treatment
against her will would be discriminatory insofar as such concessions
are not required of other people, including the parents of ailing (born)
children. Yet since parents are generally expected to provide some
types of medical care for their children—and since the only way some
serious types of prenatal harm can be treated is to invade the body of
a pregnant woman—this issue requires further discussion. In addition, because this book is concerned not only with describing what is
now the case but also with examining what should be the case, a reas-
sessment of parental duties seems in order.

Requiring a Pregnant Woman to Undergo a Cesarean Section

A cesarean section in the case of acute fetal distress could fit most of
the conditions listed here, but not all of them. The level of risk to the

mother involved in a cesarean section, for instance, is far from minor. In fact, the costs to her of undergoing a cesarean section against her will are substantial. She faces an increased risk of infection and even death (maternal mortality is two to four times higher with a cesarean section and morbidity is five to ten times higher),[2] significant discomforts of recovering from major surgery, and the negative psychological repercussions of having her judgment overruled and her body invaded against her will. The question for us is whether these costs are great enough to preclude ever requiring her to undergo the procedure.

The answer to this depends in large part on what costs we may reasonably expect parents in general to bear in order to protect their children from harm (recall that at this stage of pregnancy, a woman's duties to her future child approach the stringency of any parent's to his or her [born] child). It was mentioned earlier that a parent should act within a reasonable range of meeting a child's basic needs. But would this range also include undergoing surgery for the sake of the child? We need to compare the costs parents in general should bear with the costs to a pregnant woman of undergoing a cesarean section against her will, to ascertain that we would not be requiring pregnant women to accept significantly greater burdens than anyone else; to do otherwise would be to discriminate unfairly against pregnant women.

At present, the law does not require parents to undergo bodily invasions for the sake of their children. But looking to the state of the law will not be of much help. Not only is there no consensus about the proper scope of parental authority—and past reliance on parental authority seems to be waning as children's rights are taken more seriously—but the law itself is properly open to moral criticism. In order to clarify our thinking, then, let us consider two hypothetical cases (the details of which have been designed to correspond as closely as possible to the case of a pregnant woman who refuses a cesarean section):

> Ten-year-old Alex is dying of leukemia, and a transfusion of bone marrow offers his only chance for survival. The one compatible donor the medical team has been able to locate is the boy's mother, but she refuses to undergo the series of 150 punctures of the pelvic bone (performed under general anesthesia) needed to acquire the necessary quart of marrow. The donor faces a very small risk of death from the administration of anesthesia, and

considerable pain—as well as a small risk of infection—from the punctures. Her bone marrow would regenerate.

One-year-old Susan suffers from advanced liver disease, and she cannot survive without a liver transplant. Since approximately 50 percent of infants like Susan die before a donor organ becomes available, her physicians would like to use part of the liver of her father. Experience at this hospital has indicated that the donor's risk of death is very low, and that postoperative complications are less than 5 percent; the discomforts of recovering from the surgery are significant. With the transplantation, Susan's chances for survival soar from zero to 80 percent. Her father, however, refuses to undergo the procedure.

These cases are similar to the cesarean section cases in that: (1) a child will die unless certain medical interventions are performed; (2) the medical interventions require the parent's cooperation; and (3) this cooperation involves invasion of the parent's body.

What should the physicians in these two cases do? Should they ask a court to intervene to compel either (or both) of the parents to cooperate? Should statutes be developed requiring parents to undergo either (or both) of these procedures?

Those who would refrain from compelling the parents in these cases to undergo the procedures—and I count myself among them—would no doubt also be loathe to require a pregnant woman to undergo a cesarean section against her will. It was argued in Chapter Three that a parent's duties toward his or her child are based in large part on the interests of the child, but they are limited by the interests and rights of others (including those of the parent). Thus parents are not legally obligated to do what is in the child's absolutely best interests, but rather they must act within some acceptable, reasonable range of these interests. And while parents are expected to sacrifice more for their own child than for someone else's, there must be limits on how great a sacrifice the state may require. Although we may want the parents in the two hypothetical cases to undertake the risks necessary to save their children's lives, and although we may regard them as moral cowards for not doing so, my guess is that most people would consider such sacrifices of autonomy and bodily integrity—with the concomitant pain and risk (albeit small) of death—to go well beyond the range of what should be legally required of a parent.

Those who believe that the parents in the hypothetical cases should be legally required to undergo the procedures need to examine other features of the cesarean section cases before coming to a conclusion about whether *that* procedure should ever be compelled by the state. One problematic aspect is the high level of certainty required. In obstetrics, mistakes are not uncommon.[3] And the unexpected does occur: Chapter One noted a case in which a woman's placenta previa seemed to correct itself, allowing the child to be born naturally. A New York case was perhaps even more dramatic. A hospital petitioned the court to order a thirty-five-year-old indigent woman to have a cesarean section because the umbilical cord was wrapped around the infant's neck and would strangle the child during birth, but the court refused to issue the order, and the mother gave birth naturally—to a healthy baby.[4]

Indeed, with regard to the pregnant women who were ordered by a court to undergo a cesarean section, the statistics are rather startling: Of the first five women for whom courts mandated cesarean sections, only two underwent the operation; the other three were able to deliver live children vaginally.[5] The degree of uncertainty involved in many of these cases provides a strong argument for allowing a woman to decide what will happen to her own body.

Another problem is fulfilling the requirement of due process. Since many of these cases are treated as emergencies, a lack of time may preclude the adequate representation of the pregnant woman's interests, violating her right of due process. This is not merely an idle worry. In outlining their survey of court orders that were sought to override a pregnant woman's refusal of therapy, researchers noted that:

> In 14 of 20 cases (70 percent), hospital administrators and lawyers were aware of the situation for a day or less before a court order was pursued. In five cases (25 percent), they were aware for two to seven days, and in one case, for more than seven days. Once a court order was deemed necessary, it took six or fewer hours to obtain it in 14 of 16 cases (88 percent). In three of these cases (19 percent), the court orders were actually obtained in an hour or less; at least one order was granted by telephone.[6]

It is scandalous that a court would order the violation of a woman's body against her will after only a telephone conversation. And in fourteen cases, courts were able to decide within six hours of being contacted that invasive medical treatment should be imposed on unconsenting women. How thoroughly could the women have been represented on such short notice? Given the fundamental importance of the women's interests at stake in these cases, and given that they had no prior knowledge that medical treatment might be imposed— since there are no statutes, no well-known common-law precedents, and no administrative regulations to that effect—it is disgraceful that the courts would act so quickly to overrule them, and that they would have no appeal. This is not what is meant by due process.

Should the policy be altered? Should pregnant women be given notice that cesarean sections may be imposed upon them against their wills? No.

The death of any term fetus is certainly tragic; and the death of a term fetus who could have been saved is a very high price to pay for "protecting the rights of all competent adults, and preventing forcible, physical violations of women by coercive obstetricians and judges."[7] But while I would argue that a woman is morally obligated to undergo a cesarean section in order to save the life of her term fetus, I do not believe that the state should have the power to force her to do so. The state should not be able to override completely one person's interests in privacy and bodily autonomy in order to save the life of another. This is a sad resolution of a heartbreakingly difficult dilemma, but unfortunately there is no better option. The alternative would shatter too many important moral and legal rules and would involve an unacceptable increase of discretionary state power where the potential for abuse is high.[8]

Legally Compelling Parents to Undergo Less Invasive Medical Procedures

The determination that a cesarean section should not be legally required does not imply, however, that no medical interventions may be legally required. The claim that a parent may always refuse to undergo even the most minor of bodily invasions and thereby lose the life of her child seems to me to be intuitively wrong. Perhaps other less invasive and less risky procedures would be more commensurate with the standard of care that may be legally required of parents (including pregnant women).

The idea here is that, while the state may not order a parent to undergo major surgery for the sake of her child—for this would

totally defeat the parent's interests in bodily autonomy and privacy—
the state may sometimes be justified in setting back those interests to
a lesser degree in order to obtain a very important good (such as saving the life of a child or a term fetus). Perhaps a line can be drawn
between permissible and impermissible legal requirements, based on
the degree to which an important interest is set back (slightly thwart-
ing an interest is easier to justify than totally defeating it). Under
some circumstances, then—assuming the requirements of due process
and proportionality discussed earlier are met—it may be justifiable to
require a parent to undergo minimally burdensome procedures, such
as those involved in giving blood or ingesting a relatively safe medicine, in order to save the life of his or her child.

But although this may appear to be a small price to pay for the
life of a child, we should be very cautious about concluding that it
should always be legally required. The religious convictions of some
parents, for instance, compel them to refuse any and all medical treatment. While I would not argue that respecting a parent's religious
beliefs is more important than preserving the life of his child—and so
I agree that the state should intervene to require medical treatment
for a (born) child whose life would otherwise be lost—I do think that
respect for the parent's religious beliefs buttresses the case for not
requiring her to undergo a medical procedure in order to save the life
of her child. Her right of bodily autonomy would still be invaded
(albeit only to a minor degree), while her rights of privacy and parental authority and her right to follow the tenets of her religion would
be trampled on. The combination of factors in this case, I believe, militate against legal coercion. Thus I would also argue against requiring
a pregnant Jehovah's Witness to accept blood products. Under some
circumstances, then, a parent (or a pregnant woman) should be free to
refuse to undergo even a minor medical procedure in order to save
the life of his or her child.

But not under all circumstances. That most pregnant women love
their babies is irrelevant; the fact of the matter is that some of them
will negligently cause their future children grave and irreversible
harm while they are *in utero*. We should not excuse these women for
the harm they cause; nor should society ignore its obligations to protect these children. Hence the state may sometimes be justified in
interfering with a pregnant woman in order to prevent serious harm
to a fetus who will be carried to term.

Consider the case of a pregnant woman who is HIV-positive who refuses to take the drug AZT (zidovudine). New findings by the National Institutes of Health (NIH) indicate that HIV-positive women who take the drug during pregnancy can reduce—by two-thirds—the risk of infecting their babies with that dreadful virus. In the NIH study, half of the HIV-infected pregnant women received AZT; the other half received a placebo. Only 8.3 percent of the AZT babies contracted HIV, versus 25.5 percent in the placebo group. Reversible mild anemia in some infants was AZT's only negative side effect; the pregnant women tolerated the drug well.[9] Given that an estimated 7,000 HIV-infected women give birth each year in the United States, and that approximately 25 percent of their children are HIV-infected, use of AZT could reduce a great deal of suffering at little cost to the mothers. If long-term studies indicate continuing success, then in the future an HIV-infected pregnant woman may be required to take AZT, and if she refuses, state intervention to compel her to do so may be justifiable.

Another example involves the use of corticosteroids in women giving birth prematurely. Approximately 100,000 premature babies are born annually in the United States and about a third of them die, often because of respiratory distress (due to the immaturity of their lungs) or bleeding in the brain. When injected into the birthing woman, the hormone is carried to the fetus, where it accelerates the development of the fetus's blood vessels and lungs.[10] Widespread use of corticosteroids—which are tolerated well by the pregnant women and their children—could save thousands of lives each year.[11] In this instance as well, a pregnant woman should not be free to refuse the therapy.

This does not mean that, confronted with a noncompliant pregnant patient, a physician should turn immediately to a lawyer to begin legal proceedings to compel her to accept the AZT or the corticosteroids. That should be the last step. The first step should involve attempts to change her mind through discussion, persuasion, and rational argument. Most women do not want to cause grave harm to others—especially their own children—and are apt to acquiesce. Those few who do not, though, may be ordered by a court of law to do so. Given that the harm to them is so minimal, they should not have the right to permit such devastation to befall their children.

Yet where do we draw the line between justifiable interventions and unjustifiable ones? Robert Blank suggests that judicial intervention is warranted in cases of "negligent conduct of a high degree—a conscious and reckless disregard for the welfare of the fetus by the pregnant woman."[12] That is a start. But I doubt that any general ruling could address adequately the nuances and complexities of the issue of state-mandated medical treatment for pregnant women. Thus ultimately the question at hand—whether a parent (including a pregnant woman) should ever be coerced by the legal system into undergoing a relatively noninvasive form of medical treatment in order to save the life of his or her child—must be dealt with on a case-by-case basis. And so I agree with the conclusions of the Committee on Ethics of the American College of Obstetricians and Gynecologists that court involvement with treatment decisions should almost always—but not always—be avoided.[13]

MANDATORY TREATMENT FOR SUBSTANCE ABUSE

Given that the state is not ordinarily permitted to require substance-abusing noncriminals to enter detoxification programs, it seems reasonable to assert that there must be a compelling state interest to warrant a change in the rules with regard to pregnant women. The obvious response is that the singular vulnerability of the fetus calls for extraordinary action on its behalf. The fetuses of substance-abusing women, like the children of substance-abusing parents, are at risk of grave harm. But while a variety of people—school teachers, daycare workers, neighbors, social workers, relatives, friends—may notice the plight of these children and come to their aid, the fetus is unique in existing within and being solely dependent on its substance-abusing mother. No one can take the fetus away for a day or a week or a month while its mother goes on a binge. Thus in order to save the future child, it could be argued, the state must interfere with the activities of its mother by using its coercive power to require her to reside in a detoxification center for the duration of her pregnancy.

There are good consequentialist reasons for requiring addicted pregnant women to enter residential treatment programs. First, residential programs are more likely to be successful than outpatient programs. As outpatients, pregnant addicts continue to have access to and to use harmful substances, while inpatient programs allow closer monitoring of the woman's compliance with the treatment regimen.[14] So even if she is not permanently weaned from the substance, at least her intake of it would be controlled for the duration of her pregnancy.

Second, children impaired *in utero* can be expensive to treat medically. Exposure to a variety of substances—tobacco, cocaine, heroin, and alcohol—often increases the length of time the neonate must remain in the hospital after birth as well as the costs of that stay. One study calculated that infants born with low birthweight due to maternal smoking, for instance, add $652 million to the annual national costs for neonatal care.[15] And the problems may persist throughout the children's lives. Another study estimated that the annual cost of treating some disorders associated with fetal alcohol syndrome is $321 million in the United States alone.[16] The money might be better spent on treatment programs for substance-abusing pregnant women.

Third, breaking the mother's addiction will help her child after birth, since parental substance abuse has been consistently associated with child abuse and neglect.[17] In addition, children raised by addicts tend to have problems coping with the world; they are anxious and insecure, with disruptive behavior problems and short attention spans. And they often become substance abusers themselves.[18]

Finally, we have the appealing possibility of saving women from their thrall to a chemical and saving children who, due to their mothers' addictions, may otherwise suffer serious impairments or even death. And a great many children may be at risk. It has been estimated, for instance, that the worldwide rate of *fetal alcohol syndrome*—characterized by growth retardation, facial deformities, and central nervous system abnormalities—is 1.9 cases per 1,000 live births.[19] Even more children are born with the related but less severe set of *fetal alcohol effects*—characterized by learning and behavioral problems—which is approximately five times as common as the full-blown fetal alcohol syndrome. Experts estimate that between 50,000 and 70,000 children are born each year in the United States suffering from permanent damage caused by their mother's alcohol consumption during pregnancy.[20]

Illicit drugs also pose an enormous threat to fetal health. The National Institute on Drug Abuse estimates that 5 percent of pregnant women in the United States use one or more illegal drugs: approximately 222,000 each year.[21] And the problem is even more serious in some states (e.g., New York, California, and Florida). A study of pregnant women in one Florida county, for instance, indicated that 13.3 percent had positive results on toxicologic screening of urine for illegal drugs.[22] Another study of inner-city pregnant women estimated that 17 percent had used illegal drugs, and 70 percent of the drug

users had also smoked cigarettes.[23] While these figures are disturbing, they may not be telling the whole story, and the real figures may
indicate an even larger problem. Ira Chasnoff, an expert in the field,
believes that "substance abuse in pregnancy may be the most frequently missed diagnosis in all of obstetric and pediatric medicine."[24]

Drug use by pregnant women is not a new problem in the United
States, of course. Nineteenth-century physicians prescribed what are
now considered to be dangerous drugs for a variety of ailments:
opium and morphine for pain, fatigue, dysentery, and even hic-
coughs; cocaine for melancholia, sinus problems, and headaches; and
heroin for coughs.[25] Nor is drug use by pregnant women unique to the
United States. The problem exists in most other countries, although
the drug of choice often differs: marijuana in Jamaica, opium in the
Middle East, and betal nut (a central nervous system stimulant) in
Southeast Asia.[26]

Before we get too enthusiastic about improving the situation,
however, we need to probe more closely the realities of the cases at
hand. One very serious problem is the great difficulty of determining
precisely the long-term effects of maternal substance use on her child.
There are a variety of reasons for this:

(1) Pregnant substance abusers often fail to seek prenatal care,
    especially during the early stages of pregnancy, so the
    progress of their pregnancies cannot be monitored;

(2) of those who do seek health care, many lie about their use of
    teratogenic substances, so their physicians fail to look for that
    problem;

(3) like most substance abusers, pregnant substance abusers tend
    to use a variety of illicit substances, making it impossible to
    determine the effects of any one of them in isolation and com-
    pounding the difficulty of treatment;

(4) they frequently engage in other activities dangerous to their
    future children as well, such as smoking cigarettes and failing
    to eat properly;[27]

(5) other influences must also be considered when accounting for
    the condition of the children after birth, including family

socioeconomic status and family stability, maternal health (pregnant drug abusers tend to have a high rate of infections), and "familial patterns of temperament, intelligence, or psychopathology;"[28]

(6) follow-up studies on those children who remain in the custody of their mothers are difficult to conduct for the simple yet exasperating reason that the children cannot be located;

(7) institutional bias may skew the research; many health care institutions refuse to get involved in this type of research (usually citing concerns about patient confidentiality) and "studies showing unfavorable reproductive outcomes are more likely to be published than are studies showing no effect."[29]

In sum, the information we have about the teratogenic effects of substance abuse during pregnancy tends to be sketchy and tainted, and there is much more to be learned.[30] When during the pregnancy does the damage occur (only at certain stages or throughout)? At what amounts are the substances dangerous? How permanent and severe is the harm? How important are other factors (such as the physical and mental health of the mother and the home environment of the child) in comparison? And why do some substance-abusing pregnant women give birth to seriously impaired children while others do not?

Since details (such as the degree and probability of harm) matter, we need to focus the discussion. To do so we will concentrate at first on the use of heroin during pregnancy and then look at cocaine. Consider, for instance, the case of Margaret Reyes, which was described in the previous chapter. She was told to stop taking heroin, but she did not, and subsequently gave birth to twins suffering from drug withdrawal. Should stronger steps have been taken with her? Should she have been required to enter a residential drug treatment program until she gave birth?

Use of Heroin During Pregnancy

Chapter Three argued that the state would be justified in interfering with the activities of pregnant women only if there is a very high probability that major harms to the future child will be prevented.

While much needed information about the effects of heroin use during pregnancy is still lacking, there is a considerable amount of solid evidence that heroin use during pregnancy may damage the child while he or she is still *in utero.* One dramatic effect is drug addiction of the newborn, which can be very unpleasant and even painful for the child, involving irritability, vomiting, diarrhea, insomnia, dehydration, sweating, and convulsions.[31] Hyperactivity, impaired attention span, and the effects of low birthweight have been noted as long-term consequences.[32] Would the risk of these types of harm justify requiring pregnant heroin users to enter treatment programs against their wills?

First, let us take a closer look at the potential harm and benefits at stake. Although investigators recognize a high incidence of behavioral problems among children of heroin addicts, there is no consensus regarding the cause. The problems may be due to drug exposure *in utero*, or they may be due to being raised within a drug milieu. Requiring a woman to abstain from using heroin while pregnant, therefore, may do very little to improve her child's chances of succeeding in school if she later returns to heavy drug use.

And the newborn's drug dependence—while unpleasant and disturbing—typically only lasts several weeks (although cases of its enduring for as long as four months have been recorded), and usually can be treated effectively.[33] Thus it alone does not constitute a serious enough harm to warrant coercive state action.

The low birthweight of these infants, however, does involve risk of significant harm. Low-birthweight children (under 2,500 grams) are much more likely than normal-weight children to have neurodevelopmental handicaps, congenital anomalies, and learning disorders, and are almost forty times more likely to die during their first month of life.[34] Should the state have the power to coerce pregnant heroin abusers into entering drug treatment programs in order to prevent low-birthweight children?

If so, then perhaps the state should also intervene to prevent this problem in general. The goal of mandating drug rehabilitation for pregnant women, after all, is to protect the future children, not to punish the mothers. And many children are at risk. Over 7 percent of all children born in the United States in 1992 weighed less than 2,500 grams.[35]

According to the Institute of Medicine, among the "principal risk factors for low birthweight" infants are the mother's low socioeconomic status, African descent, low level of education, unmarried status, and age (under seventeen or over thirty-four).[36] Any one of these factors has a clear correlation with low birthweight; several together indicate a very high risk indeed—and poor, single, uneducated, African-American teenagers are precisely those at greatest risk of having low-birthweight infants. Many of these females do not want to get pregnant, and of those who do, most wish to bear healthy children.

These facts point to the need for a variety of social interventions: providing sex and health education in schools, making contraception more widely available and more easily affordable, and offering inexpensive and convenient prenatal care. But should stronger measures be taken as well? Should the state compel all females at high risk of bearing a growth-retarded child to take steps to reduce the risk? Should pregnant women, in other words, be legally required to seek prenatal care and to follow medical advice? Instituting such a policy might significantly reduce the number of impaired infants, since lack of prenatal care is a common factor among a large proportion of severely impaired children.

As Chapter Four pointed out, however, this strategy suffers from serious shortcomings. First, the doctrine of informed, voluntary consent—which is applied universally to all competent patients—would be abrogated in these cases, giving physicians an unacceptable degree of control over their patients' lives. Second, the intimate lives of anyone at risk of giving birth to a low-birthweight child would be open to state inspection. This would include not only poor, unmarried, uneducated women—an already downtrodden group—but a large number of others as well. Also among those at high risk of having a low-birthweight child are women whose deliveries are spaced close together, women who fail to gain weight during pregnancy, women who suffer from hypotension or hypertension, women over the age of thirty-four, and anemic women.[37]

In addition, the response of the legal system could well be problematic. Under one possible scenario, the courts would be overwhelmed with cases involving women who are likely to bear low-birthweight children, and judges will choose to invade the privacy and limit the liberty of these individuals to an extent not usually tolerated. Under a more likely scenario, the state would use its coercive force to interfere with the lifestyles of those pregnant females of whom society already disapproves (such as heroin abusers) or who lack social status (such as uneducated, unmarried teenagers). One need recall only the parallel fact that the women compelled by courts to undergo cesarean sections to date tended to be poor and members of minorities. Neither of these alternatives—oppressing a great many women or unfairly discriminating against a few—is acceptable. A more promising approach is to expand the social benefits available to these women and to offer them incentives to take advantage of them.

A final strategy is to concede that use of the state's power to coerce pregnant heroin abusers into lifestyle changes—while over-looking other women who have a similarly high risk of delivering low-birthweight babies—is discriminatory, but at least this particular discrimination has a rational basis. After all, this country's official pol-icy is one of "zero tolerance" for the use of the illegal substance. Why not, then, enforce the ordinary criminal drug possession laws against pregnant women, sentencing them to a sojourn in a residential drug treatment program? Perhaps this strategy would also be appropriate for pregnant women who use a purportedly even more dangerous drug: cocaine.

The Use of Cocaine During Pregnancy

If the popular media are to be trusted, cocaine (including crack, its less expensive, smokable sibling) is the scourge of the nation, destroy-ing individuals and families, schools, and communities. It also is sin-gled out for causing grave and irreparable prenatal harm. A typical article on the subject appeared in *Time* magazine in 1991. Under the headline, "Innocent Victims," the caption read: "Damaged by the drugs their mothers took, crack kids will face social and educational hurdles and must count on society's compassion."[38] While alluding in passing to other teratogenic substances, the article gives the impres-sion that having been exposed to crack/cocaine *in utero* is the one big problem in these children's lives.

A woman's use of cocaine during pregnancy can damage her fetus. The most frequently noted effects are low birthweight (espe-cially very low birthweight—under 1,500 grams), complications dur-ing pregnancy (such as precipitate labor and poor oxygen supply to the infant during labor), a higher than average infant mortality rate, and drug withdrawal symptoms. Watching an infant withdraw from cocaine exposure can be very difficult. The child appears to have been revved up: his breathing is faster than normal and his muscles are tense, he is fussy and jittery, he is easily startled and has difficulty sleeping. He is clearly uncomfortable, and he is uncomfortable to be around. Other negative effects have also been noted: brain lesions, cardiac abnormalities, and behavior problems (such as a short attention span and problems bonding emotionally).[39]

Which of these types of harm are caused by cocaine and which are due to other factors? And what are the chances that any of these problems will befall a particular child? No one knows. Consider the evidence. First, many infants exposed to cocaine show no withdrawal symptoms at all, and for those who do, the drug withdrawal usually lasts only a couple of weeks, at most a few months. Second, although the infant mortality rate is higher than normal, "Even among children heavily exposed to drugs *in utero*, more than 95 percent survive."[40] Third, the long-term behavioral effects are unknown; the studies are simply inconclusive. Many of the problems noted could be due to other causes: growing up with a drug-addicted mother, for instance, or insufficient nutrition before and after birth. One study of children whose behavior problems were believed to have been caused by their *in utero* exposure to cocaine showed that in fact the problems had other roots entirely: for instance, a death in the family, homelessness, or abuse.[41] Fourth, there are many other factors associated with low birthweight, so curbing maternal cocaine use will not significantly decrease the number of low-birthweight children—especially given that most children born to cocaine addicts fall within the normal weight limits.[42] And finally, most substance-abusing pregnant women, including those who use crack and cocaine, give birth to normal children.[43] Recall the case of Jennifer Johnson, who was criminally prosecuted because she used cocaine while pregnant; the American Public Health Association came to her defense because, association representatives claimed, her two children appeared healthy.

It is also unclear whether maternal cocaine use is associated with congenital abnormalities. In a study of 18,000 infants born in New York City, for instance, 1,300 were identified as having been exposed to cocaine, but there was no significant increase in congenital abnormalities among that group. And despite what has come to be regarded as a cocaine epidemic, "there has been no over-all increase in the number of malformations" in the United States.[44] Nor is it clear that cocaine exposure causes serious learning impairments. Therefore teachers working with children who had been exposed to cocaine *in utero* are less concerned with that fact than the public at large tends to be. Explains Vicki Ferrara, a special education teacher in Los Angeles,

"When I go into a classroom, I never ask if the child is drug-exposed. I don't care. I say, 'What's the problem?' Drugs cause problems but what happens afterward can be just as important."[45]

In short, there is little conclusive evidence about the extent of damage to children exposed *in utero* to cocaine. And while cocaine may sometimes cause very serious prenatal harm, it is impossible to predict which children will be harmed and how extensive the damage will be. This does not mean the problems are not there; it means that to date there is little consensus about exactly what the problems are, how they are caused, and the likelihood of their occurring.

This level of uncertainty militates against adopting a strategy of enforcing the criminal drug possession laws against pregnant women and sentencing them to a sojourn in a residential drug treatment program. There is another countervailing consideration as well: Such a strategy is not likely to work. The problem is not the failure of addicts to respond to treatment if they are coerced into it; coerced patients often do as well as patients who have sought treatment voluntarily.[46] The problem is that too many vital questions about the process of drug rehabilitation remain, especially with regard to pregnant women. Because of the power of the addictions, the prevalence of illegal drugs in some communities, and our insufficient knowledge about addictions, it is enormously difficult to break addictions. And with addicts often abusing a variety of substances—cocaine, heroin, alcohol, cigarettes—all of which may be teratogenic, the challenge of providing comprehensive and effective treatment is increased.

As a further complication, pregnant women have usually been excluded from hospital and community drug rehabilitation centers, so there is a serious dearth of knowledge about how best to treat them. And treating drug-abusing pregnant women is uniquely complicated. Substituting methadone for heroin, for instance, would not be enough to reduce the risk of harm to the future child because methadone itself causes prenatal damage, and it may not be wise to eliminate all drugs from the mother's system (having her go "cold turkey"), for that may do more harm than good to the fetus.[47]

In addition, pregnant women who want help often cannot find it, for there is a grave shortage of programs willing to treat them.[48] Before we could expect pregnant women to get treatment for their addictions, we first must guarantee that the help is there. And right now it is not.

Thus under present conditions—where the level of information about the harmful effects of most drugs is low, the level of uncertainty about how best to treat pregnant substance abusers is high, and the number of centers willing to treat pregnant women is woefully inadequate—the state would not be justified in requiring pregnant drug abusers to enter residential drug rehabilitation programs against their wills. Placing a drug-abusing pregnant woman who has been convicted of a crime in a residential treatment facility instead of in jail, however, makes a great deal of sense. Providing treatment programs on a voluntary basis, and entreating pregnant women to participate in them, is certainly a reasonable alternative. The programs might help some women and their children in the short run, and might offer valuable information about treating addictions to help others in the long run.

A Future Scenario

No doubt our profound ignorance will be replaced at some point with a real understanding about the mechanics and effects of these drugs when ingested during pregnancy. And hopefully more resources will be invested in rehabilitation programs for substance-abusing pregnant women. Some states are taking this responsibility seriously. Wisconsin, for instance, provides grants to public and private agencies to develop programs designed to help pregnant substance abusers, and gives pregnant women first priority for state services such as drug rehabilitation. And since 1988 Oregon has utilized a multidisciplinary program to help jailed pregnant substance abusers.

This raises a very important question: What if future data indicate conclusively that drug use during pregnancy causes severe and long-lasting damage to the developing organism, and that drug detoxification programs are successful in preventing this harm?

In this case, the harm at stake is grave as well as permanent, affecting fundamentally important interests of the child; the agent of harm is the mother, and in ingesting the drug, she shows reckless disregard for the risk of harm which her conduct poses for the child she intends to bear; the harm to the child can be prevented only by interfering with an already illegal activity of the mother; successful methods for preventing this harm exist; fulfilling the requirements of due process does not appear to be problematic in these cases (they are not emergencies); in this special case it should be possible to draft a law that is neither unconstitutionally vague nor unduly open to abuse; we need not worry too much about instituting a policy which discourages drug-abusing pregnant women from seeking prenatal care, since they tend to forgo seeking prenatal care anyway; and finally, removing their addictions might help their bonding with their children. Together these facts offer strong reasons for coercing a woman who ingests heroin or cocaine to cease this activity during pregnancy.

But such a policy exhibits a real bias with regard to pregnant drug abusers, certainly insofar as we allow other pregnant women with high-risk pregnancies to conduct themselves as they wish, and insofar as we continue to refrain from prosecuting nonpregnant possessors of illegal drugs or at least continue to sentence them more lightly. Although questionable, our intolerance of a pregnant woman's drug addiction—while allowing other pregnant women to cause similarly serious prenatal harm and other drug addicts to go free—might be justifiable on the basis of a greater social good. This means, however, that requiring pregnant drug abusers to enter residential drug treatment programs would be appropriate only if we are certain that instituting such a program will prevent prenatal harm and will not in fact create more harm than it is intended to prevent. And it is not clear that these conditions can be met.

A variety of concerns are relevant here. First, the process may hinder rather than help the bonding between mother and child; a coerced denial of freedom may foster the mother's resentment toward the child and thus shatter the bonding that might otherwise occur. Second, it may jeopardize other aspects of the woman's life: she may lose her home, her job, and her other children if placed in a treatment center for several months. Third, pregnant addicts—fearing that they would be compelled to enter residential treatment programs and craving the freedom to pursue their habits—may be even less likely to seek medical care, perhaps thereby placing their offspring at even greater risk of harm.

In addition, the timing of the coercion matters. If the woman is ordered to enter a drug treatment program during the early stage of pregnancy, she may well choose instead to have an abortion (after all, she is in the grip of an addiction); but if she is not required to enter a program until she is near term, it may be too late to do any real good, since considerable damage may have been done during the first few months of gestation. Finally, since not all pregnant drug abusers give birth to seriously impaired children, a policy of coercing all of them into entering residential treatment facilities would be open to the charge of unjustifiably limiting the liberty of certain individuals (i.e., those whose drug habits ultimately cause no significant damage).

These pros and cons are difficult to assess conclusively, given the dearth of relevant data. However, on the basis of what we know and what we can anticipate, it seems reasonable to conclude that pregnant drug abusers should not be coerced by the state into entering residential drug treatment programs. Such a policy would create more harm than good. It should be clear by now that a policy of putting these women in jail (where little medical treatment is available) is even less reasonable.

A Compromise Solution

Does this mean, then, that our hands are tied? After all, these women are taking illicit substances to the detriment of their children. And certainly their drug addictions do not reflect autonomous decisions. Thus the prospect of limiting their liberty may be less troubling than the prospect of limiting the liberty of other pregnant women.

As a compromise measure, then, we should consider requiring those pregnant drug abusers who are likely to cause significant harm to their offspring to participate in outpatient substance abuse programs. This assumes, of course, that we have acquired the appropriate expertise in treating pregnant addicts, we have developed the ability to predict which children will be harmed, and we have created the necessary number of treatment centers.

The penalty for refusing to take part in the outpatient program would be a sojourn in a residential treatment facility. And using the coercive force of the state to back the policy puts pregnant drug abusers on notice that society will not tolerate the harm they cause. This may lead some women to seek treatment who otherwise would not.

Since the purpose here is to prevent harm to the future person, not to punish the pregnant woman, it would make sense to avoid the distress of a criminal trial, the stigma of a criminal record, and the threat of jail. Rather than proceeding via the criminal justice system, then, a variation on the traditional civil commitment process could be implemented.[49]

But civil commitment—even to an outpatient program—is still a denial of liberty; and the defiance of a commitment once ordered can be credibly enforced only by confinement to a residential treatment center, which is an even greater denial of liberty. Therefore strict principles of due process must apply: The woman's rights to counsel, to hearing, to proper notice, to trial, and to appeal must be respected. These procedures are obviously costly, but they may not be suspended or abridged.

In addition, the treatment protocols must be carefully regulated. Two concerns are especially germane here. The first is that "systems of benevolent coercion" sometimes lose their treatment function and degenerate instead into "social monitoring functions."[50] The second is that, because the right to refuse treatment generally does not extend to those who are considered dangerous to others, the doctrine of informed, voluntary consent would be abrogated in these cases.[51] To guard against potential abuse, the range of therapeutic interventions must be limited in several ways: (1) only a pregnant woman whose first trimester has passed and who continues the harmful activity may be coerced into treatment; (2) there is clear and convincing evidence that her behavior will cause grave and long-lasting harm to her future child;[52] (3) a specific and widely approved set of treatment protocols is likely to reduce the risk of this harm; (4) only these demonstrably effective treatments are mandated; (5) this treatment will be provided; and (6) clinical decisions are carefully monitored.

It should be noted that, since the illegality of the substance is not the controlling issue here—the issue is the fact that the mother is causing grave and irreversible harm to her offspring—pregnant alcoholics should be subject to similar coercion by the state. By providing treatment in the least restrictive setting available, this policy offers a decent compromise between two competing claims: a pregnant woman's liberty and the welfare of her future child.

NOTES

1. A cesarean section is warranted for fetal problems (such as myelomeningocele, respiratory distress, and abnormal presentation) as well as maternal problems (e.g., the pregnant woman has placenta previa or certain infections, such as herpes or AIDS).

2. E. L. Shearer, "Cesarean Section: Medical Benefits and Costs," *Social Science and Medicine* 37, pp. 1223–31, 1993.

3. For instance, physicians prescribed diethylstilbestrol (DES) to many pregnant women to prevent miscarriages, not knowing that it could cause cancer in their children. For an exploration of the reasons behind the widespread and "uncritical embrace" of DES, see D. Dutton, *Worse than the Disease:*

Pitfalls of Medical Progress, Cambridge University Press, N.Y.: 1988. See also A. Oakley, *The Captured Womb: A History of Medical Care of Pregnant Women*, N.Y.: Oxford University Press, 1984.

   4. T. Lewin, "Courts Acting to Force Care of the Unborn," *New York Times*, November 23, 1987, A1.

   5. N. K. Rhoden, "Judges in the Delivery Room," *California Law Review* 74, pp. 1951–2030, 1986.

   6. V. E. B. Kolder et al., "Court-Ordered Obstetrical Interventions," p. 1193, 1987.

   7. G. J. Annas, "Forced Caesareans: The Most Unkindest Cut of All," *Hastings Center Report* 12, pp. 16–18, 1982.

   8. Either a concern for upholding fundamental moral and legal principles or a concern about the negative consequences of such a policy would be enough, I believe, to justify rejecting it; together, these elements seem compelling.

   9. "AZT Reduces Rate of Maternal Transmission of HIV," *NIAID News* February 21, 1994; D.S. Pinkley, "AZT Found to Reduce Perinatal HIV Transmission Risk," *American Medical News* March 14, 1994; E. M. Connor et al., "Reduction of Maternal–Infant Transmission of Human Immunodeficiency Virus Type 1 with Zidovudine Treatment," *New England Journal of Medicine* 331, pp. 1173–80, 1994.

   10. M. Mugford et al., "Cost Implications of Different Approaches to the Prevention of Respiratory Distress Syndrome," *Archives of Disease in Childhood* 66, pp. 757–64, 1991.

   11. National Institute of Child Health and Human Development, *Report of the Consensus Development Conference on the Effect of Corticosteroids for Fetal Maturation on Perinatal Outcomes*, Rockville, MD.: U.S. Department of Health and Human Services, MH Pub. No. 95–3784, 1994.

   12. R. H. Blank, "Maternal–Fetal Relationship: The Courts and Social Policy," *Journal of Legal Medicine* 14, pp. 73–92, 1993, at p. 90.

   13. The Committee on Ethics of the American College of Obstetricians and Gynecologists concludes that:

   (1) With the advances in medical technology, the fetus has become more accessible to diagnostic and treatment modalities. The maternal–fetal relationship remains a unique one, requiring a balance of maternal health, autonomy, and fetal needs. Every reasonable effort should be made to protect the fetus, but the pregnant woman's autonomy should be respected.

   (2) The vast majority of pregnant women are willing to assume significant risk for the welfare of the fetus, a problem arising only when this potentially beneficial advice [the physician's recommendation] is rejected. The role of the obstetrician should be one of an informed educator and counselor, weighing the risks and benefits to both patients, as well as realizing that tests, judgments, and decisions are fallible. Consultation with others,

including an institutional ethics committee, should be sought when appropriate to aid the pregnant woman and obstetrician in making decisions. The use of the courts to resolve these conflicts is almost never warranted.

(3) Obstetricians should refrain from performing procedures unwanted by the pregnant woman. The use of judicial authority to implement treatment regimens in order to protect the fetus violates the pregnant woman's autonomy. Furthermore, inappropriate reliance on judicial authority may lead to undesirable societal consequences such as the criminalization of noncompliance with medical recommendations.

American College of Obstetricians and Gynecologists, Committee on Ethics, "Statement of the Committee on Ethics," Washington, D.C., 1987.

The Committee on Bioethics of the American Academy of Pediatrics came to a similar conclusion:

If a fetal intervention is one of proven efficacy and has concomitant low maternal risk, the physician should recommend the procedure and stress, if necessary, the responsibility of the mother to accept some personal risk for the potential benefit to her fetus. Should the woman refuse to undergo an intervention that poses a personal risk, her autonomous choice and risk to bodily integrity should, in general, be respected.

In unusual cases, a physician may be unsympathetic to the woman's refusal of treatment. Under the following conditions a physician might consider actively opposing the woman's choice: (1) there is substantial likelihood that the fetus will suffer irrevocable harm without the intervention; (2) the intervention is clearly appropriate and will likely be efficacious; and (3) the risk to the woman is low. When these conditions are present, the woman's physician should inform her that the decision creates a moral dilemma for the physician and should try to persuade her to consent. If refusal persists, the physician may wish to inform the woman that he believes her decision is unreasonable and that consultation with a hospital ethics committee or others within the institution might be sought. Finally, in rare cases, recourse to the courts might be considered. Court intervention should be seen as a last resort to be undertaken with great caution because of the potentially regrettable consequences of forced medical or surgical procedures.

American Academy of Pediatrics, Committee on Bioethics, "Fetal Therapy: Ethical Considerations," *Pediatrics* 81, pp. 898–99, 1988.

14. L. S. Chan et al., "Differences Between Dropouts and Active Participants in a Pediatric Clinic for Substance Abuse Mothers," *American Journal of Drug and Alcohol Abuse* 12, pp. 89–99, 1986; J. Fitzsimmons et al., "Pregnancy in a Drug-abusing Population," *American Journal of Drug & Alcohol Abuse* 12, pp. 247–55, 1986.

15. W. G. Manning et al., "The Taxes of Sin: Do Smokers Pay Their Way?" *Journal of the American Medical Association* 262, pp. 901–06, 1989.

16. Treating fetal alcohol syndrome involves "providing special services for pre- and postnatal growth retardation requiring neonatal intensive care, some specific organic disorders (e.g., cleft palate and hearing loss) requiring surgical repair and subsequent treatment, and mental retardation relative to FAS." E. L. Abel and R. J. Sokol, "Incidence of Fetal Alcohol Syndrome and Economic Impact of FAS-related Anomalies," *Drug and Alcohol Dependence* 19, pp. 51–70, 1987.

17. C. P. Barnard, "Alcoholism and Incest," *Focus on Family and Chemical Dependency* 7, pp. 27–29, 1984; C. H. Kempe and R. Helfer, eds., *The Battered Child*, Chicago: University of Chicago Press, 1980; J. Howard, "Chronic Drug Users as Parents," *Hastings Law Journal* 9, pp. 130–60, 1992; Institute for Health Policy, Brandeis University, *Substance Abuse: The Nation's Number One Health Problem*, Princeton: Robert Wood Johnson Foundation, 1993.

18. J. Howard, *Hastings Law Journal* 43, pp. 645–68 1992; L. Rubenstein, *Yale Law and Policy Review* 9, pp. 130–60 1991; Institute for Health Policy, Brandeis University, *Substance Abuse: The Nation's Number One Health Problem*, 1993.

19. E. L. Abel and R. J. Sokol, "Incidence of Fetal Alcohol Syndrome and Economic Impact of FAS-related Anomalies," *Drug and Alcohol Dependence* 19, pp. 51–70, 1987.

20. M. Dorris, "The Tragedy of Fetal Alcohol Syndrome," *1994 Medical and Health Annual*, Chicago: Encyclopedia Britannica, Inc., p. 120, 1994.

21. L. Johnson, *National Survey Results on Drug Use from the Monitoring the Future Study, 1975–1993*, Rockville, MD.: DHHS, 1994.

22. I. J. Chasnoff et al., "The Prevalence of Illicit-drug or Alcohol Use During Pregnancy and Discrepancies in Mandatory Reporting in Pinellas County, Florida," *New England Journal of Medicine* 322, pp. 1202–06, 1990.

23. J. G. Feldman et al., "A Cohort Study of the Impact of Perinatal Drug-Use on Prematurity in an Inner City Population," *American Journal of Public Health* 82, 726–28, 1992.

24. Ira Chasnoff notes that, "The reported incidence of substance abuse in pregnancy rose with the increased thoroughness of the assessment utilized by the hospital staff and physicians." Hospitals with a low level of assessment—in which pregnant women were not questioned about their drug use, and newborns were tested only if they exhibited symptoms of distress—reported a 3 percent rate of substance use; while hospitals with a high level of assessment—in which every pregnant woman and/or neonate was tested—reported a 15.7 percent rate of substance use (and several reported a 24 percent or higher rate). I. J. Chasnoff, "Drug Use and Women: Establishing a Standard of Care," in D. E. Hutchings (ed.), *Prenatal Abuse of Licit and Illicit Drugs*, N.Y.: The New York Academy of Medicine, pp. 208–10, 1989.

25. See S. R. Krandall and W. Chavkin, "Illicit Drugs in America," *Hastings Law Journal* 43, pp. 615–43, 1992; D. F. Musto, "Opium, Cocaine and Marijuana in American History," *Scientific American*, July 1991, pp. 40–47.

26. L. N. Robins et al., "Effects of In Utero Exposure to Street Drugs," *American Journal of Public Health* 83(Supplement), pp. 3–31, 1993.

27. I. J. Chasnoff, "Perinatal Effects of Cocaine," *Contemporary Obstetrics and Gynecology,* 29, pp. 163–79, 1987; D. A. Frank et al., "Cocaine Use During Pregnancy: Prevalence and Correlates," *Pediatrics* 82, pp. 888–95, 1988; T. R. Kosten et al., "Cocaine Abuse Among Opioid Addicts: Demographic and Diagnostic Factors in Treatment," *American Journal of Drug and Alcohol Abuse* 12, pp. 1–16, 1986; B. B. Little et al., "Patterns of Multiple Substance Abuse During Pregnancy," *Southern Medical Journal* 83(5), pp. 507–09, 1990; L. N. Robbins et al., "Effects of In Utero Exposure to Street Drugs," *American Journal of Public Health* 83(Supplement), pp. 3–31, 1993.

28. J. Marcus, S. Hans, and R. J. Jeremy, "A Longitudinal Study of Offspring Born to Methadone-maintained Women. III. Effects of Multiple Risk Factors on Development at 4, 8, and 12 Months," *American Journal of Drug and Alcohol Abuse* 10, pp. 195–207, 1984.

29. L. N. Robins *op cit.*, p. 13. See also G. Koren et al., "Bias Against the Null Hypothesis: The Reproductive Hazards of Cocaine," *Lancet* 2, pp. 1440–42, 1989.

30. Researchers justifiably complain about the "overwhelming number of confounding prenatal and environmental influences and the small number of drug-exposed subjects who have been carefully evaluated in a prospective fashion." G. S. Wilson, "Clinical Studies of Infants and Children Exposed Prenatally to Heroin," in D. E. Hutchings (ed.), *Prenatal Abuse of Licit and Illicit Drugs*, N.Y.: The New York Academy of Medicine, pp. 183–94, 1989. See also Krandall and Chavkin, *op cit.* 1992; Robins et al., *op cit.* 1993.

31. A. A. Flandermeyer, "A Comparison of the Effects of Heroin and Cocaine Abuse upon the Neonate," *Neonatal Network*, pp. 42–48, 1987; Krandall and Chavkin, *op cit.* 1992.

32. Other teratogenic effects of heroin have been reported, but not consistently. See L. G. Alroomi et al., "Maternal Narcotic Abuse and the Newborn," *Archives of Disease in Childhood* 63, pp. 81–83, 1986; S. Deren, "The Children of Substance Abusers: A Review of the Literature," *Journal of Substance Abuse Treatment* 3, pp. 77–94, 1986; L. P. Finnegan, "Outcome of Children Born to Women Dependent upon Narcotics," *Advances in Alcohol and Substance Abuse*, pp. 55–101, 1982; G. S. Wilson, "Clinical Studies of Infants and Children Exposed Prenatally to Heroin," in D. E. Hutchings (ed.), *Prenatal Abuse of Licit and Illicit Drugs*, N.Y.: The New York Academy of Medicine, pp. 183–94, 1989; Robins, *op cit.* 1993.

33. Krandall and Chavkin, *op cit.* 1992; Robins et al. *op cit.* 1993.

34. R. E. Behrman, "Premature Births Among Black Women," *New England Journal of Medicine* 312 pp. 763–65, 1987; Committee to Study the Prevention of Low Birthweight, Institute of Medicine, *Preventing Low Birthweight*, Washington, D.C.: National Academy Press, 1985; M. C. McCormick, "The

Contribution of Low Birth Weight to Infant Mortality and Childhood Morbidity," *New England Journal of Medicine* 312, pp. 82–90, 1985.

   35. Annie E. Casey Foundation, *Kids Count Data Book*, Baltimore, MD.: Annie E. Casey Foundation, 1995.

   36. Committee to Study the Prevention of Low Birthweight, Institute of Medicine *op cit.*, 1985.

   37. Ibid.

   38. "Innocent Victims," *Time*, May 13, 1991, pp. 56–63.

   39. I. J. Chasnoff et al., "Prenatal Drug Exposure: Effects on Neonatal & Infant Growth & Development," *Neurobehavioral Toxicology and Teratology* 8, pp. 357–62, 1986; S. Deren, "The Children of Substance Abusers: A Review of the Literature," *Journal of Substance Abuse Treatment* 3, pp. 77–94, 1986; T. M. Doberczak et al., "Neonatal Neurologic & Electroencephalographic Effects of Intrauterine Cocaine Exposure," *Journal of Pediatrics* 113, pp. 354–58, 1988; A. A. Flandermeyer, "A Comparison of the Effects of Heroin and Cocaine Abuse upon the Neonate," *Neonatal Network*, pp. 42–48, 1987; D. A. Frank et al., "Cocaine Use During Pregnancy: Prevalence and Correlates," *Pediatrics* 82, pp. 888–95, 1988; S. N. MacGregnor et al., "Cocaine Use During Pregnancy: Adverse Perinatal Outcome," *American Journal of Obstetrics and Gynecology* 1587, pp. 686–89, 1987; J. D. Madden et al., "Maternal Cocaine Abuse and Effect on the Newborn," *Pediatrics* 77, pp. 209–11, 1986; A. S. Oro and S. D. Dixon, "Perinatal Cocaine and Metamphetamine Exposure: Maternal and Neonatal Correlates," *Journal of Pediatrics* 222, pp. 571–78, 1987; C. S. Phibbs et al., "The Neonatal Costs of Maternal Cocaine Use," *Journal of the American Medical Association* 266(11), pp. 1521–26, 1991; Robins et al., *op cit.*, 1993; B. Zuckerman et al., "Effects of Maternal Marijuana and Cocaine Use on Fetal Growth," *New England Journal of Medicine* 320, pp. 762–68, 1989.

   40. Robins et al., *op cit.*, p. 17.

   41. S. Daley, "Born on Crack and Coping With Kindergarten," *New York Times*, February 7, 1991.

   42. Robins et al., *op cit.*, p. 16.

   43. L. S. Chan et al., "Differences Between Dropouts and Active Participants in a Pediatric Clinic for Substance Abuse Mothers," *American Journal of Drug and Alcohol Abuse* 12, pp. 89–99, 1986; J. Fitzsimmons et al., "Pregnancy in a Drug-abusing Population," *American Journal of Drug & Alcohol Abuse* 12, pp. 247–55, 1986; Robins et al., *op cit.*

   44. Robins et al., p. 14.

   45. Vicki Ferrara, quoted by S. Daley, "Born on Crack and Coping With Kindergarten," *New York Times*, February 7, 1991.

   46. Collins and Allison, for instance, conclude that, "The evidence presented here suggests that the use of legal threat to pressure individuals into drug treatment is a valid approach for dealing with drug abusers and their undesirable behaviors. Legal threat apparently helps keep these individuals constructively involved in treatment and does not adversely affect long-term treatment goals." J. J. Collins and M. Allison, "Legal Coercion and Retention in Drug Abuse Treatment," *Hospital and Community Psychiatry* 34, pp. 1145–49, 1983. See also S. M. Ehrenkranz et al. (eds.), *Clinical Social Work with Maltreated Children and Their Families*, N.Y.: New York University Press, 1989; F. Mark, "Does Coercion Work? The Role of Referral Source in Motivating Alcoholics in Treatment," *Alcoholism Treatment Quarterly* 5, pp. 5–22, 1988; J. Westermeyer, "Nontreatment Factors Affecting Treatment Outcomes in Substance Abuse," *American Journal of Drug & Alcohol Abuse* 15, pp. 13–29, 1989.

47. I. J. Chasnoff et al., "Prenatal Drug Exposure: Effects on Neonatal & Infant Growth & Development," *Neurobehavioral Toxicology and Teratology* 8, pp. 357–62, 1986; K. C. Edelin et al., "Methadone Maintenance in Pregnancy: Consequences to Care and Outcome," Obstetrics and Gynecology 7, pp. 399–404, 1988; T. R. Kosten et al., "Cocaine Abuse Among Opioid Addicts: Demographic and Diagnostic Factors in Treatment," *American Journal of Drug and Alcohol Abuse* 12, pp. 1–16, 1986; M. Kreek, "Opioid Disposition and Effects During Chronic Exposure in the Perinatal Period in Man," *Advances in Alcohol & Substance Abuse* 34, pp. 21–53, 1982.

48. The shortage of rehabilitation programs willing to treat pregnant women in the United States is well-documented. W. Chavkin, "Drug Addiction and Pregnancy: Policy Crossroads," *American Journal of Public Health* 80, pp. 483–87, 1990; M. R. Golden, "When Pregnancy Discrimination Is Gender Discrimination: The Constitutionality of Excluding Pregnant Women From Drug Treatment Programs," *New York University Law Review* 66(6), pp. 1832–80, 1991; J. Schachter, "Help Is Hard to Find for Addict Mothers: Drug Use 'Epidemic' Overwhelms Services," *Los Angeles Times*, 1986 II–1; R. Sherman, "Keeping Babies Free of Drugs," *The National Law Journal* 1, 28–29, 1989; C. Trost, "Born to Lose," *Wall Street Journal*, 1989.

49. For more on this proposal, see D. Mathieu, "Mandating Treating for Pregnant Substance Abusers: A Compromise," *Politics and the Life Sciences* 14, 1–10, 1995.

50. E. P. Mulvey et al., "The Promise and Peril of Involuntary Outpatient Commitment," *American Psychologist* 42, pp. 571–84, 1987.

51. B. A. Arrigo, "Paternalism, Civil Commitment and Illness Politics," *Journal of Law and Health* 7, pp. 131–68, 1992–3; D. F. Chavkin, "'For Their Own Good': Civil Commitment of Alcohol and Drug-Dependent Pregnant Women," *South Dakota Law Review* 37, pp. 224–88, 1992; E. P. Mulvey et al., *op cit.*

52. The Supreme Court has ruled that clear and convincing evidence is constitutionally required before an adult can be civilly committed to treatment in a residential facility (*Addington v. Texas*, 441 U.S. 418, 1979). The Court thus rejected the higher standard, beyond a reasonable doubt, as well as the lower standard, preponderance of the evidence.

6

Interventions Before and After Pregnancy

REPRODUCTIVE HAZARDS IN THE WORKPLACE

An assortment of chemicals that are widely used in the workplace—lead, benzene, formaldehyde, vinyl chloride, carbon tetrachloride, chloroform, carbon disulfide, fluorocarbon-22, carbon monoxide, mercury, and dioxin—can be reproductive hazards. Exposure to some of these chemicals can harm the developing fetus directly (teratogenic damage), while others harm the parents' reproductive systems and so indirectly harm the fetus (mutagenic damage); and exposure to still others (lead, ethylene oxide, and vinyl chloride) may cause both kinds of damage.[1]

As a result, workers who participate in the manufacture of a variety of goods—rubber, plastics, pesticides, nylons, gasoline, adhesives, batteries, pigments, pipes, laminates, and bullets—may be at risk of some sort of reproductive damage. In response, many major companies instituted fetal protection policies barring women from certain jobs that involve working with toxic substances.[2] Although in some instances only pregnant women were prohibited from working with specific materials, another common policy was to prohibit all females between the ages of sixteen and fifty from working with substances believed to be reproductive hazards—unless the women could prove that they were sterile.

Employers have a variety of reasons for excluding all fertile women from working in certain jobs. First, some substances can cause a great deal of teratogenic damage during the very early stages of pregnancy, before a woman knows that she is pregnant. Second, some substances can damage the woman's reproductive system itself, causing fetal malformations or death when she eventually conceives. Third, some companies respond conservatively to the indication of risk of harm. Although there is evidence that a certain chemical

129

causes genetic damage, for instance, the evidence may be unclear as to when the damage occurs, so all women are barred from working with the chemical as a precautionary measure. And companies often appeal to economic considerations, including a potential litigation explosion. It is prohibitively expensive to reduce exposure levels to the point at which there are no reproductive risks, they claim, so they need to exclude women from the workplace in order to avoid costly suits brought by damaged children. And finally, companies assert a moral obligation to prevent future children from being injured by workplace toxicants.

Although the expressed intention of these exclusionary policies is laudable—protecting future generations from harm (and protecting the companies from economic harm)—one of the effects was damaging: women were excluded from many skilled and lucrative jobs and either relegated to more menial and lower-paying tasks or precluded from working in certain industries altogether. The repercussions of these exclusionary policies were far from minor: millions of jobs were closed to women, regardless of their plans to have children or their career goals.[3] Denying women equal participation in the workforce—barring them from jobs and relegating them to low-paying jobs—not only may violate their rights, but may harm them and their children. The extent to which women's interests can be seriously undermined by policies prohibiting them from working in certain jobs should not be underestimated, and the fact that some women chose to be sterilized in order to keep their jobs indicates the importance of these positions to them.[4]

The best solution to the problems created by the existence of reproductive hazards in the workplace is to remove the hazards and make the workplace safe for all workers. But companies claim that this is not always feasible. Thus there seems to be a basic conflict between two desirable but incompatible social benefits: preventing serious reproductive harm and providing equal employment opportunities for women. As with the imposition of fetal therapies, the choice is between causing harm to some women in order to prevent harm to their offspring, or permitting harm to befall children in order to avoid harming their mothers.

But there may be something else at issue here as well. Some commentators contend that the protection of future generations is not the only concern of employers, and that employers have used the existence of reproductive hazards in the workplace as an excuse to continue unfair patterns of sex discrimination.[5] One cogent charge is that if the type of job in question had traditionally been occupied by males, then it was much more common for women to be excluded than if the type of job had typically been filled by females—even if both types of job were shown to involve significant reproductive risk. An example of this disparity involves female operating room personnel who are exposed to significant levels of anesthetic gases, which have long been considered to be reproductive hazards.[6] Women, however, have not been excluded from the operating theater. This failure to exclude may be due to the traditional acceptance of women in (at least some aspects of) medicine, so removing them from that arena would be difficult indeed, and certainly more difficult than prohibiting other women from holding jobs that women have not traditionally occupied.[7]

And even if the existence of reproductive hazards in the workplace was not used as a smokescreen to hide an insidious prejudice against them, the fact was that women were excluded from working with substances that may cause reproductive damage while men were not. Perhaps one assumption that helps to explain policies which excluded women and not men from working in certain jobs is that the risks of harm befall the reproductive systems of female employees to a much greater extent than that of male employees. This assumption, however, is unwarranted. In fact, both men and women are at risk of reproductive harm. As a former director of the National Institute of Occupational Safety and Health wrote to the B.F. Goodrich Company,

> We must stand firm on the principle that if an exposure is sufficiently toxic to produce genetic damage in an unborn child or in a fertile female, then it must be considered to be equally toxic to the fertile male worker and to his unborn child. . . . There is *a priori* no reason to believe that the genetic material of a male worker is in any way more resistant to toxic occupational injury than that of the female.[8]

And studies fail to support the conclusion that men are not as susceptible to reproductive damage as women. There is growing evidence, for instance, that paternal exposure to certain substances in the workplace is linked to an assortment of reproductive harms: increased rates of stillbirths, preterm deliveries, cancers, and low birthweights.[9]

Yet because most studies are conducted on women and not on men,
too little evidence exists to indicate the level of risk to the offspring of
male workers.[10]

This is not to suggest that any policy which excluded women and
not men is unjustifiable. Such a policy may be acceptable, but only if
it can be shown that a particular substance causes serious reproductive harm through the mother and not through the father. Yet while it
may be reasonable to exclude at least some women and no men under
these circumstances, it does not follow that it would be reasonable to
exclude all women from working with that substance. Simply because
a woman is fertile does not mean that she intends to reproduce: Some
women are celibate, some are gay, some use birth control, and some
would get abortions. Further, many women who are of child-bearing
age, and believe themselves to be fertile, are not. And some desperately need the money offered by the riskier jobs in order to care adequately for their families. To treat all fertile women (or all who are
presumed to be fertile) as though they were potential mothers—and
ignore the relevant differences in their goals, needs, lifestyles, and
responsibilities—is to demean them, to deny them not just the right to
equal employment opportunities but also the right to be rational
adults, to weigh their risks and obligations as they see fit.

Indeed, one can raise an effective argument against permitting
any fetal protection policy that excludes at least some women and no
men. Thomas Murray reminds us of the unfortunate reality that morally responsible parents may sometimes have good reasons for exposing their children to risk of significant harm.

> Near the medical school in Galveston is a massive collective of
> petrochemical plants in a community known as Texas City. Texas
> City is a "cancer corridor"—people who live there have a statisti-
> cally higher risk of developing cancer than those who live in
> neighboring towns, presumably because of their proximity to the
> plants and their emissions. Suppose a man living elsewhere were
> offered a higher paying job in Texas City. Accepting it and living
> there would mean exposing himself and his family to a low but
> still increased risk of cancer. But it would also mean a higher stan-
> dard of living for them all, better schools, and other advantages.
>
> Would we say of a man who accepted that job that he has
> done something morally wrong? Should we deny jobs in Texas

City to men and women with children on the grounds they are
exposing their unconsenting offspring to the risk of harm?[11]

Those who believe that this man would be wrong to accept the job in
Texas City—who believe that parents in general should never expose
their children to risk of serious harm—could consistently hold that a
woman who intends to bear children would be wrong to accept a job
working with vinyl chloride or methotrexate. But they would also
have to agree that many other desirable and socially valuable positions should not be given to men or women who have or intend to
have or can have children. Some jobs—such as administering anesthesia—carry the risk of reproductive harm, while others—such as cut-
ting timber and conducting police drug busts—carry the risk of
orphaning the children of those who engage in them.[12] Meat-packing
is also dangerous, as is making semiconductor chips.[13] Farming is
especially hazardous; in 1988, 140,000 agricultural workers in the
United States suffered disabling injuries and 1,500 died.[14] Were we to
be consistent, we would have to agree that these positions, with their
inherent risks of serious harm to children, should be given only to
adults who do not have and who do not intend to have children.

But is this conclusion really tenable? Adopted as public policy
and consistently applied, this position could cause a great deal of
social disruption, not the least of which would involve a drastic rise
in the unemployment rate as well as a severe reduction in many use-
ful commodities. A more realistic stance would recognize the sad reality that, like the man who moves his family to Texas City, parents
often have to make difficult choices among imperfect options. The
choice between accepting a decent-paying albeit risky job in order to
support your family and working in a lower-paying job in order to
avoid all risks of reproductive harm—when what you really want is
the chance to earn a good salary without risking harm to your children—is a tragic choice. And some individuals' options are precisely
so constrained. They do not have the freedom to take another job
(since no other jobs for which they are qualified exist nearby); they do
not have the freedom to move elsewhere (since they are held to the
location by family obligations); and they do not have the freedom to
stop working (unless they are willing to go on welfare). The choice
here is between different kinds of responsibilities—responsibilities to
one's present family versus responsibilities to future additions to

one's family—both of which cannot be satisfied. I see no reason to conclude that choosing to act in the interests of the present members of one's family is in any way a morally blameworthy choice.

In addition, working in a job which carries a small risk of reproductive harm may be preferable in many ways to the available alternatives. As Judge Cudahy pointedly asks,

> What is the situation of the pregnant woman, unemployed or working for the minimum wage and unprotected by health insurance, in relation to her pregnant sister, exposed to an indeterminate lead risk but well-fed, housed, and doctored? Whose fetus is at greater risk?[15]

The consequentialist claim that we would do more good overall if we prevented harm to future generations caused by workplace hazards is true only if the benefits to these individuals outweigh the harm caused to them and to the women who wish to work in the jobs from which they are excluded. And in many instances this simply may not be the case. Thus it seems quite plausible to posit that a woman may be acting in a morally responsible manner when she chooses to work in a job that carries a small risk of reproductive harm. To deny her this morally acceptable option—to further limit her already constrained freedom to choose—is to deny her too much, and to discriminate against her unfairly. The decision, then, should be hers to make.

Fetal Protection Policies and the Courts

Title VII of the Civil Rights Act of 1964 and its 1978 Pregnancy Amendment prohibit employers from discriminating on the basis of sex and/or pregnancy.[16] Yet the courts continued to allow employers to maintain policies excluding millions of women from certain jobs until 1991, when the U.S. Supreme Court struck down exclusionary policies.

One reason for the persistence of exclusionary policies is an ambiguity inherent in Title VII. While barring discrimination on the basis of sex, it allows differential treatment in those instances where sex "is a bona fide occupational qualification [BFOQ] reasonably necessary to the normal operation of that particular business or enterprise."[17] So in the 1980s three U.S. circuit courts of appeals agreed that, while fetal protection policies barring women but not men from working with toxic substances are discriminatory, they may be justified if the employer can demonstrate that: (1) considerable (i.e., not speculative although not necessarily conclusive) objective evidence exists to indicate that there is a substantial risk of harm to the potential offspring of female employees from their exposure to toxic substances in the workplace; (2) scientific evidence also indicates that the hazard does not apply to the offspring of male employees; (3) the program instituted by the employer is effective in obtaining the goal of preventing harm to workers' offspring; and (4) no other, less restrictive alternatives exist which would accomplish this goal.[18] Two of the circuit courts ruled that the fetal protection policies under consideration failed these tests; but the Seventh Circuit Court of Appeals upheld the policy used by Johnson Controls, a California firm.

Johnson Controls had instituted a fetal protection policy at its battery manufacturing plants in 1977 because of the workers' exposure to lead, which has been linked with serious reproductive harm: impaired intelligence and motor abilities, low birthweight, and stillbirth. The policy required that all workers be informed of these risks and that women who intended to get pregnant be encouraged to take another job. In 1982, however, Johnson Controls switched from warning to excluding. The new policy stated that no fertile woman could be hired for a job in which an employee had been found to have a certain level of lead in his or her blood anytime during the previous year; nor could fertile women be hired for a job which might lead to a promotion to the lead-exposed job. In effect, this meant that no production jobs were open to fertile women. Yet there was no exclusionary policy for men, even though paternal exposure may also be harmful to the fetus. This was entirely contrary to the recommendations of the Occupational Safety and Health Administration (OSHA).

> OSHA had issued regulations in 1978 stating that both male and female reproductive functions could be adversely affected by exposure to lead and that "both men and women are subject to genetic damage which may affect both the course and outcome of pregnancy." The agency avoided gender-neutral policies regarding lead exposure in the workplace and said there was no "basis whatsoever for the claim that women of childbearing age should be excluded from the workplace in order to protect the fetus or the course of pregnancy."[19]

Nonetheless, the Seventh Circuit Court of Appeals ruled that Johnson Control's policy was appropriate.

The U.S. Supreme Court, however, disagreed. In 1991 the Court ruled unanimously that the exclusionary policy instituted by Johnson Controls discriminated against women in violation of Title VII. That Johnson Controls was sincerely trying to prevent harm to future generations is irrelevant, the Court noted, because "The absence of a malevolent motive does not convert a facially discriminatory policy into a neutral policy with a discriminatory effect."[20] A majority of justices also contended that almost no fetal protection policy could withstand judicial scrutiny. Although protecting fetuses is morally commendable, it is not the essence of most businesses and therefore cannot be sustained as a business necessity. Their position is straightforward: "Title VII, as amended by the Pregnancy Discrimination Act, forbids sex-specific fetal-protection policies."[21] A minority, however, refused to rule out all fetal protection policies in principle, on the grounds that such a sweeping conclusion is not implied by Title VII.[22]

It is difficult to predict the impact of the Court's ruling in the *Johnson* case. Although the justices unanimously agreed that Johnson Control's exclusionary policy was unfair, they were sharply divided over whether some other exclusionary policy could be sustained in the future. Given the changes in the composition of the Court since this ruling—two of the five majority-opinion justices have left the Court—the fate of fetal protection policies remains an open question.[23]

In response to the Supreme Court's decision, however, Johnson Controls abandoned its exclusionary policy and instituted a policy of warning workers of the dangers of working with lead and having them sign waivers.[24] Full disclosure is of course a good idea; it is an essential element in a worker's ability to make an informed choice. But its combination with waivers can be problematic; Robert Blank sees it as "a type of employment blackmail." His concern is that the use of waivers will shift the burden of responsibility from the employer to the worker, and this "would undermine the very moral responsibility for fetal health that many industries have used to defend FPPs [fetal protection policies] in the first place."[25] Employers may even become less concerned about cleaning up the workplace, making it more dangerous for workers as well as their offspring.

Joseph Losco and Mark Shublak surmise that, if waivers successfully shield employers from civil suits, the repercussions may be far-reaching:

If this use of waivers turns out to blunt suits against employers with workplace hazards, it is not unreasonable to speculate that physicians, hospitals, medical providers, insurance companies, and others may use such devices to limit their own liability in cases where individuals do not live up to a prescribed standard of care. This could force parents either to assume the full cost of raising a child with a serious defect traceable to a workplace hazard or to quit their jobs. In either case, the burden of workplace hazards will have been removed from the company where the hazards exist and transferred to individuals who suffer consequences.[26]

These concerns, however, may be overstated. After all, getting an employee's signature on a waiver does not release the employer from responsibility for providing a safe working environment. OSHA safety rules for the protection of the worker will continue to apply to the manufacturer's production process. And OSHA legislation could be amended to apply specifically to substances causing fetal damage.

In addition, arguments which reject both exclusionary fetal protection policies and employee waivers leave employers in a precarious spot: The employers are legally liable for knowingly hiring women to work in inherently dangerous jobs. The employers' best response, of course, is to remove the hazards from the workplace, or at least to reduce workers' exposure to the hazards to acceptable levels. Where that is possible, an employer should be held accountable for doing so. But that may not always be the case. And then it seems likely that courts would permit waivers, so long as they are carefully framed and limited in scope. In these instances it would be reasonable for the courts to negate any company's attempt to require an employee to waive the company's negligence (where company practices have created a risk of employee harm higher than that which would otherwise be preventable through employer precautions, manufacturing techniques, and safety measures), and to recognize only those waivers which bar claims for injury caused solely by the inherently dangerous nature of the work product. This use of limited waivers should militate against some of the negative repercussions foreseen by Losco and Shublak.

But not all of them. In some instances children who were damaged *in utero* may not be allowed to sue their parents' employers and so will sue their parents instead. This is the subject of the next section.

RESPONDING TO PRENATAL HARMS AFTER THE FACT

Given the host of complexities raised by efforts to control the conduct of pregnant women who cause prenatal harm, perhaps the best answer is to wait until the child is born before taking legal action. The possibility of responding successfully to an impaired child after birth is an important issue, since conclusions regarding appropriate actions during pregnancy would be affected profoundly if we believed that some of the legal and ethical problems of pregnancy could be addressed more successfully after pregnancy.

One increasingly common way of addressing prenatal harm after the fact is through mandatory reporting requirements.[27] States have passed a variety of laws requiring physicians to report purported instances of neglect and abuse. In some states, any newborn whose urine test is positive for illegal drugs is considered by law to be a victim of child abuse or neglect, and hospitals are required to alert local child welfare agencies. In other states, newborns are considered neglected or abused only if they actually exhibit signs of drug addiction or alcohol abuse, and these cases must be reported to state authorities. While in still other states, affected newborns are considered to be at high risk of being abused or neglected in the future, so they too are reported to child protective agencies. As a result, many drug-affected newborns do not leave the hospitals with their mothers but instead are placed with another relative (such as a grandmother) or in a foster home.

Whether or not an infant is released to its mother's custody depends in large part on others' perceptions of the mother's fitness to care for her child. Not all drug-exposed newborns are separated from their mothers, of course; not all drug-abusing women are judged to be incompetent parents. But a woman with a history of many years of drug abuse who has not entered a drug treatment program, who has shown no signs of attempting to deal with her addiction or properly nurture her other children, and who gives birth to an addicted child is likely to leave the birth facility alone.

The concerns raised by removing newborns from their mothers are not fundamentally different from the problems confronted every day by child welfare workers who respond to evidence of past child abuse or neglect and who try to predict and prevent future cases, and by parents who face losing custody of their children. Indeed, children raised by addicts tend to have a variety of problems coping with the world—they tend to be anxious and insecure, for instance, evincing behavior problems and short attention spans—regardless of whether they were exposed to drugs *in utero*. Since procedures and standards for removing children from their parents have been widely debated, and there is an impressive array of current literature on the subject, the issues involved need no further exploration in this book.[28]

There is another method of addressing prenatal harm after the fact: prosecuting mothers for having done something wrong while pregnant. Several states have statutes that allow criminal prosecution of pregnant women who abuse certain illegal substances. But as pointed out here, the criminal approach is fraught with such serious difficulties that it simply cannot be championed as a viable solution to the problem.[29] Therefore we will investigate a relatively new and untested way of responding to prenatal harm after the fact: expanding the realm of private law to allow children to sue their parents for having caused them harm while *in utero*.

Legal Suits to Remedy Prenatal Harm

Rather than allowing the state to intervene in the lives of pregnant women in order to prevent prenatal harm, we might do better to permit children who had been harmed *in utero* to sue their parents later.[30] Conceivably, invoking the private law might well have as much deterrent effect on the injurious activities of pregnant women as would invoking the criminal law, with the added benefit of providing compensation for the impaired child. In addition, the tort approach would be superior to the other methods examined. Unlike proposals to require pregnant women to behave in certain ways, the tort approach is immune to the disapproving charge of unfair discrimination against pregnant women, since fathers too may be sued. Recent evidence that a father's alcohol consumption and cigarette use may cause a variety of problems in his offspring, for instance, could support suits brought by impaired children against their fathers.[31] And unlike the use of criminal sanctions, tort remedies avoid the negative consequences of jailing mothers and branding them with criminal records. Tort law, then, may be the best method for dealing with these situations.

It was mentioned in Chapter Two that prenatal negligent acts or omissions which show up as injuries later are widely accepted as legitimate causes for civil legal action. That is, courts recognize claims made for compensation on behalf of children who suffered unwarranted prenatal injuries and were born alive. Although some jurisdictions recognize as prenatal harms only those injuries inflicted on a viable fetus who is subsequently born alive, most courts allow claims to be made on behalf of a person who was injured at any point during his fetal period. And according to some courts, a person may even be harmed by events that occurred before he was conceived.[32] The harm in these cases is considered to befall the child, not the fetus, as Leonard Glantz explains:

> In compensating those infants who have been harmed as the result of prenatal injuries and were born alive, the courts have implicitly found that the true damage is suffered after birth, i.e., having to go through life with some defect or deformity. Thus, the damage has not actually been suffered by the viable or nonviable fetus, but by the human being who must now live with the handicap caused by the tortfeasor.[33]

One significant conclusion to be drawn from this brief review of the courts' treatment of prenatal harms is that the fetus as such need not be considered to have any moral or legal standing in order for the courts to recognize a prenatal harm, since it is the person after birth who actually suffers.

The type of private law response to prenatal harm with which we are concerned here is a straightforward tort suit: The child who had been harmed while *in utero* sues the person who negligently caused the harm.[34] As with other torts, there are four necessary elements to suits involving prenatal harm: (1) the defendant had a duty of due care to the child; (2) the defendant's act or omission was negligent; (3) the child was harmed (made worse off than he otherwise would have been); and (4) the negligent breach of duty was the proximate cause of harm to the child.

Before we can conclude that allowing children to sue their parents for prenatal injuries is good policy, however, we first must explore the relevant countervailing considerations. There are two types of objections: (1) arguments against allowing children to sue their parents in general, and (2) arguments against allowing children to sue their parents specifically for prenatal harm.

Allowing Children to Sue Their Parents

For the first half of this century, American courts generally were persuaded that children's suits against their parents should not be recognized, believing that such suits would have seriously detrimental
effects on the parent-child relationship. Courts feared that, by allowing children to sue their parents, the state would thereby officially
sanction the blame that children may place on their parents, and thus
would create a means for destroying the family relationship—a relationship the state usually seeks to encourage and protect. Similarly,
courts worried that recognizing such suits would undermine parental
authority and control over their children, and that easy availability of
a legal remedy might encourage people to go too quickly into an
adversarial arena rather than attempting in good faith to work out
their differences between themselves.

But while these are legitimate concerns, there are good reasons to
believe that they should not be determinative. One reasonable
response is that the courts misplace the responsibility for the disinte-
gration of the family. It is not the legal system's recognition of legitimate claims for compensation that creates difficulties within a family,
but the other way around—that is, the existence of serious family
strife leads one member to seek compensation from another through
the courts. In one of the first cases brought by a child against his or
her parent, for instance, a daughter sued her father to compensate her
for injuries suffered when he raped her; but the court rejected her
claim in the interests of preserving domestic harmony.[35] It is difficult
to see the logic of the court's response to this tragic situation, for it
should be clear that an already troubled family will not be saved by
denying one member legal remedy for harm inflicted by another.

A different type of argument against recognizing suits brought by
children against their parents is that the children would not really
benefit. Parents usually care for and support their children; if money
were taken away from them and put into a trust fund for the child,
for instance, the parents would have less to spend on the child, and
the child's care might suffer thereby. Harming the plaintiff in order to
"compensate" him for his injuries clearly makes no sense.

It does not follow from this, however, that children should not be
allowed to sue their parents. It simply means that these matters need
to be decided on a case-by-case basis, and monetary compensation

awarded only in those cases in which it will benefit the child. In addition, a sharp distinction is usually drawn in tort law between the question of liability and the question of damages. For instance, minor children above a certain age can be sued, even though they usually have very shallow pockets and even though their parents are not generally liable for what they do (although some state statutes make parents liable for a limited amount).

There are instances, of course, in which the plaintiff child might benefit monetarily from the suit. A trust could be set up for the child, and the amount of money the parent is compelled to make available for the child's support through the trust might be considerably more than the parent would spend on the child had there been no court award. But this too might backfire insofar as it could create enormous practical difficulties with regard to the child's care should the child remain with his or her parent, since a guardian *ad litem* would have to be appointed by the court to oversee the expenditures from the trust. Would the guardian be expected to select and purchase the child's clothes, for example, or simply pay for the clothes the parent selects? Would the guardian be expected to oversee the child's diet and schooling and extracurricular activities? The guardian *ad litem*'s responsibility for making the support decisions would no doubt infringe in some substantial ways on the parent's autonomy over his or her child, increasing the chances of a further rift between parent and child.

There remains another sort of concern as well. Some courts have worried that recognizing claims brought by children against their parents would create a means for defrauding insurance companies. As one court noted, "We all know that realistically such actions are never thought of, let alone commenced, unless there is an insurance policy."[36] And another court added that, "A parent [with liability insurance coverage] may encourage his minor child to bring such an action against him."[37] In order to protect against such fraudulent claims, some courts have decided to deny all suits brought by children against their parents. This could perhaps best be characterized as the throwing-the-baby-out-with-the-bath-water theory of case disposition, and it could be applied equally well—with obviously disastrous consequences—to many other types of liability insurance cases.

Courts have been moving away from the doctrine of parental immunity, however, and are recognizing a large range of suits brought by children against their parents; indeed, the majority of states have either abandoned or severely restricted parental immunity. In addition to the reasons already given, this change of attitude has been motivated by the recognition that to deny a cause of action by children against their parents is to discriminate unfairly against the children. A related reason involves a concern for consistency in the law: Since courts recognize contract and property disputes between children and their parents, it seems reasonable to recognize torts as well. As one court noted, "[I]t is difficult to argue that the law should protect the property rights of a minor more zealously than the rights of his person."[38] Thus most U.S. courts now conclude that there is no convincing reason—either of logic or of policy—to prohibit children from suing their parents.

Allowing Children to Sue Their Parents for Prenatal Injuries

There are four good reasons for allowing children to sue their parents for having negligently caused them harm while *in utero*. The first is that our society already recognizes prenatal harm in general as a legitimate cause for legal action, so it is unfair to prohibit a tort to go forward on the grounds that the alleged tortfeasor is the parent of the injured party. To do so would be to deny equal protection of the law to the person who has been harmed.

Second, the knowledge that children are allowed to sue their parents for prenatal harm may deter some parents from acting in ways that are likely to cause harm, while still allowing the parents the freedom to choose for themselves (unlike the coercive measures previously discussed). Of course, the deterrent effect would not always exist. It is not likely that the possibility of a legal suit by her child would stop an alcoholic pregnant woman from imbibing large quantities of alcohol or a heroin addict from continuing to use the drug during pregnancy. And in any case, the deterrent effect will only work where the woman is mentally alert and educated enough to understand the very idea of torts and lawsuits, so that this knowledge can prompt her to take suitable actions during pregnancy in order to avoid the prospect of a later court battle. When deterrence fails, however, the third reason for allowing these suits arises: compensation can be provided to the injured child.

Finally, this method escapes the charge of unfair discrimination, since in principle both sexes may be held liable for a prenatal negligent act or omission which later shows up as injury to the child. It is expected that mothers would be sued more frequently, since they have more opportunities for causing prenatal harm, but men too can cause prenatal harm.[39] Take, for instance, the case of Pamela Rae Stewart, described in the previous chapter. Ms. Stewart was accused of harming her son by having intercourse with her husband while she was pregnant and failing to seek medical care after she started to bleed. It could be argued, however, that her husband was also responsible for the child's condition, since he participated in these events even though he was (or so the prosecution claimed) aware of the physician's admonitions.[40] Had the boy lived, he might have had a cause of action against both parents.

These four arguments offer strong support in favor of recognizing a legal duty of due care on the part of both parents that is enforceable after birth in a tort action by the child. But of course there are countervailing considerations.

One concern is that this would create an untenable burden on the pregnant woman, since even her most mundane activities—such as ingesting cough medicine or aspirin or taking an airplane trip or exercising vigorously—could cause prenatal harm. In recognition of this, reasonable standards of care are needed (such as those discussed earlier). When applied to the pregnant woman, these standards of care would involve refraining from acts which a reasonably prudent pregnant person would avoid when that person knows or, in the exercise of reasonable care, should know that such acts cause prenatal harm. The pregnant woman's duty would also extend to the provision of those benefits that a reasonably careful pregnant person would provide. Chapter Three argued that this standard would be different in some important respects from the standard applied to reasonably prudent parents in general (since the fetus exists within the woman's body), and that her duty would be more or less stringent depending on the stage of her pregnancy. Using such standards would free a woman from civil liability for having engaged in potentially risky conduct which the reasonably prudent pregnant person would pursue, as well as for having caused relatively minor prenatal harm.

Another concern is that, while the use of the private law to compensate victims of prenatal harm is theoretically acceptable, it is far from being a real solution to the problem of prenatal harm since it is likely to be applicable only to those few cases in which the child has access to enough money to bring a lawsuit and/or the parent has enough money to provide compensation. And the question of money raises another, even more problematic, consideration: The "deep pockets" elements of our tort system could well induce some child-plaintiffs to sue their mothers' physicians as well as their mothers. In that case, obstetricians would have an incentive to become more coercive toward their patients—using the courts to compel pregnant women to accept certain treatments or to undergo certain lifestyle changes—in order to reduce their own long-range legal liability.

The Illinois Supreme Court found an additional problem with such suits: "Mother and child would be legal adversaries from the moment of conception until birth."[41] While holding a third party liable for prenatal injuries may make sense, the court asserted, holding a mother liable for similar injuries does not: "No other defendant must go through biological changes of the most profound type...in order to bring forth an adversary into the world." The court concluded that a child should not be able to sue her mother for having caused prenatal injuries—due to an automobile accident in this case—because such suits would infringe too much on the mother's rights of privacy and bodily autonomy.

There is one more countervailing consideration: A pregnant woman who fears that the child she intends to bear will eventually bring suit against her in court might choose instead to have an abortion. While this does not trouble everyone, it is enough to deter some from advocating the tort remedy. Illinois state Senator Richard Kelly, for instance, has stated that although a child ought to have the right to sue her mother for prenatal harm, he is unwilling to introduce a bill permitting such action for fear that abortions would increase as a result.[42]

Conclusion

The risk of these unappealing side effects militates against allowing children to sue their parents for prenatal harm, and it provides us with yet another reason for seeking a less adversarial method for responding to the problem of prenatal harm. Indeed, all of the proposals we have examined have serious problems. They are either ineffective, unfair, or too costly (in terms of both their burdens on individuals and their negative social consequences). We remain, then, without a good legal solution to the problem of avoidable prenatal harm. There is no good solution. But there is a set of relatively unintrusive approaches that ought to be tried: intensifying educational efforts, making contraceptive methods more available and affordable, providing free prenatal care, offering positive rewards for pregnant women who change their lifestyles, and so on. This is the subject of the final chapter.

NOTES

1. Reproductive damage includes, e.g., infertility, impotence, and spontaneous abortion, as well as various birth defects and genetic disorders. T. W. Clarkson et al., *Reproductive and Developmental Toxicity of Metals*, N.Y.: Plenum Press, 1983; M. Kirsch-Volders (ed.), *Mutagenicity, Carcinogenicity and Teratogenicity of Industrial Pollutants*, N.Y.: Plenum Press, 1984; P. R. Sager et al., "Reproductive and Developmental Toxicity of Metals," in L. Friberg et al. (eds.), *Handbook on the Toxicology of Metals, Volume II*, N.Y.: Elsevier, 1986.

2. Companies that instituted fetal protection policies include Olin Corporation, Eastman Kodak, Goodyear, B.F. Goodrich, DuPont, General Motors, Johnson Controls, and American Cyanamid.

3. Judge Frank H. Easterbrook estimated that as many as 20 million jobs would be closed to women. *International Union, UAW v. Johnson Controls*, 886 F2d 871 (7th Cir., 1989). But precisely determining the impact on women is exceedingly difficult, as Alan Blanco explains:

> A further estimate of potential impact can be made by considering the range of products processed with substances which form the basis of exclusionary policies. About 835,000 workers are affected by the OSHA lead standard, about two million workers are exposed to benzine, and hundreds of thousands of workers are exposed to vinyl chloride. Aggregation of these figures results in a very incomplete estimate of the potential exclusionary effects of fetal protection policies because the list of hazardous substances is very incomplete.

A. C. Blanco, "Fetal Protection Programs Under Title VII—Rebutting the Procreation Presumption," *University of Pittsburgh Law Review* 46, 755–794, pp. 763–64.

4. R. Bayer, "Women, Work, and Reproductive Hazards," *The Hastings Center Report* 12, pp. 14–19, 1982; R. Retshesky, "Workers, Reproductive Hazards, & the Politics of Protection: An Introduction," *Feminist Studies* 5, pp. 233–46, 1979. For a discussion of the importance of work, the role of women in the workforce, and the value of "good and fulfilling work" to the individual, see A. R. Gini, and T. J. Sullivan, *It Comes with the Territory: An Inquiry Concerning Work and the Person*, N.Y.: Random House, 1986.

5. S. Faludi, *Backlash: The Undeclared War Against American Women*, N.Y.: Crown, 1991; K. J. Maschke, "From the Workplace to the Delivery Room: Protecting the Fetus in the Post-*Roe* Era," *Politics and the Life Sciences* 12, 53–60, 1993; R. Retshesky, "Workers, Reproductive Hazards, & the Politics of Protection: An Introduction," *Feminist Studies* 5, 233–46, 1979; W.W. Williams, "Firing the Woman to Protect the Fetus: The Reconciliation of Fetal Protection with Employment Opportunity Goals Under Title VII," *The Georgetown Law Review* 69, pp. 641–704, 1981.

6. American Society of Anesthesiologists, "Occupational Disease Among Operating Room Personnel: A National Study," *Anesthesiology* 41, pp. 321–40, 1974; Baker and Dalrymple, "Radiation and the Fetus," in W. R. Hendee, (ed.), *Health Effects of Low-Level Radiation*, Norwalk, CT.: Appleton-Century-Croft, pp. 127–30, 1984; E. N. Cohen et al., "Anesthesia, Pregnancy, and Miscarriage: A Study of Operating Room Nurses and Anesthetists," *Anesthesiology* 34, 343–47, 1971; R. P. Knill-Jones et al., "Anesthetic Practice and Pregnancy: Controlled Study of Women Anesthetists in the United Kingdon," *Lancet* 1, pp. 1326–28, 1972; T. Tannenbaum and R. J. Goldberg, "Exposure to Anesthetic Gases and Reproductive Outcome—A Review of the Epidemiologic Literature," *Journal of Occupational Medicine* 27, pp. 659–68, 1985.

7. W. W. Williams, "Firing the Woman to Protect the Fetus: The Reconciliation of Fetal Protection with Employment Opportunity Goals Under Title VII," *The Georgetown Law Review* 69, 641–704, 1981.

8. A. C. Blanco, "Fetal Protection Programs Under Title VII—Rebutting the Procreation Presumption," p. 30.

9. Office of Technology Assessment: *Reproductive Health Hazards in the Workplace: Summary*, Washington, D.C.: Government Printing Office, 1985; D. Savitz et al., "Effect of Parents' Occupational Exposures on Risk of Stillbirth, Preterm Delivery, and Small-for-gestational-age Infants," *American Journal of Epidemiology* 129, pp. 1201–18, 1989; J. R. Wilklins and R. A. Koutras, "Paternal Occupation and Brain Cancer in Offspring," *American Journal of Industrial Medicine* 14, pp. 299–318, 1988.

10. This high degree of uncertainty is a regular feature in dealing with reproductive hazards in the workplace. A great deal remains unknown about reproductive hazards in general: What substances do in fact cause damage to the offspring of workers? At what levels are these substances safe or unsafe to fetuses? What are the probabilities that damage will occur? Does the damage occur to the parent (and hence indirectly to the fetus) or directly to the fetus? Do the substances affect both men and women, and to what extent? Improving this state of affairs is exceedingly difficult. The damage, for instance, may not be caused by a substance used in isolation, but instead may be caused by one ingredient within a mixture of chemicals—and we have no simple, effective method for determining toxicity for complex chemical mixtures. In addition, the harm may have a multitude of contributing causes that are impossible to isolate. Or the harm may be the result of cumulative or synergistic influences, each individual instance of which goes unnoticed.

Furthermore, the difficulty of assigning probabilities to one potentially harmful factor among many will remain a serious problem, since experiments designed to isolate one variable while controlling others may themselves be unethical. An experiment designed to determine the level at which a particular substance is harmful would be unethical, for example, because it would deliberately expose people to substances known to increase the probability of harm, presumably in doses large enough to be able to determine the degree of the probability. In other words, the experiment would involve intentionally harming innocent people. So the uncertainty involved in ascertaining reproductive hazards in the workplace seems to be as intractable as it is pervasive.

11. T. M. Murray, "Who Do Fetal-Protection Policies Really Protect?" *Technology Review* 88, pp. 12–13, 20, 1988 at p. 20.

12. Not only does the death of a parent frequently put the child at considerable financial risk, but evidence shows that the emotional damage to the child is often severe and long-lasting; indeed, the early loss of a parent may be instrumental in precipitating self-destructive conduct by the child years afterward. H. I. Kushner, *Self-Destruction in the Promised Land: A Psychocultural History*, N.J.: Rutgers University Press, 1989.

13. "Blood, Sweat and Fears," *Time* 9/28/87, pp. 50–51.

14. "Danger on the Job," *Newsweek*, pp. 42–46, 1989.

15. Circuit Court Judge Cudahy dissented in (*U.A.W. v. Johnson Controls op cit.*, p. 902).

16. Section 703(a) of the Civil Rights Act of 1964, 78 Stat. 255. Title VII prohibits employers from discriminating against any individual on the basis of that person's race, color, religion, sex, or national origin. In 1978 Congress passed the Pregnancy Discrimination Act (P.L. 95–555), which included the Pregnancy Amendment to Title VII; this amendment prohibits employers from discriminating against "women affected by pregnancy, childbirth, or related medical conditions."

17. Section 703(e) of Title VII, Civil Rights Act of 1964.

18. *Hayes v. Shelby Memorial Hospital* 726 F.2d 1543, 1984; *International Union, UAW v. Johnson Controls op cit.*; *Wright v. Olin Corp* 697 F.2d 1172, 1982.

19. K. J. Maschke, *op cit.*, p. 54.

During the 1980s, however, OSHA played a minor role in the development of fetal protection policies. "During this period . . . OSHA did not fulfill its statutory mandate to ensure that workers be safeguarded from reproductive hazards. It was barred from utilizing its general duty clause to prohibit employers from conditioning employment on sterilization. Moreover, the agency was lax in enforcing existing standards and in formulating new standards to regulate reproductive hazards in the workplace. Where OSHA did attempt to regulate these policies, its efforts were thwarted by the courts, which determined that fetal protection policies were not within the scope of the Occupational Safety and Health Act." S. U. Samuels, "To Furnish a Workplace Free From Recognized Hazards," *Politics and the Life Sciences* 12, pp. 243–54, 1993.

20. *International Union, UAW v. Johnson Controls*, p. 188.

21. *International Union, UAW v. Johnson Controls*, p. 187.

22. Five justices—Blackmun, Marshall, Stevens, O'Connor, and Souter—interpreted Title VII to exclude fetal protection policies; four justices—Kennedy, Rehnquist, Scalia, and White—agreed that Title VII might permit some fetal protection policies.

23. Since the *Johnson* ruling, Justices Marshall, Blackmun, and White have been succeeded by Justices Thomas, Ginzberg, and Breyer.

24. J. Losco and M. Shublak, "Paternal–Fetal Conflict: An Examination of Paternal Responsibilities to the Fetus," *Politics and the Life Sciences* 13, pp. 63–75, 1994.

25. R. Blank, *Fetal Protection in the Workplace*, N.Y.: Columbia University Press, p. 161, 1993.

26. J. Losco and M. Shublak, *op cit.*, p. 71.

27. See N. K. Schiff, "Legislation Punishing Drug Use During Pregnancy," *Hastings Constitutional Law Quarterly* 19, pp. 197–234, 1991; T. L. Pelham and A. R. DeJong, "Nationwide Practices for Screening and Reporting Prenatal Cocaine Abuse," *Child Abuse and Neglect* 16, pp. 763–70, 1992.

28. See, e.g., M. Bush, *Families in Distress*, Berkeley: University of California Press, 1988; S. M. Ehrenkranz et al. (eds.), *Clinical Social Work with Maltreated Children and Their Families*, N.Y.: New York University Press, 1989; A. M. Haralambie, *Handling Child Custody, Abuse, and Adoption Cases, 2nd edition*, N.Y.: McGraw-Hill, 1993.

29. See also J. C. Merrick, "Maternal Substance Abuse During Pregnancy," *Journal of Legal Medicine* 14, pp. 57–71, 1993; L. Rubenstein, "Prosecuting Maternal Substance Abusers: An Unjustified and Ineffective Policy," *Yale Law and Policy Review* 9, pp. 130–60, 1991; D. E. Roberts, "Punishing Drug Addicts Who Have Babies: Women of Color, Equality, and the Right of Privacy," *Harvard Law Review* 104(7), pp. 1419–82, 1991; D. W. Greene, "Abuse Prosecutors: Gender, Race, and Class Discretion and the Prosecution of Drug-Addicted Mothers," *Buffalo Law Review* 39, pp. 737–802, 1991; N. K. Schiff, "Legislation Punishing Drug Use During Pregnancy: Attack on Women's Rights in the Name of Fetal Protection," *Hastings Constitutional Law Quarterly* 19, pp. 197–234, 1991.

30. See, e.g., M. W. Shaw, "Conditional Prospective Rights of the Fetus," *The Journal of Legal Medicine* 5, pp. 63–116, 1984; C. Simon, "Parental Liability for Prenatal Injury," *Columbia Journal of Law and Social Problems* 14, pp. 47–92, 1978.

31. Ervin et al.; E. M. John et al.; R. E. Little; and C. F. Sing.

32. In *Renslow v. Mennonite Hospital*, for instance, the Illinois Supreme Court held that a child who suffered permanent disability to her brain, nervous system, and various organs had a legitimate claim for compensation as the result of the negligent transfusion of her Rh-negative mother with Rh-positive blood—over seven years prior to the child's conception. The court found that the child was harmed by the negligent transfusion because she was made worse off than she otherwise would have been, even though she did not exist at the time the harmful activity (the transfusion) occurred. The court reasoned that,

> The cases allowing relief to an infant for injuries incurred in its previable state make it clear that a defendant may be held liable to a person whose existence was not apparent at the time of his act. We therefore find it illogical to bar relief for an act done prior to conception where the defendant would be liable for this same conduct had the child, unbeknownst to him, been conceived prior to his act. We believe that there is a right to be born free from prenatal injuries forseeably caused by a breach of duty to the child's mother.
>
> The extension of duty in such a case is further supported by sound policy considerations. Medical science has developed various techniques which can mitigate or, in some cases, totally alleviate a child's prenatal harm. In light of these substantial medical advances it seems to us that sound social policy requires the extension of duty in this case *Renslow v. Mennonite Hospital* 367 N.E.2d 1250, 1977, at p. 1255).

See also *Bergstresser v. Mitchell* 577 F.2d 22, 1978, *Jorgensen v. Meade Johnson Laboratories, Inc.* 483 F.2d 237, 1973.

This reasoning is not universally accepted, however. In *Albala v. City of New York* (434 N.Y.S.2d 400, 1981), for instance, the court refused to recognize a cause of action brought on behalf of a brain-damaged child whose injuries had resulted from a perforation of the uterus which had been suffered by the child's mother during an abortion performed prior to the child's conception.

33. L. H. Glantz, "The Legal Aspects of Fetal Viability," in A. Milunsky and G. J. Annas (eds.), *Genetics and the Law,* N.Y.: Plenum Press, p. 36, 1976.

34. A complex variation on this is the "wrongful life" suit. In a wrongful life suit, a child claims that, but for the conduct of another, she would not have been conceived or, once conceived, would not have been born alive, and that her being born with serious impairments (even though there was no possibility that she could be born without the impairments) was a harm that calls for compensation. The child states, in effect, that she never should have been born, and she claims damages for having to live with her permanent and severe handicaps.

The first "wrongful life" suit was brought forward in 1963. In that case, the son of an unwed woman sued his father for creating his illegitimate state. The court refused to allow the child to recover, however, for fear that the judicial system would be inundated with suits brought by disgruntled children [*Zepeda v. Zepeda* 41 Ill. Ap.2d 240, 190 N.E.2d 849, *cert denied* 379 U.S. 945, 1964]. Most wrongful life cases, however, differ from this one in that a party other than the parent is the defendant (usually a health care professional), and the child's condition is worse than illegitimacy (for example, the child suffers from cystic fibrosis or Tay–Sachs disease). Nonetheless, many courts have refused to allow the children any recovery for damages, usually on the grounds that "there is no rational way to measure non-existence with the pain and suffering of the child's impaired existence" [*Goldberg v. Ruskin* 499 N.E.2d 406, 1986]—and therefore there is no way to measure appropriate compensation for the child.

Other courts, however, have recognized that medical professionals may be liable for damages to children in wrongful life suits, although the damages awarded in these cases have not included pain and suffering awards but instead have been limited to medical expenses *Curlender v. Bio-Science Laboratories* 106 Cal. App.3d 811, 165 Cal Rptr. 477, 1980, *Procanik v. Cillo* 97 N.J. 339, 478 A.2d 755, 1984. And as a California court noted, wrongful life suits against parents may also be appropriate:

> One of the fears expressed in the decisional law is that, once it is determined that such infants have rights cognizable at law, nothing would prevent such a plaintiff from bringing suit against its own parents for allowing plaintiff to be born. In our view, this fear is groundless. The 'wrongful-life' cause of action with which we are concerned is based upon negligently caused failure by someone under a duty to do so to inform the prospective parents of facts needed by them to make a conscious choice *not* to become parents. If a case arose where, despite due care by the medical profession in transmitting the necessary warnings, parents made a conscious choice to proceed with a pregnancy, with full knowledge that a seriously impaired infant would be born, that conscious choice would provide an intervening act of proximate cause to preclude liability insofar as defendants other than the parents were concerned. Under such circumstances, we see no sound public policy which should protect those parents from being answerable for the pain, suffering and misery which they have wrought upon their offspring [*Curlender v. Bio-Science Laboratories*].

Notably, the California legislature responded to this case by enacting Civil Code Section 43.6, which ensures that children cannot sue their parents for bringing them into the world. And other states—including Minnesota, South Dakota, and Utah—have passed laws prohibiting wrongful life suits in general.

In contrast are torts brought by the parents. Parents may sue a health care provider for "wrongful birth" due to the provider's failure to warn them of the risks of birth defects or for giving them inaccurate information about the risks. The charge here is that the parents would not have brought the fetus to term had they realized its damaged state, and they sue for the expenses of caring for a seriously impaired child and compensation for their suffering in doing so. A similar type of case is "wrongful conception" (also referred to as "wrongful pregnancy"), in which parents sue health care providers over the failure of their attempts to avoid pregnancy (i.e., unsuccessful sterilizations, abortions, or birth control measures) and the resultant birth of an unwanted child. Parents may also sue the person who negligently causes the death of a wanted fetus ("wrongful death").

For more on the complex subject of "wrongful life," see J. R. Botkin, "The Legal Concept of Wrongful Life," *Journal of the American Medical Association* 259, 1541–45, 1988; H. T. Engelhardt, Jr., "Current Controversies in Obstetrics: Wrongful Life and Forced Fetal Surgical Procedures," *American Journal of Obstetrics and Gynecology* 151, 313–18, 1985; J. Feinberg, "Wrongful Life and the Counterfactual Element in Harming," *Social Philosophy and Policy* 4, 145–78, 1986; E. H. Morreim, "The Concept of Harm Reconceived: A Different Look at Wrongful Life," *Law and Philosophy* 7, 3–33, 1988; T. D. Rogers, "Wrongful Life and Wrongful Birth," *South Carolina Law Review* 33, pp. 713–57, 1982; B. Steinbock, "The Logical Case for Wrongful Life," *Hastings Center Report* 16, 15–20, 1986.

35. *Roller v. Roller*, 37 Wash. 242, 79 P. 788, 1905.

36. *Hastings v. Hastings*, 33 N.J. 247, 163 A.2d 147, 1960, at 150.

37. *Dennis v. Walker*, 284 F. Supp. 413, 1968, at 417.

38. *Goller v. White*, 20 Wis.2d 402, 122 N.W.2d 193, 1963.

39. J. Losco and M. Shublak, *op. cit.*

40. Criminal charges were not brought against the father because he denied knowledge of the doctor's recommendations and the prosecutor could not prove otherwise.

41. *Stallman v. Youngquist*, No. 6457 (Ill. Sup. Ct., 1988).

42. P. Marcotte, "Crime and Pregnancy," *ABA Journal*, 14–15, 1989.

7

Social Reform

INTRODUCTION

Social disadvantages—such as low socioeconomic status, lack of education, inaccessibility of prenatal care, and stress—significantly increase the risk of serious prenatal harm.[1] Thus an effective, and non-coercive, way to reduce the incidence of avoidable prenatal harm is to improve women's general quality of life. The opportunities for improvement exist on many fronts in the United States. George Annas, for instance, argues that,

> The best chance the state has to protect fetuses is through actions to enhance the status of all women by fostering reasonable pay for the work they do and equal employment opportunities, and providing a reasonable social safety net, quality prenatal services, and day care programs.[2]

And Dawn Johnsen adds that,

> Guaranteeing pregnant women adequate food, housing, and medical care would go very far toward improving the health of the children they bear. Also, accommodating pregnancy in the workplace through paid disability leave, liberal parental leave for both parents, part-time employment, and flexible hours, all without hidden penalties on career advancement, would enable women to give more consideration to the health of their fetuses, as well as to their own health.[3]

Proposals for providing a comprehensive set of social benefits to women and children should be taken seriously. They are in some countries. In Sweden, for example, the government subsidizes day-care centers and health care programs, and employers offer fifteen

153

months of paid parental leave from work; the citizens of the Nether-
lands enjoy an extensive social security net which offers financial
assistance throughout their lives. Indeed, the social benefits offered to
pregnant women throughout Europe are far more bountiful than
those in the United States. And the infant mortality/morbidity statistics are far better in those countries than in the United States.[4]

Although the United States is far from having a generous network of support programs, it has continued to show at least a modest
commitment to providing social services. Congress has consistently
supported antipoverty programs (at least to the extent that it has not
cut funding to these programs as deeply as it could have), and it
recently widened pregnant women's eligibility for Medicaid benefits;
the vast majority of Americans have some form of health insurance
(either public or private); a variety of municipalities have passed com-
parable-worth laws (evening out the wage levels of male and female
workers); more and more corporations offer leaves to new parents
(with assurances of comparable jobs when they return); the federal
government (through its Social Services Block Grant) as well as many
companies provide day-care benefits; and so on.

It is highly unlikely, however, that this country will soon provide
a secure social safety net under which its citizens need not fall, or that
American businesses will become significantly more sensitive to the
needs and concerns of parents. Certainly the necessary set of social
programs will not be established soon enough to prevent the impairment of thousands of infants.[5] But recognizing that these benefits will
be withheld is one thing; believing that these benefits should be withheld turns all declarations of concern for healthy babies and healthy
children—and certainly all statements of concern for preventing prenatal harm—into empty (and suspect) pronouncements.

Given that major American social institutions will not soon be
transformed, this country can at least increase its efforts to enhance
some of its current programs. I noted that one area in which there is
considerable room for improvement is the treatment of pregnant drug
addicts, and there are other methods as well which have the potential
for greatly reducing the incidence of prenatal harm and improving
the health of infants. Two will be explored here: improving women's
access to medical care and nutritional support.

An alternative view—one this book rejects—is that the only legitimate role of the state is to protect the negative rights of individuals,
and this does not include the conferral of positive benefits such as

health care and nutritional support. Proponents of this libertarian stance contend that the only social structure compatible with it is the competitive market, and all resources should be distributed by free-market processes.

But there are serious problems with this position. The interplay of legitimate voluntary exchanges in the marketplace may lead to injustices. One countervailing consideration is that cumulative harmful effects on welfare and liberty created by unfettered market processes may be serious enough to provide strong ethical grounds for challenging the virtually unlimited right to private property and free exchange championed by libertarians. A second argument against the unchecked market is that because everyone has an extended period of dependence in childhood, how well one fares will be determined to a large extent by the voluntary exchanges of one's parents, not by one's own voluntary exchanges. A final argument against the libertarian position is that the market simply transmits the unfairness of the initial distribution of assets that people bring to the market. For all of these reasons, the moral and social costs of an unchecked market may be too high, and interference may be warranted in some circumstances.

Health care is frequently invoked as a legitimate exception to allowing market forces to operate freely. Using the ability to pay to decide which patients receive health care is, many argue, unfair discrimination against the poor, and need for health care should instead be the primary distributive criterion. This basically is the position assumed in this book—with the caveat that, because resources are finite and health is not the only good, not all health care "needs" can be met.

MEDICAL CARE

There is an impressive array of evidence indicating that prenatal care is effective in reducing infant mortality and morbidity.[6] While most pregnant women in the United States have access to prenatal care in theory—the majority of large and medium sized companies provide prenatal care as part of their health insurance benefits, while all state Medicaid programs cover prenatal care—in fact millions of pregnant women find it difficult to receive adequate medical care.[7] Those most likely to receive little or no prenatal care are indigent, unmarried teen-agers of African descent; and these are precisely the individuals who are at greatest risk of having low-birthweight babies.

Some women do not receive medical care because they do not seek it. They are stymied by a lack of transportation, or an inability to find someone to care for their other children, or a fear of the medical establishment, or a lack of knowledge about the importance of prenatal care and/or the availability of services, or an unwillingness to cope with the inconveniences and long waits at many clinics.[8] Many other pregnant women go without medical care because it is not available. This is due in part to a dearth of physicians in some areas, and in part to the reluctance of some physicians to treat Medicaid patients and patients with no health insurance.[9]

One result of the dearth of prenatal care is that many children are born handicapped who could have been born healthy. In one recent case, a woman who had not received prenatal care before delivery bore a child suffering from cataracts as well as liver and heart problems caused by her syphilis—all of which could have been prevented had she been given a $20 injection of penicillin. The child survived for a only a month, at a cost of over $70,000 for hospital care.[10] And the incidence of low birthweight (2,500 grams or less), which is a major determinant of infant mortality and morbidity, could be reduced significantly with adequate prenatal care. In its 1985 study on low-birthweight infants, the Institute of Medicine concluded that,

> Efforts to reduce the nation's incidence of low birthweight must include a commitment to enrolling all pregnant women in prenatal care. Many of the women who now receive inadequate prenatal care are those at greater than average risk of a low birthweight delivery. Moreover, participation in a system of prenatal care is a prerequisite for many individual interventions that help reduce the risk of low birthweight.
>
> In reaching this conclusion, the committee reviewed carefully the data documenting the effectiveness of prenatal care and concluded that, although a few studies have not been able to demonstrate a positive effect of prenatal care, the overwhelming weight of the evidence indicates that prenatal care reduces low birthweight and that the effect is greatest among high-risk women. This finding is strong enough to support a broad national commitment to ensuring that all pregnant women, especially those at socioeconomic or medical risk, receive high-quality prenatal care.[11]

I concur that the medical benefits offered to pregnant women should be as comprehensive as possible. Admittedly this would require expanding the current system of benefits significantly, and thus spending considerably more money on prenatal care, but several programs have confirmed the value of this approach:

> Key reforms in such successful demonstration programs have included early, stable, and continuous enrollment; an expansion of benefits to include preventive health and patient support services as well as traditional medical and hospital care; adequate reimbursement; and extensive utilization of community-based providers skilled in caring for low-income patients and trained in the management of persons with medical and social risks. When such changes have been made, impressive results have followed, and sizable cost savings have been realized.[12]

An example is the Family Center Program, which has provided comprehensive prenatal and postnatal care of drug-dependent women since 1969. The program utilizes nurses, neonatologists, perinatologists, psychiatrists, and social workers in a team approach to treatment. In addition to medical care and drug detoxification, the Family Center Program offers individual counseling, support groups, nutrition education, parenting classes, and home visits. Although the program has had little success in keeping its patients from taking teratogenic substances—it is an outpatient program—it has had considerable success in reducing the incidence of low-birthweight infants and premature births.[13]

Of course, it is naive to think that simply making adequate medical care available to pregnant women would solve the problem of avoidable prenatal harm. There are many reasons a pregnant woman does not seek prenatal care, such as lack of transportation or babysitters, fear of physicians, or ignorance about the value of prenatal care. Simply making the services available, therefore, would fall short of the goal of substantially reducing the incidence of prenatal harm. Hence supplementary public education programs are also needed, as well as incentive programs to encourage pregnant women to seek care. Money could be offered for each prenatal visit, for example.[14] And services—such as transportation to the health care institution and child care—could be provided. Many European countries offer these and other services—such as home visits to provide educational services and social support—to pregnant women, with impressive results: almost all pregnant women participate in early and continuous prenatal care. Indeed, it is clear that European policy makers have realized that merely offering prenatal medical care is not enough. To be effective, medical services must be embedded in a "generous spectrum of social supports and financial benefits."[15]

If our society is serious about reducing the incidence of prenatal harm, serious enough to consider criminalizing some actions of pregnant women, then extending these benefits makes sense as a first step. Indeed, extending these benefits should be required as a first step.

IMPROVED NUTRITION

There is no doubt that maternal nutrition during pregnancy has an enormous impact on the health of the child after birth. Improper maternal nutrition may cause congenital malformations, may impair the development of the brain, and may produce low-birthweight infants, who have higher infant mortality and disability rates.[16] One fairly straightforward means of accomplishing the goal of increasing the number of healthier babies, then, is to increase the number of pregnant women who have adequate and appropriate diets.

The most common problem is presented by pregnant women who cannot afford a nutritious diet, and much is already being done to help them. In 1972, for instance, Congress revised the Child Nutrition Act to include the Special Supplemental Food Program for Women, Infants and Children (WIC), which provides supplemental food (such as milk, cheese, eggs, cereal, and juice) to low-income mothers with infants and to children below the age of six with nutritional problems. This program, which was implemented in 1974, has been successful in reducing the number of low-birthweight babies and the number of newborns who require treatment in neonatal intensive care units—and has also been successful in reducing Medicaid costs.[17] Unfortunately, many members of Congress are trying to dismantle the program.

And much more remains to be accomplished. Many poor families either cannot obtain nutritional support or receive a supply inadequate to meet their needs. There are many reasons for this: Some people live in remote areas and do not have easy access to social service agencies; some people are intimidated by the bureaucratic rules involved; some people still do not realize that these benefits are available. Many people, though, are poor but not poor enough to qualify for assistance, and this number increases as financial cuts in social services are made. And cuts in other social service programs—such as housing subsidies and assistance with utility bills—leaves the beneficiaries with less money to spend on food. In addition, the WIC program continues to fall far short of providing benefits to all who are eligible.[18]

There is a different type of problem here as well: Some pregnant women have the means to obtain nutritional foods but eat badly anyway. Many of these women simply are not aware of what they should and should not be eating, and some of them would respond positively to educational efforts. But not all of them; it is surprisingly difficult to entice some pregnant women to change their eating habits.[19] Reaching these women would involve more effort, such as offering individual counseling and reinforcement sessions.

Although providing these sessions would be considerably more expensive than distributing pamphlets or showing films, the costs would be offset by the savings in neonatal intensive care.[20] Many low-birthweight babies spend the first month of their lives in a neonatal intensive care unit, at a cost of approximately $60,000 each. For considerably less than this amount of money, a full-time nutritionist could be hired to counsel pregnant women regarding their eating habits. If only two mothers per year were persuaded to maintain appropriate diets, so two infants escaped the problems of low birthweight—and the cost of two months' treatment in a neonatal intensive care unit was thereby eliminated—the savings would be considerable.

Some women, however, would be deaf to the entreaties of a counselor. Take, for instance, the case of Adrienne Robinson, mentioned at the beginning of Chapter One:

> On a return visit to the hospital, Adrienne Robinson tells of how, three months pregnant, she began living alone in an abandoned car after her cocaine-smoking boyfriend beat her with a baseball bat, whipped her with an extension cord, and tried to move in another woman-friend.
>
> Ms. Robinson saw doctors once, after contracting pneumonia, then moved into a motel with another homeless woman, who hallucinated, beat her and traded Ms. Robinson's federal pregnancy-related milk and food supplies for cocaine. Ms. Robinson ate

potato chips and smoked cocaine. 'I knew I was killing my baby, but I couldn't stop,' she says, rocking Christian, born with syphilis and cocaine addiction.[21]

Could a counselor have persuaded Ms. Robinson to change her ways? It is impossible to say. It is likely, though, that merely increasing food benefits to her—without any further help—would simply have improved her access to illegal drugs. Hence even stronger measures— such as intensive efforts to get her to enter a drug treatment program (assuming one is available)—might have been appropriate.

The basic point, however, should not be lost. Providing indigent women with the means for obtaining nutritious diets would go further in reducing the number of low-birthweight babies than would, for instance, committing drug-addicted women to jail (where they are more likely to receive the drugs to which they are addicted than they are to receive treatment for their addictions). And if we as a society are so concerned about preventing prenatal harm, it makes more sense for us to ensure equitable access to basic health care services than to bring the coercive mechanisms of state criminal statutes to bear. Making these benefits available would save the lives as well as improve the health of many children, without infringing on their mothers' rights of bodily integrity and private decision making. Indeed, the existence of these less intrusive and cost-effective means of preventing prenatal harm stands as a strong reason against allowing the state to intrude into a pregnant woman's life in more invasive ways.

CONCLUSION

I have argued that, while a pregnant women has moral obligations to act in the interests of her future child throughout her pregnancy, there are compelling reasons against legally requiring her to meet certain standards of due care before it is uncontroversially clear that she will bring the pregnancy to term. Hence the state would not be justified in intervening to prevent some very troubling types of prenatal harm because they are caused during the early stage of pregnancy.

However, there still may be instances in which the state's interests in preventing prenatal harm may be strong enough to warrant overriding a pregnant woman's freedom of choice (which, after all, is not unlimited, even in principle) when it is uncontroversially clear that she will go to term. But an intervention would have to meet certain fundamental tests before it would be justifiable: (1) The harm to be prevented to the future person is grave and irreversible; (2) the harm to the mother is relatively minor; (3) the intervention involves the least intrusive means available; (4) the intervention will be successful in preventing or at least ameliorating serious prenatal harm; (5) requirements of due process and equal protection of the law are met; and (6) the benefits of adopting this type of state intervention as social policy will greatly outweigh the disbenefits.

There are, however, a variety of countervailing considerations: (1) A woman's fundamental rights of bodily integrity and private decision making should not be subordinated to the welfare of someone else; (2) state intervention into the activities of pregnant women will have seriously negative consequences (pregnant women will be unwilling to be candid with their physicians, for instance, or they will not seek prenatal care at all); (3) a few reasonable limitations on the activities of pregnant women may lead inevitably to many unjust and onerous limitations (the "slippery slope" arguments); (4) it is not fair to demand things of pregnant women that are demanded of no one else in society, so requiring pregnant women to behave in certain ways or risk legal penalties is unfairly discriminatory; and (5) it is sometimes impossible to draft fair, workable laws.

It is difficult at this early stage of the debate to evaluate conclusively the pros and cons of allowing the state to intervene in the lives of pregnant women in order to prevent prenatal harm. Good policy choices require reliable empirical data analyzing the consequences of institutionalizing the type of action in question, and many of the requisite sociological, historical, medical, and psychological studies have not yet been completed (or, in some cases, even undertaken). Arguments on both sides of the issue appeal to likely consequences, but no one really knows whether and to what extent these consequences will actually materialize. Hence my conclusions are necessarily preliminary and theoretical, and even a bit tentative. It does seem clear, though, that few, if any, coercive state interventions to prevent prenatal harm could meet the conditions stated here.

Although I have highlighted the substantial problems encountered in legally forcing pregnant women to act in certain ways for the sake of their future children, my analysis does not by any means imply that society should ignore the future persons who are avoidably harmed in the prenatal stage. There is considerable room for

reform in the area between the extremes of instituting coercive measures backed by the power of the state —threat of criminal sanction,
for instance, or direct court orders to undergo medical treatment —
and giving pregnant women *carte blanche* to behave any way they
wish.

Since many pregnant women in America cannot afford nutritious
diets and have little or no access to adequate medical care or treatment for addictions, their chances are low of meeting acceptable standards of care toward their future children. If we as a society wish to
require that people meet certain standards of due care, then we
should make it possible for them to do so. And one real opportunity
for compliance will come through improved social benefits, a method
that can be expected to more successful and less intrusive than using
threats of criminal sanction or tort liability, forcing medical treatment,
or mandating drug detoxification. Hence, before we consider initiat-
ing coercive state mechanisms to punish women who fail to maintain
what we judge to be proper standards of care during pregnancy, we
should at least give them a meaningful chance to do better voluntarily.

The proposal is, therefore, that we expand the level of benefits
designed to promote healthy pregnancies: Increase the availability of
prenatal care programs, offer incentives and inducements to women
to enroll in programs designed to change behavior patterns, send out
more social workers to educate women of childbearing age, provide
counselors to attempt to persuade the more recalcitrant pregnant
women to amend their ways, and so on.[22] And since those women
who are pregnant even though they do not want to be are likely to fail
to act in the interests of children they do not want to have, improving
their chances of not getting pregnant would be an important step in
the direction of reducing prenatal harm. Sex and health education in
the schools should be expanded and required, and methods of contraception should be made more widely available and affordable.[23] The
success of similar programs in a variety of European countries adds
strength to the argument that they should be introduced here.

An increase in the level of social benefits will not be effective in
eliminating all preventable prenatal harm, of course, and some pregnant women will continue to fall below the minimum standard of
care of a reasonably prudent pregnant person. That most pregnant
women love their babies is irrelevant; the fact of the matter is that
some of them will negligently cause their children grave and irreversible harm while the children are *in utero*. We should not pretend that

these women are not responsible for the harm they cause; nor should society ignore its obligation to protect these children.

Hence I believe that the state may sometimes be justified in interfering with a pregnant woman in order to prevent prenatal harm. One suggestion, for instance, is that pregnant substance abusers may be committed by civil courts to outpatient treatment centers (assuming certain conditions—of due process, access, efficacy, and ability to predict which addicts are likely to harm their offspring—can be met).

There may be rare instances in which the state may justifiably override the decision of a mentally competent pregnant woman in order to provide medical care to her fetus. As examples, I have suggested the case of an HIV-infected pregnant woman who refuses AZT treatments and the case of a woman giving birth prematurely who refuses a corticosteroid injection.[24] I hasten to add, however, that given the considerable obstacles to administering any intervention fairly and well, the choices of the state should be very severely constricted. Finally, if our goal is to prevent harm to innocent children— not to punish their mother—then providing more social welfare and incentive programs should be the first step; instituting coercive measures should be the last.

NOTES

1. Committee to Study the Prevention of Low Birthweight, Institute of Medicine, *Preventing Low Birthweight*, Washington, D.C.: National Academy Press, 1985; M. Sulvetta et al., *International Infant Mortality Rankings: A Reflection of Public Policies*, Washington, D.C.: Urban Institute, 1993.

2. G. J. Annas, "Pregnant Women as Fetal Containers," *Hastings Center Report*, 16, pp. 13–14, 1986, at p. 14.

3. D. Johnsen, "A New Threat to Pregnant Women's Autonomy," *Hastings Center*, 17, pp. 33–40, 1987, at p. 39.

4. C. A. Miller, "Maternal and Infant Care: Comparisons Between Western Europe and the United States," *International Journal of Health Services* 23, pp. 655–64, 1993; M. Sulvetta et al., *op cit*.

5. One problem is that the first step—raising sufficient funds to support these social benefits—will not be taken. Few United States legislators are willing to propose something so unpopular as a tax increase.

6. P. A. Buescher et al., "A Comparison of Women in and out of a Prematurity Prevention Project in a North Carolina Perinatal Care Region," *American Journal of Public Health* 78, pp. 264–71, 1988; Committee to Study the

Prevention of Low Birthweight, Institute of Medicine, *op cit.*; J. J. Fangman et al., "Prematurity Prevention Programs: An Analysis of Successes and Failures," *American Journal of Obstetrics and Gynecology* 170, pp. 744–50, 1994; E. S. Fisher et al., "Prenatal Care and Pregnancy Outcomes During the Recession: The Washington State Experience," *American Journal of Public Health* 75, pp. 866–69, 1985; T. R. Moore et al., "The Perinatal and Economic Impact of Prenatal Care in a Low-Socioeconomic Population," *American Journal of Obstetrics and Gynecology* 154, pp. 29–33, 1986; J. L. Murray and M. Bernfield, "The Differential Effect of Prenatal Care on the Incidence of Low Birth Weight Among Blacks and Whites in a Prepaid Health Plan," *New England Journal of Medicine* 319, pp. 1385–91, 1988; F. Rahbar et al., "Prenatal Care and Perinatal Mortality in a Black Population," *Obstetrics and Gynecology* 65, pp. 327–29, 1985; A. L. Wilson et al., "Does Prenatal Care Decrease the Incidence and Cost of Neonatal Intensive Care Admissions?" *American Journal of Perinatology* 9, pp. 281–84, 1992; B. P. Yawn and R. A. Yawn, "Preterm Birth Prevention in a Rural Practice," *Journal of the American Medical Association* 262, pp. 230–33, 1989.

7. B. M. Aved, "Barriers to Prenatal Care for Low-Income Women," *Western Journal of Medicine* 158, pp. 493–98, 1993; R. E. Behrman, "Preventing Low Birthweight: A Pediatric Prospective," *Journal of Pediatrics* 107, pp. 842–54, 1985; Committee to Study the Prevention of Low Birthweight, Institute of Medicine, *op cit.*, 1985; Alan Guttmacher Institute, *Blessed Events and the Bottom Line: Financing Maternity Care in the United States*, N.Y.: Alan Guttmacher Institute, 1988; J. L. Johnson et al., "Factors that Prevent Women of Low Economic Status from Seeking Prenatal Care," *Journal of the American Academy of Nurse Practitioners* 6, pp. 105–11, 1994; S. L. Nazario, "High Infant Mortality Is a Persistent Blotch On Health Care in U.S.," *Wall Street Journal*, 1988, p. B1.

8. B. M. Aved, *op cit.*; M. L. Poland et al., "Barriers to Receiving Adequate Prenatal Care," *American Journal of Obstetrics and Gynecology* 157, pp. 297–303, 1987.

9. B. M. Aved, *op cit.*; J. L. Johnson et al., *op cit.*

10. S. L. Nazario, *op cit.*

11. Committee to Study the Prevention of Low Birthweight, Institute of Medicine: *op cit.*

12. S. Rosenbaum et al., "Incantations in the Dark: Medicaid, Managed Care, and Maternity Care," *Milbank Quarterly* 1988, 4, pp. 661–93, at p. 667.

13. J. Fitzsimmons et al., "Pregnancy in a Drug-abusing Population," *American Journal of Drug & Alcohol Abuse* 12, pp. 247–55, 1986. Another innovative program is Project CONNECT, a joint venture of New York City and New York State, which uses case managers to improve pregnant women's access to a variety of services: medical care, substance abuse/alcohol treatment, education, and child care. See L. A. Randolph and B. R. Sherman, "Project CONNECT: An Interagency Partnership to Confront New Challenges Facing At-

Risk Women and Children in New York City," *Journal of Community Health* 18, pp. 73–81, 1993.

14. It has been calculated, for instance, that were the Kaiser system—a large health maintenance organization in California—to offer a $100 incentive to each enrolled pregnant woman for seeking prenatal care throughout her pregnancy, the HMO would save millions of dollars annually in reduced hospital costs. J. L. Murray and M. Bernfield, *op cit.*

15. C. A. Miller, *op cit.*

16. C. Phillips and N. Johnson, "The Impact of Quality of Diet and Other Factors on Birth Weight of Infants," *American Journal of Clinical Nutrition* 30, pp. 215–21, 1977; R. Rosso, "Nutrition and Maternal–Fetal Exchange," *American Journal of Clinical Nutrition* 34, pp. 744–81, 1981.

17. L. Ku et al., "Full Funding for WIC: A Policy Review," *Urban Institute Research Paper*, Washington, D.C.: Urban Institute, 1994; D. Rush et al., "The National WIC Evaluation: Evaluation of the Special Supplemental Food Program for Women, Infants, and Children, III, Historical Study of Pregnancy Outcomes," *American Journal of Clinical Nutrition* 48, pp. 412–28, 1988; W. F. Schramm, "WIC Prenatal Participation and Its Relationship to Newborn Medical Costs in Missouri: A Cost/Benefit Analysis," *American Journal of Public Health* 75, pp. 851–57, 1985.

18. L. Ku et al., *op cit.* WIC currently covers approximately two-thirds of those eligible; President Clinton has resolved to increase funding to WIC by the end of fiscal year 1996 in order to include more people.

19. C. D. Allen and C. R. Ries, "Smoking, Alcohol and Dietary Practices During Pregnancy: Comparison Before and After Prenatal Education," *Journal of the American Dietic Association* 85, pp. 607–08, 1985; Y. Robitaille and M. S. Kramer, "Does Participation in Prenatal Courses Lead to Heavier Babies?" *American Journal of Public Health* 75, pp. 1186–89, 1985.

20. C. Orstead et al., "Efficacy of Prenatal Nutrition Counseling: Weight Gain, Infant Birth Weight, and Cost-Effectiveness," *Journal of the American Dietic Association* 85, pp. 40–45, 1985.

21. S. L. Nazario, *op cit.*

22. Some communities have already instituted such measures. Washington, D.C., operates a van (the Maternity Outreach Mobile) to transport pregnant women to and from medical clinics (as well as to remind them of their appointments).

23. The Committee to Study the Prevention of Low Birthweight of the Institute of Medicine recommends that Title X of the Public Health Service Act be more generously funded in order to make contraception more accessible.

> Title X authorizes project grants to public and private nonprofit organizations for the provision of family planning services to all who need and want them, including sexually active teenagers, but with

> priority given to low-income persons. The Committee urges that federal funds be made generously available to meet the documented need for family planning. The Title X program and family planning services generally should be regarded as important parts of the public effort to prevent low birthweight.

Committee to Study the Prevention of Low Birthweight, Institute of Medicine, *op cit.*, p. 18.

> It is important also to make more methods of contraception available. There are several highly successful methods used in other countries but not available in the United States; examining these measures for possible use in the United States should be given a higher priority.

24. These cases, I believe, meet the requirements of the American Medical Association's Board of Trustees:

> If an exceptional circumstance could be found in which a medical treatment poses an insignificant or no health risk to the woman, entails a minimal invasion of her bodily integrity, and would clearly prevent substantial and irreversible harm to her fetus, it might be appropriate for a physician to seek judicial intervention.

H. M. Cole, "Legal Interventions During Pregnancy," *Journal of the American Medical Association* 264, pp. 2663–70, 1990.

Bibliography

Abel, E. L.: 1984, *Fetal Alcohol Syndrome and Fetal Alcohol Effects*, New York: Plenum Press.

Abel, E. L. and R. J. Sokol: 1987, "Incidence of Fetal Alcohol Syndrome and Economic Impact of FAS-related Anomalies," *Drug and Alcohol Dependence* 19, pp. 51–70.

Ahmann, S.: 1989, 'Mother-to-be Tried for Exposing Fetus to Cocaine,' *Ob Gyn News*, 1 & 26.

Alan Guttmacher Institute: 1988, *Blessed Events and the Bottom Line: Financing Maternity Care in the United States*, New York: Alan Guttmacher Institute.

Allen, C. D. and C. R. Ries: 1985, 'Smoking, Alcohol and Dietary Practices During Pregnancy: Comparison Before and After Prenatal Education,' *Journal of the American Dietic Association* 85, pp. 607–08.

Alroomi, L. G. et al.: 1986, 'Maternal Narcotic Abuse and the Newborn,' *Archives of Disease in Childhood* 63, pp. 81–83.

American Academy of Pediatrics, Committee on Bioethics: 1988, 'Fetal Therapy: Ethical Considerations,' *Pediatrics* 81, pp. 898–99.

American College of Obstetricians and Gynecologists Committee on Nutrition: 1974, *Nutrition in Maternal Health Care*, American College of Obstetricians and Gynecologists, Chicago.

American College of Obstetricians and Gynecologists: 1987 'Statement of the Committee on Ethics,' Washington, D.C.: American College of Obstetricians and Gynecologists.

American Medical Association Council on Scientific Affairs: 1983, 'Fetal Effects of Maternal Alcohol Use,' *Journal of the American Medical Association* 249, pp. 2517–21.

American Society of Anesthesiologists: 1974, 'Occupational Disease Among Operating Room Personnel: A National Study,' *Anesthesiology* 41, pp. 321–40.

Anderson, C. E.: 1989, 'When Faith Healing Fails,' *ABA Journal*, 22–23.

Annas, G. J.: 1982, 'Forced Caesareans: The Most Unkindest Cut of All,' *Hastings Center Report* 12, pp. 16–18.

_____: 1986, 'Pregnant Women as Fetal Containers,' *Hastings Center Report*, 16, pp. 13–14.

Annie E. Casey Foundation: 1995, *Kids Count Data Book*, Baltimore, MD: Annie E. Casey Foundation.

Aronson, M. and R. Olegard: 1987, 'Children of Alcoholic Mothers,' *Pediatrician* 14, pp. 57–61.

Arrigo, B. A.: 1992–3, "Paternalism, Civil Commitment and Illness Politics," *Journal of Law and Health* 7, pp. 131–68.

Aved, B. M., 1993: "Barriers to Prenatal Care for Low-Income Women," *Western Journal of Medicine* 158, pp. 493–8.

"AZT Reduces Rate of Maternal Transmission of HIV," *NIAID News* February 21, 1994;

Baker, M. L. and Dalrymple: 1984, 'Radiation and the Fetus,' in W. R. Hendee, (ed.), *Health Effects of Low-Level Radiation*, Norwalk, CT: Appleton-Century-Croft, pp. 127–30.

Barnard, C. P.: 1984, 'Alcoholism and Incest,' *Focus on Family and Chemical Dependency* 7, pp. 27–29.

Bayer, R.: 1982, 'Women, Work, and Reproductive Hazards,' *The Hastings Center Report* 12, pp. 14–19.

Bayles, M. D.: 1984, *Reproductive Ethics*, N.J.: Prentice-Hall, Inc., Englewood Cliffs.

Beal, R.:, 1984 'Can I Sue Mommy? An Analysis of a Woman's Tort Liability for Prenatal Injuries to her Child Born Alive,' *San Diego Law Review* 21, pp. 325–70.

Becker, B. L.: 1991, "Order in the Court," *Hastings Constitutional Law Quarterly* 19, pp. 235–59.

Behrman, R. E.: 1987, 'Premature Births Among Black Women,' *New England Journal of Medicine* 312, pp. 763–65.

_____: 1985, 'Preventing Low Birthweight: A Pediatric Prospective,' *Journal of Pediatrics* 107, pp. 842–54.

Bertin, J. E.: 1989, 'Reproductive Hazards in the Workplace,' in S. Cohen and N. Taub (eds.), *Reproductive Laws for the 1990s*, Clifton, N.J.: Humana Press.

Blanco, A. C.: 1985, 'Fetal Protection Programs Under Title VII—Rebutting the Procreation Presumption,' *University of Pittsburgh Law Review* 46, pp. 755–94.

Blank, R.: 1988, *Life, Death and Public Policy*, DeKalb, Ill.: Northern Illinois University Press.

_____: 1992, 'Fetal Protection Policies in the Workplace,' *Politics and the Life Sciences* 11, pp. 215–29.

_____: 1993, "Maternal-Fetal Relationship: The Courts and Social Policy," *Journal of Legal Medicine* 14, pp. 73–92.

_____: 1993, *Fetal Protection in the Workplace*, N.Y.: Columbia University Press.

"Blood, Sweat and Fears," *Time*, September 28, 1987, pp. 50–51.

Blume, S. B.: 1986, 'Is Social Drinking During Pregnancy Harmless? There is Reason to Think Not.' *Advances in Alcohol & Substance Abuse* 5, pp. 209–19.

_____: 1987, 'Public Policy Issues Relevant to Children of Alcoholics,' *Advances in Alcohol & Substance Abuse* 6, pp. 5–15.

Borowski, T. A., Jr.: 1988, 'No Liability for the Wrongful Death of Unborn Children—the Florida Legislature Refuses to Protect the Unborn,' *Florida State University Law Review* 16, pp. 835–61.

Botkin, J. R.: 1988, 'The Legal Concept of Wrongful Life,' *Journal of the American Medical Association* 259, pp. 1541–45.

Bowes, W. A. and B. Salgestad: 1981, 'Fetal Versus Maternal Rights: Medical and Legal Perspectives,' *Obstetrics and Gynecology* 58, pp. 209–14.

Buescher, P. A. et al.: 1988, "A Comparison of Women in and out of a Prematurity Prevention Project in a North Carolina Preinatal Care Region," *American Journal of Public Health* 78, pp. 264–71.

Burkett et al.: 1990, "Perinatal Implications of Cocaine Exposure," *Journal of Reproductive Medicine* 35, p. 35.

Bush, M.: 1988, *Families in Distress*, Berkeley, CA: University of California Press.

Capron, A. M.: 1980, 'The Continuing Wrong of 'Wrongful Life,'' in A. Milunsky and G. J. Annas (eds.), *Genetics and the Law II*, N.Y.: Plenum Press, pp. 81–93.

Catz, C. S. and S. J. Yaffee: 1976, 'Environmental Factors: Pharmacology,' in National Institutes of Health, *Prevention of Embryonic, Fetal and Perinatal Disease*, Washington, D.C.: Government Printing Office, pp. 119–45.

Chan, L. S. et al.: 1986, 'Differences Between Dropouts and Active Participants in a Pediatric Clinic for Substance Abuse Mothers,' *American Journal of Drug and Alcohol Abuse* 12, pp. 89–99.

Chang, D. and J. Holahan: 1990, *Medicaid Spending in the 1980s: The Access-Cost Containment Trade-Off Revisted*, University Press of America.

Chasnoff, I. J.: 1987, 'Perinatal Effects of Cocaine,' *Contemporary Obstetrics and Gynecology,* 29, pp. 163–179.

_____: 1989, 'Drug Use and Women: Establishing a Standard of Care,' in Donald E. Hutchings (ed.), *Prenatal Abuse of Licit and Illicit Drugs*, N.Y.: The New York Academy of Medicine, pp. 208–10.

Chasnoff, I. J. et al.: 1986, 'Prenatal Drug Exposure: Effects on Neonatal & Infant Growth & Development,' *Neurobehavioral Toxicology and Teratology* 8, pp. 357–362.

_____: 1989, "Temporal patterns of cocaine use in pregnancy," *Journal of the American Medical Association* 261, pp. 1741–44.

_____: 1990, 'The Prevalence of Illicit-drug or Alcohol Use During Pregnancy and Discrepancies in Mandatory Reporting in Pinellas County, Florida,' *New England Journal of Medicine* 322, pp. 1202–06.

Chavkin, D. F.: 1992, "'For Their Own Good': Civil Commitment of Alcohol and Drug-Dependent Pregnant Women," *South Dakota Law Review* 37, pp. 224–88.

Chavkin, W.: 1990, "Drug Addiction and Pregnancy: Policy Crossroads," *American Journal of Public Health* 80, pp. 483–87.

Childress, J. F.: 1982, *Who Should Decide? Paternalism in Health Care*, N.Y.: Oxford University Press.

Churchville, V.: 1988, 'D.C. Judge Jails Woman as Protection for Fetus,' *Washington Post*, A1 and 8.

Clarkson, T. W. et al., eds.: 1988, *Biological Monitoring of Toxic Metals*, N.Y.: Plenum Press.

_____: 1983, *Reproductive and Developmental Toxicity of Metals*, N.Y.: Plenum Press.

Clarren, S. K. and D. W. Smith: 1978, 'The Fetal Alcohol Syndrome," *New England Journal of Medicine* 298, pp. 1063–67.

Cnattingius, S.: 1992, 'Smoking During Pregnancy," *International Journal of Technology Assessment in Health Care* 8 (Supplement 1), pp. 91–95.

Cnattingius, S. et al.: 1985, 'Smoking, Maternal Age, and Fetal Growth,' *Obstetrics and Gynecology* 66, pp. 449–52.

'Cocaine Babies: The Littlest Victims:' *Newsweek*, November 13, 1989, p. 55.

Cohen, E. N. et al.: 1971, 'Anesthesia, Pregnancy, and Miscarriage: A Study of Operating Room Nurses and Anesthetists,' *Anesthesiology* 34, pp. 343–47.

Cole, C. D. et al.: 1984, 'Neonatal Ethanol Withdrawal: Characteristics in Clinically Normal, Nondysmorphic Neonates,' *Journal of Pediatrics* 105, pp. 445–71.

Cole, H. M.: 1990, "Legal Interventions During Pregnancy," *Journal of the American Medical Association* 264, pp. 2663–70.

Collins, J. J. and M. Allison: 1983, 'Legal Coercion and Retention in Drug Abuse Treatment,' *Hospital and Community Psychiatry* 34, pp. 1145–49.

'Comment: Criminal Liability of a Prospective Mother for Prenatal Neglect of a Viable Fetus,' *Whittier Law Review* 9, 1987, pp. 363–96.

Committee to Study the Prevention of Low Birthweight, Institute of Medicine: 1985, *Preventing Low Birthweight*, Washington, D.C.: National Academy Press.

Connor, E. M. et al.: 1994, "Reduction of Maternal-Infant Transmission of Human Immunodeficiency Virus Type I With Zidovudine Treatment," *New England Journal of Medicine* 331, pp. 1173–80.

Cook, W.: 1970, 'Incompetent Donors: Was the First Step or the Last Taken in Strunk v. Strunk?' *California Law Review* 58, pp. 754–74.

Curriden, M.: 1990, 'Holding Mom Accountable,' *ABA Journal*, March pp. 51–53.

Daley, S.: "Born on Crack and Coping With Kindergarten," February 7, 1991, *New York Times*.

'Danger on the Job:' *Newsweek*, December 11, 1989, pp. 42–46.

D'Arcy, E.: 1963, *Human Acts: An Essay in Their Moral Evaluation*, Oxford: Clarendon Press.

Deren, S.: 1986, 'The Children of Substance Abusers: A Review of the Literature,' *Journal of Substance Abuse Treatment* 3, pp. 77–94.

'Disease the Focus of Programs to Reduce Infant Mortality,' *Infectious Diseases in Children*, 1988, p. 20.

Doberczak, T. M. et al.: 1988, 'Neonatal Neurologic & Electroencephalographic Effects of Intrauterine Cocaine Exposure,' *Journal of Pediatrics* 113, pp. 354–58.

Dorris, M.: 1994, "The Tragedy of Fetal Alcohol Syndrome," *1994 Medical and Health Annual*, Chicago: Encyclopedia Britannica, Inc., pp. 120–23.

Dutton, D. B.: 1988, *Worse than the Disease: Pitfalls of Medical Progress*, N.Y.: Cambridge University Press.

Dworkin, R.: 1977, *Taking Rights Seriously*, Cambridge, MA: Harvard University Press.

_____: 1979, "We Do Not Have a Right to Liberty," in R. Cunningham (ed.), *Liberty and the Rule of Law*, College Station, TX: Texas A & M University Press.

Edelin, K. C. et al.: 1988, 'Methadone Maintenance in Pregnancy: Consequences to Care and Outcome,' *Obstetrics and Gynecology* 7, pp. 399–404.

Ehrenkranz, S. M. et al., (eds.): 1989, *Clinical Social Work with Maltreated Children and Their Families*, N.Y.: New York University Press.

Elias, S. and Annas, G. J., (eds.): 1987, *Reproductive Genetics and the Law*, Chicago: Chicago Year Book.

Engelhardt, H. T., Jr.: 1985, 'Current Controversies in Obstetrics: Wrongful Life and Forced Fetal Surgical Procedures,' *American Journal of Obstetrics and Gynecology* 151, pp. 313–18.

Enthovan, A. and R. Kronick: 1989, 'A Consumer-Choice Health Plan for the 1990s,' *New England Journal of Medicine* 320, pp. 29–37.

Ershoff, D. H. et al.: 1990, "Pregnancy and Medical Cost Outcome of a Self-Help Prenatal Smoking Cessation Program in a HMO," *Public Health Reports—Hyattsville* 105, pp. 340–47.

Ervin, C. et al.: 1984, "Alcoholic Fathering and Its Relation to Child's Intellectual Development," *Alcoholism: Clinical and Experimental Research* 8, pp. 362–65.

Evans, R. W. et al.: 1984, *The National Heart Transplantation Study: Final Report*, Seattle: Battelle Human Affairs Research Centers.

Faden, R. R. and T. L. Beauchamp: 1986, *A History and Theory of Informed Consent*, N.Y.: Oxford University Press.

Fadiman, A.: 1983, 'The Unborn Patient,' *Life* vol. 6, pp. 38–44.

Faludi, S.: 1991, *Backlash: The Undeclared War Against American Women*, N.Y.: Crown.

Fangman, J. J. et al.: 1994, "Prematurity Prevention Programs: An Analysis of Successes and Failures," *American Journal of Obstetrics and Gynecology* 170, pp. 744–50.

Feinberg, J.: 1970, 'The Expressive Function of Punishment,' in *Doing and Deserving*, Princeton: Princeton University Press, pp. 95–118.

_____: 1980, 'Is There a Right to be Born?' *Rights, Justice, and the Bounds of Liberty*, Princeton: Princeton University Press, pp. 207–20.

_____: 1984, *The Moral Limits of the Criminal Law, Volume One, Harm to Others*, N.Y.: Oxford University Press.

_____: 1984, *The Problem of Abortion*, 2nd ed., Belmont, CA: Wadsworth.

_____: 1986, 'Abortion,' in Tom Regan (ed.) *Matters of Life and Death* 2nd ed., N.Y.: Random House, pp. 257–93.

_____: 1986, 'Wrongful Life and the Counterfactual Element in Harming,' *Social Philosophy and Policy* 4, pp. 145–78.

Feldman, J. G. et al.: 1992, "A Cohort Study of the Impact of Perinatal Drug-Use on Prematurity in an Inner-City Population," *American Journal of Public Health* 82(5), pp. 726–28.

Field, M. A.: 1989, 'Controlling the Woman to Protect the Fetus,' *Law, Medicine and Health Care* 17, pp. 114–29.

Finnegan, L. P.: 1982, 'Outcome of Children Born to Women Dependent upon Narcotics,' *Advances in Alcohol and Substance Abuse*, pp. 55–101.

Fisher, E. S. et al.: 1985, 'Prenatal Care and Pregnancy Outcomes During the Recession: The Washington State Experience,' *American Journal of Public Health* 75, pp. 856–69.

Fitzsimmons, J. et al.: 1986, 'Pregnancy in a Drug-abusing Population,' *American Journal of Drug & Alcohol Abuse* 12, pp. 247–55.

Flandermeyer, A. A.: 1987, 'A Comparison of the Effects of Heroin and Cocaine Abuse upon the Neonate,' *Neonatal Network*, pp. 42–48.

Fleisher, L. D. P.: 1987, 'Wrongful Births: When Is There Liability for Prenatal Injury?' *American Journal of the Diseases of Children* 141, pp. 1260–65.

Fletcher, J.: 1981, 'The Fetus as Patient: Ethical Issues,' *Journal of the American Medical Association* 246, pp. 772–73.

_____: 1986, 'Drawing Moral Lines in Fetal Therapy,' *Clinical Obstetrics and Gynecology* 29, pp. 595–602.

Fost, N. et al.: 1980, "The Limited Moral Significance of 'Fetal Viability,'" *Hastings Center Report* 10, pp. 10–13.

Frank, D. A. et al.: 1988, 'Cocaine Use During Pregnancy: Prevalence and Correlates,' *Pediatrics* 82, pp. 888–95.

Freudenheim, M.: 'Company Programs to Avoid 'Preemies',' *New York Times*, December 28, 1988, C1, 3.

Gallagher, J.: 1985, 'Fetal Personhood and Women's Policy,' in V. Shapiro (ed.) *Sage Yearbooks in Women's Policy Studies*, Beverly Hills, CA: Sage Publications.

_____: 1989, 'Position Paper: Fetus as Patient,' in S. Cohen & N. Taub (eds.), *Reproductive Laws for the 1990s,* Clifton, N.J.: Humana Press, pp. 185–236.

Garfield, J. and P. Hennessey (eds.): 1984, *Abortion: Moral and Legal Perspectives* Amherst, Mass.: University of Massachusetts Press.

Gini, A. R. and T. J. Sullivan: 1989, *It Comes with the Territory: An Inquiry Concerning Work and the Person*, N.Y.: Random House.

Glantz, L. H.: 1976, 'The Legal Aspects of Fetal Viability,' in A. Milunsky and G. J. Annas (eds.), *Genetics and the Law,* N.Y.: Plenum Press, pp. 29–43.

Golden, M. R.: 1991, "When Pregnancy Discrimination Is Gender Discrimination: The Constitutionality of Excluding Pregnant Women From Drug Treatment Programs," *New York University Law Review* 66, pp. 1832–80.

Goldstein, J.: 1982, 'Medical Care for the Child at Risk: On State Supervision of Parental Autonomy,' in W. Gaylin and R. Macklin (eds.), *Who Speaks for the Child? The Problem of Proxy Consent*, N.Y.: Plenum Press, pp. 153–88.

Greene, D. W.: 1991, "Abuse Prosecutors: Gender, Race, and Class Discretion and the Prosecution of Drug-Addicted Mothers," *Buffalo Law Review* 39, pp. 737–802.

Hansen, M.: 1992, "Courts Side With Moms in Drug Cases," *ABA Journal*, Nov. p. 18.

Hanson, J. W. et al.: 1978, 'The Effects of Moderate Alcohol Consumption During Pregnancy on Fetal Growth and Morphogenesis,' *Journal of Pediatrics* 93, pp. 457–60.

Haralambie, A. M.: 1993, *Handling Child Custody, Abuse, and Adoption Cases, 2nd edition*, N.Y.: McGraw-Hill.

Harrison, M. R.: 1982, 'Unborn: Historical Perspective of the Fetus as Patient,' *The Pharos* 45, pp. 19–24.

_____: 1993, 'Fetal Surgery,' *Western Journal of Medicine* 159, pp. 341–349.

Harrison, M. R. et al.: 1982, 'Fetal Treatment 1982,' *The New England Journal of Medicine* 307, pp. 1651–52.

Hart, H. L. A.: 1976, *Punishment and Responsibility*, N.Y.: Oxford University Press.

Henig, R. M.: 'Saving Babies Before Birth,' *New York Times Magazine*, February 28, 1982.

Hill, R. M. et al.: 1977, 'Utilization of Over-the-Counter Drugs During Pregnancy,' *Clinical Obstetrics and Gynecology* 20, pp. 381–94.

Himaka, M.: 'Judge Drops Prenatal Care Case Against Mother,' *The San Diego Union*, February 27, 1989, A1.

Honoré, A. M.: 1966, 'Law, Morals, and Rescue,' in J.M. Ratcliffe (ed.), *The Good Samaritan and the Law*, N.Y.: Doubleday and Co., Inc., pp. 225–42.

Howard, J.: 1992, "Chronic Drug Users as Parents," *Hastings Law Journal* 43, pp. 645–68.

"Innocent Victims," May 13, 1991, *Time* pp. 56–63.

Institute for Health Policy, Brandeis University: 1993, *Substance Abuse: The Nation's Number One Problem*, Princeton: Robert Wood Johnson Foundation.

International Surgery Registry: 1986, 'Catheter Shunts for Fetal Hydronephrosis and Hydrocephalus,' *New England Journal of Medicine* 315, pp. 336–40.

John, E. M. et al.: 1991, "Prenatal Exposure to Parents: Smoking and Childhood Cancer," *American Journal of Epidemiology* 133, pp. 123–32.

Johnsen, D.: 1986, 'The Creation of Fetal Rights: Conflicts with Women's Constitutional Rights to Liberty, Privacy, and Equal Protection,' *Yale Law Journal* 95, pp. 599–625.

_____: 1987, 'A New Threat to Pregnant Women's Autonomy,' *Hastings Center Report* 17, pp. 33–40.

_____: 1992, "Promoting Healthy Births Without Sacrificing Women's Liberty," *Hastings Law Journal* 43, pp. 569–614.

Johnson, J. L. et al.: 1994, "Factors That Prevent Women of Low Economic Status from Seeking Prenatal Care." *Journal of the American Academy of Nurse Practitioners* 6, pp. 105–11.

Johnson, K.: "Child Abuse Is Ruled Out in Birth Case," *New York Times*, August 18, 1992, pp. B1, B4.

Johnson, L.: 1994, *National Survey Results on Drug Use from the Monitoring the Future Study, 1975–1993*. Rockville, MD: DHHS.

Joyce, K. et al.: 1983, 'Internal and External Barriers to Obtaining Prenatal Care,' *Social Work and Health Care* 9, pp. 89–96.

Jurow, R. and R. H. Paul: 1984, 'Cesarean Delivery for Fetal Distress Without Maternal Consent,' *Obstetrics and Gynecology* 63, pp. 596–98.

Kempe, C. H. and R. Helfer (eds.): 1980, *The Battered Child*, Chicago: University of Chicago Press.

Kirsch-Volders, M. (ed.): 1984, *Mutagenicity, Carcinogenicity and Teratogenicity of Industrial Pollutants*, N.Y.: Plenum Press.

Knill-Jones, R. P. et al.: 1972, 'Anesthetic Practice and Pregnancy: Controlled Study of Women Anesthetists in the United Kingdom,' *Lancet* 1, pp. 1326–28.

Kolder, V. E. B. et al.: 1987, 'Court-Ordered Obstetrical Interventions,' *The New England Journal of Medicine* 316, pp. 1192–96.

Koren, G. et al.: 1989, "Bias Against the Null Hypothesis: The Reproductive Hazards of Cocaine," *Lancet* 2, pp. 1440–42.

Kosten, T. R. et al.: 1986, 'Cocaine Abuse Among Opioid Addicts: Demographic and Diagnostic Factors in Treatment,' *American Journal of Drug and Alcohol Abuse* 12, pp. 1–16.

Krandall, S. R. and W. Chavkin: 1992, "Illicit Drugs in America," *Hastings Law Journal* 43(3), pp. 615–43.

Kreek, M.: 1982, 'Opioid Disposition and Effects During Chronic Exposure in the Perinatal Period in Man,' *Advances in Alcohol & Substance Abuse* 34, pp. 21–53.

Ku, L. et al.: 1994, "Full Funding for WIC: A Policy Review," *Urban Institute Research Paper* Washington, D.C.: Urban Institute.

Kushner, H. I.: 1989, *Self-Destruction in the Promised Land: A Psychocultural History*, N.J.: Rutgers University Press.

Laird, J. and A. Hartman (eds.): 1985, *A Handbook of Child Welfare*, N.Y.: The Free Press.

Lappé, M.: 1975, 'The Moral Claims of the Wanted Fetus,' *The Hastings Center Report* 5, pp. 11–13.

Levmore, S.: 1986, 'Waiting for Rescue: An Essay on the Evolution and Incentive Structure of the Law of Affirmative Obligations,' *Virginia Law Review* 72, pp. 879–941.

Lewin, T.: 'Courts Acting to Force Care of the Unborn,' *New York Times*, November 23, 1987, A1.

Little, B. B. et al.: 1990, "Patterns of Multiple Substance Abuse During Pregnancy," *Southern Medical Journal* 83(5), pp. 507–09.

Little, R. E.: 1977, 'Moderate Alcohol Use During Pregnancy and Decreased Infant Birth Weight,' *American Journal of Public Health* 67, pp. 1154–56.

Little, R. E. et al.: 1982, 'Fetal Alcohol Effects in Humans and Animals,' *Advances in Alcohol & Substance Abuse*, pp. 103–25.

Little, R. E. and Sing, C. F.: 1987, 'Father's Drinking and Infant Birthweight: Report of an Association,' *Teratology* 36, pp. 59–65.

LoBue, C. C.: 1983, 'Effects of Drugs on the Fetus,' in Kenneth R. Niswander (ed.), *Manual of Obstetrics*, Boston: Little Brown, pp. 281–304.

Lomansky, L. E.: 1987, *Persons, Rights, and the Moral Community*, N.Y: Oxford University Press.

Longo, L. M.: 1980, "Environmental Pollution and Pregnancy," *American Journal of Obstetrics and Gynecology* 137, p. 162.

_____: 1982, 'Health Consequences of Maternal Smoking,' in the National Research Council, *Alternative Dietary Practices and Nutritional Abuses in Pregnancy*, Washington, D.C: National Academy Press.

Losco, J., and M. Shublak: 1994, "Paternal-Fetal Conflict: An Examination of Paternal Responsibilities to the Fetus," *Politics and the Life Sciences* 13, pp. 63–75.

Luker, K.: 1984, *Abortion and the Politics of Motherhood*, Berkeley: University of California Press.

MacGregnor, S. N. et al.: 1987, 'Cocaine Use During Pregnancy: Adverse Perinatal Outcome,' *American Journal of Obstetrics and Gynecology* 1587, pp. 686–89.

Mackenzie, T. M. and T. C. Nagel: 1986, 'Commentary: When a Pregnant Woman Endangers Her Fetus,' *Hastings Center Report* 16, pp. 24–25.

Madden, J. D. et al.: 1986, 'Maternal Cocaine Abuse and Effect on the Newborn,' *Pediatrics* 77, pp. 209–11.

Mahowald, M.: 1989, 'Beyond Abortion: Refusal of Caesarean Section,' *Bioethics* 3, pp. 106–21.

Manning, W. G. et al.: 1989, "The Taxes of Sin: Do Smokers Pay Their Way?" *Journal of the American Medical Association* 262, pp. 901–06.

Marcotte, P.: 1989, 'Crime and Pregnancy,' August *ABA Journal*, pp. 14–15.

Marcus, J. et al.: 1984, 'A Longitudinal Study of Offspring Born to Methadone-maintained Women. III. Effects of Multiple Risk Factors on Development at 4, 8, and 12 Months,' *American Journal of Drug and Alcohol Abuse* 10, pp. 195–207.

Mark, F.: 1988, 'Does Coercion Work? The Role of Referral Source in Motivating Alcoholics in Treatment,' *Alcoholism Treatment Quarterly* 5, pp. 5–22.

Maschke, K. J.: 1993, "From the Workplace to the Delivery Room: Protecting the Fetus in the Post-*Roe* Era," *Politics and the Life Sciences* 12 (1), pp. 53–60.

Mathieu, D.: 1985, 'Respecting Liberty and Preventing Harm: Limits of State Intervention in Prenatal Choice,' *Harvard Journal of Law & Public Policy* 8, pp. 19–55.

_____: 1992, "Crime and Punishment: Abortion as Murder?" *Journal of Social Philosophy* 23 (2), pp. 5–22.

_____: 1995, "Mandating Treatment for Pregnant Substance Abusers: A Compromise," *Politics and the Life Sciences* 14, pp. 1–10.

McCormick, M. C.: 1985, 'The Contribution of Low Birth Weight to Infant Mortality and Childhood Morbidity,' *New England Journal of Medicine* 312, pp. 82–90.

McElveen, J. C., Jr.: 1985, 'Reproductive Hazards in the Workplace,' *The Forum* 20, pp. 547–71.

Merkatz, I. R. et al.: 1980, "Ritodrine Hydrochloride: A Betamimetic Agent for Use in Preterm Labor. II. Evidence of Efficacy." *Obstetrics and Gynecology* 56, pp. 7–13.

Merrick, J. C.: 1993, "Maternal Substance Abuse During Pregnancy," *Journal of Legal Medicine* 14, pp. 57–71.

Miller, C. A.: 1993, "Maternal and Infant Care: Comparisons Between Western Europe and the United States," *International Journal of Health Services* 23, pp. 655–64.

Mills, J. L., et al.: 1984, 'Maternal Alcohol Consumption and Birth Weight,' *Journal of the American Medical Association* 252, pp. 1875–79.

Moore, T. R. et al.: 1986, 'The Perinatal and Economic Impact of Prenatal Care in a Low-Socioeconomic Population,' *American Journal of Obstetrics and Gynecology* 154, pp. 29–33.

Morreim, E. H.: 1988, 'The Concept of Harm Reconceived: A Different Look at Wrongful Life,' *Law and Philosophy* 7, pp. 3–33.

"Mother Sentenced for Exposing Fetus to Cocaine," *Washington Post*, July 2, 1991, p. A4.

Mugford, M. et al.: 1991, "Cost Implications of Different Approaches to the Prevention of Respiratory Distress Syndrome," *Archives of Disease in Childhood* 66, pp. 757–64.

Mulvey, E. P. et al.: 1987, "The Promise and Peril of Involuntary Outpatient Commitment," *American Psychologist* 42, pp. 571–84.

Murray, J. L. and M. Bernfield: 1988, 'The Differential Effect of Prenatal Care on the Incidence of Low Birth Weight Among Blacks and Whites in a Prepaid Health Plan,' *New England Journal of Medicine* 319, pp. 1385–91.

Murray, T. M.: 1985, 'Who Do Fetal-Protection Policies Really Protect?' *Technology Review* 88, pp. 12–13, 20.

Musto, D. F.: 1991, "Opium, Cocaine and Marijauna in American History," July *Scientific American*, pp. 40–47.

Nadel, M.: 1985, 'Offspring with Fetal Alcohol Effects,' in D. Cook et al. (eds.), *Psychosocoial Issues in the Treatment of Alcoholism*, N.Y.: Haworth Press.

Naeye, R. L. et al.: 1973, 'Effects of Maternal Nutrition on the Human Fetus,' *Pediatrics* 52, pp. 494–500.

National Center on Child Abuse and Neglect, U.S. Children's Bureau, U.S. Department of Health and Human Services: 1978, *Substance Abuse and Child Abuse and Neglect*, Washington, D.C.: Government Printing Office:

National Institute of Child Health and Human Development: 1994, *Report of the Consensus Development Conference on the Effect of Corticosteroids for Fetal Maturation on Perinatal Outcomes*, Washington, D.C.: U.S. Department of Health and Human Services, NIH Pub. No. 95–3784.

Nazario, S. L.: 'High Infant Mortality Is a Persistent Blotch On Health Care in U.S.,' *Wall Street Journal*, October 9, 1988.

Nelson, L. J. and N. Milliken: 1988, 'Compelled Medical Treatment of Pregnant Women: Life, Liberty and Law in Conflict,' *Journal of the American Medical Association* 259, pp. 1060–66.

Note: 1985, 'Faith Healing Exemptions to Child Protection Laws: Keeping the Faith Versus Medical Care for Children,' *Journal of Legislation* 12, 1985, pp. 243–63.

Oakley, A.: 1984, *The Captured Womb: A History of Medical Care of Pregnant Women*, N.Y.: Oxford University Press.

Office of Technology Assessment: 1985, *Reproductive Health Hazards in the Workplace: Summary*, Washington, D.C.: Government Printing Office.

Olegard, R.: 1992, "Alcohol and Narcotics: Epidemiology and Pregnancy Risks," *International Journal of Technology Assessment in Health Care* 8 (Supplement 1), pp. 101–05.

Olson, J. et al.: 1983, 'Alcohol Use, Conception Time and Birthweight,' *Journal of Epidemiology and Community Health* 37, pp. 63–75.

Oro, A. S. and S. D. Dixon: 1987, 'Perinatal Cocaine and Metamphetamine Exposure: Maternal and Neonatal Correlates,' *Journal of Pediatrics* 222, pp. 571–78.

Orstead, C. et al.: 1985, 'Efficacy of Prenatal Nutrition Counseling: Weight Gain, Infant Birth Weight, and Cost-Effectiveness,' *Journal of the American Dietic Association* 85, pp. 40–45.

Parness, J.: 1985, 'Crimes Against the Unborn,' *Harvard Journal on Legislation* 22, pp. 97–172.

Pelham, T. L. and A. R. DeJong: 1992, "Nationwide Practices for Screening and Reporting Prenatal Cocaine Abuse," *Child Abuse and Neglect* 16(5), pp. 763–70.

Phibbs, C. S. et al.: 1991, "The Neonatal Costs of Maternal Cocaine Use," *Journal of the American Medical Association* 266(11), pp. 1521–26.

Phillips, C. and N. Johnson: 1977, 'The Impact of Quality of Diet and Other Factors on Birth Weight of Infants,' *American Journal of Clinical Nutrition* 30, pp. 215–21.

Plant, M. L. and M. A. Plant: 1987, 'Family Alcohol Problems Among Pregnant Women: Links with Maternal Substance Use and Birth Abnormalities,' *Drug & Alcohol Dependence* 20, pp. 213–19.

Pinkley, D. S.: "AZT Found to Reduce Perinatal HIV Transmission Risk," March 14, 1994, *American Medical News*.

Poland, M. L. et al.: 1987, 'Barriers to Receiving Adequate Prenatal Care,' *American Journal of Obstetrics and Gynecology* 157, pp. 297–303.

_____: 1993, "Punishing Pregnant Drug Users: Enhancing the Flight from Care," *Drug and Alcohol Dependence* 31, pp. 199–203.

'Pregnant Teen Held for Safety of Fetus,' *St. Paul Pioneer Press and Dispatch*, August 16, 1985, A3.

Prentice, R. A.: 1985: 'Expanding the Duty to Rescue," *Suffolk University Law Review* 19, pp. 15–54.

President's Commission for the Study of Ethical Problems in Medicine and Biomedical and Behavioral Research: 1983, *Securing Access to Health Care, Volume One: Report*, Washington, D.C.: Government Printing Office.

Rahbar, F. et al.: 1985, 'Prenatal Care and Perinatal Mortality in a Black Population,' *Obstetrics and Gynecology* 65, pp. 327–29.

Randolph, L. A. and B. R. Sherman: 1993, "Project CONNECT: An Interagency Partnership to Confront New Challenges Facing At-Risk Women
and Children in New York City," *Journal of Community Health* 18, pp. 73–
81.
Retshesky, R.: 1979, 'Workers, Reproductive Hazards, & the Politics of Protection: An Introduction,' *Feminist Studies* 5, pp. 233–46.
Rhoden, N. K.: 1986, 'Judges in the Delivery Room,' *California Law Review* 74,
pp. 1951–2030.
_____: 1987, 'Caesareans and Samaritans,' *Law, Medicine and Health Care* 15,
pp. 118–25.
Robins, L. N. et al.: 1993, 'Effects of In Utero Exposure to Street Drugs,' *American Journal of Public Health* 83 (Supplement), pp. 3–31.
Roberts, D. E.: 1991, "Punishing Drug Addicts Who Have Babies: Women of
Color, Equality, and the Right of Privacy," *Harvard Law Review* 104(7), pp.
1419–82.
Robertson, J. A.: 1976, 'Organ Donations by Incompetents and the Substituted
Judgment Doctrine,' *Columbia Law Review* 76, pp. 48–78.
_____: 1982, 'The Right to Procreate and *in Utero* Fetal Therapy,' *Journal of
Legal Medicine* 3, pp. 333–66.
_____: 1983, 'Procreative Liberty and the Control of Conception, Preg-
nancy, and Childbirth,' *Virginia Law Review* 69, pp. 405–64.
Robitaille, Y. and M. S. Kramer: 1985, 'Does Participation in Prenatal Courses
Lead to Heavier Babies?' *American Journal of Public Health* 75, pp. 1186–89.
Rogers, T. D.: 1982, "Wrongful Life and Wrongful Birth," *South Carolina Law
Review* 33, pp. 713–57.
Rosenbaum, S. et al.: 1988, 'Incantations in the Dark: Medicaid, Managed
Care, and Maternity Care,' *Milbank Quarterly* 4, pp. 661–93.
Rosso, R.: 1981, 'Nutrition and Maternal-Fetal Exchange,' *American Journal of
Clinical Nutrition* 34, pp. 744–81.
Rothenberg, K.: 1988, 'Medical Decision Making for Children,' *BioLaw, Volume
I*, Frederick, MD.: University Publications of America, pp. 149–76.
Rothman, B. K.: 1986, 'When a Pregnant Woman Endangers Her Fetus: Com-
mentary,' *Hastings Center Report* 16, p. 25.
Roy, D. J.: 1988, 'Fetal Therapy: Ethical Considerations,' in Carl Nimrod and
Glenn Griener (eds.), *Biomedical Ethics and Fetal Therapy*, Ontario, Canada:
Wilfrid Laurier University Press, pp. 59–66.
Rubenstein, L.: 1991, "Prosecuting Maternal Substance Abusers: An Unjusti-
fied and Ineffective Policy," *Yale Law and Policy Review* 9(1), pp. 130–60.
Ruffenach, G.: "Trying to Cure Shortage of Organ Donors," March 13, 1991,
Wall Street Journal, p. B1.
Rush, D. et al.: 1988, 'The National WIC Evaluation: Evaluation of the Special
Supplemental Food Program for Women, Infants, and Children, III, His-
torical Study of Pregnancy Outcomes,' *American Journal of Clinical Nutri-
tion* 48, pp. 412–28.
Sager, P. R. et al.: 1986, 'Reproductive and Developmental Toxicity of Metals,'
in L. Friberg et al. (eds.), *Handbook on the Toxicology of Metals, Volume II*,
N.Y.: Elsevier.

Samuels, S. U.: 1993, "To Furnish a Workplace Free From Recognized Hazards," *Politics and the Life Sciences* 12(2), pp. 243–54.

Savitz, D. et al.: 1989, 'Effect of Parents' Occupational Exposures on Risk of Stillbirth, Preterm Delivery, and Small-for-gestational-age Infants,' *American Journal of Epidemiology* 129, pp. 1201–18.

Schachter, J.: 'Help is Hard to Find for Addict Mothers: Drug Use 'Epidemic' Overwhelms Services,' *Los Angeles Times*, December 12, 1986, II–1.

Schiff, N. K.: 1991, "Legislation Punishing Drug Use During Pregnancy," *Hastings Constitutional Law Quarterly* 19, pp. 197–234.

Schramm, W. F.: 1985, 'WIC Prenatal Participation and Its Relationship to Newborn Medical Costs in Missouri: A Cost/Benefit Analysis,' *American Journal of Public Health* 75, pp. 851–57.

Shaw, M. W.: 1977, 'Genetically Defective Children: Emerging Legal Considerations,' *American Journal of Law & Medicine* 3, pp. 333–40.

_____: 1980, 'The Potential Plaintiff: Preconception & Prenatal Torts,' in A. Milunsky & A. J. Annas (eds.) *Genetics and the Law, II*, N.Y.: Plenum Press.

_____: 1984, 'Conditional Prospective Rights of the Fetus,' *The Journal of Legal Medicine* 5, pp. 63–116.

Shaw, M. W. and A. E. Doudera (eds.): 1983, *Defining Human Life: Medical, Legal & Ethical Implications*, Ann Arbor, Mich.: AUPHA Press.

Shearer, E. L.: 1993, "Cesarean Section: Medical Benefits and Costs," *Social Science and Medicine* 37, pp. 1223–31.

Sherman, R.: 1988, 'Keeping Baby Safe From Mom,' *The National Law Journal* October 3, pp. 1, 24–25.

_____: 1989, 'Keeping Babies Free of Drugs,' *The National Law Journal* October 16 1, pp. 28–29.

Shiono, P. H. et al.: 1986, 'Smoking and Drinking During Pregnancy,' *Journal of the American Medical Association* 255, pp. 82–84.

Simon, C.: 1978, 'Parental Liability for Prenatal Injury,' *Columbia Journal of Law and Social Problems* 14, pp. 47–92.

Spital, A.: 1991, "The Shortage of Organs for Transplantation," *New England Journal of Medicine* 325, pp. 1243–46.

Spohr, H. L. et al.: 1993, "Prenatal Alcohol Exposure and Long-Term Developmental Consequences,' *Lancet* 341, pp. 907–10.

Starfield, B.: 1985, 'Motherhood and Apple Pie: The Effectiveness of Medical Care for Children,' *Milbank Memorial Fund Quarterly* 63, pp. 523–46.

Starozewski, M.: 1986, 'Wrongful Death of a Fetus: Does a Cause of Action Arise When There is No Live Birth?' *Villanova Law Review* 31, pp. 659–95.

Stein, Z. and J. Kline: 1983, 'Editorial: Smoking, Alcohol and Reproduction,' *American Journal of Public Health* 73, pp. 1154–56.

Steinbock, B.: 1986, 'The Logical Case for Wrongful Life,' *Hastings Center Report* 16, pp. 15–20.

_____: 1992, *Life Before Birth*. N.Y.: Oxford University Press.

Sulvetta, M. et al.: 1993, "International Infant Mortality Rankings: A Reflection of Public Policies," Washington, D.C.: Urban Institute Press.

Sumner, L. W.: 1981, *Abortion and Moral Theory*, Princeton: Princeton University Press.

Tannenbaum, T. and R. J. Goldberg: 1985, 'Exposure to Anesthetic Gases and Reproductive Outcome—A Review of the Epidemiologic Literature,' *Journal of Occupational Medicine* 27, pp. 659–68.

Terry, D.: "A Child is Born in Court Case Over Cesarean," December 31, 1993, *New York Times*, p. A12.

Trost, C.: 'Born to Lose,' *Wall Street Journal*, July 18, 1989.

Veatch, R.: 1984, 'Limits of Guardian Treatment Refusal: A Reasonableness Standard,' *American Journal of Law and Medicine* 9, pp. 427–70.

Warren, M. A.: 1973, 'On the Moral and Legal Status of the Fetus,' *The Monist*, pp. 43–61.

Weinrib, E. J.: 1980, 'The Case for a Duty to Rescue,' *Yale Law Journal* 90, pp. 247–93.

Westermeyer, J.: 1989, 'Nontreatment Factors Affecting Treatment Outcomes in Substance Abuse,' *American Journal of Drug & Alcohol Abuse* 15, pp. 13–29.

'When the Courts Take Charge of the Unborn': *New York Times*, April 27, 1989, A–1.

Wilkins, J. R. and R. A. Koutras: 1988, "Paternal Occupation and Brain Cancer in Offspring," *American Journal of Industrial Medicine* 14, pp. 299–318.

Williams, W. W.: 1981, 'Firing the Woman to Protect the Fetus: The Reconciliation of Fetal Protection with Employment Opportunity Goals Under Title VII,' *The Georgetown Law Review* 69, pp. 641–704.

Wilson, A. L. et al.: 1992, "Does Prenatal Care Decrease the Incidence and Cost of Neonatal Intensive Care Admissions?" *American Journal of Perinatology* 9, pp. 281–84.

Wilson, G. S.: 1989, 'Clinical Studies of Infants and Children Exposed Prenatally to Heroin,' in Donald E. Hutchings (ed.), *Prenatal Abuse of Licit and Illicit Drugs*, N.Y.: The New York Academy of Medicine, pp. 183–94.

Wilson, G. S. et al.: 1981, 'Follow-up of Methadone-treated and Untreated Narcotic-dependent Women and Their Infants: Health, Developmental, and Social Implications,' *Journal of Pediatrics* 98, pp. 716–22.

Yawn, B. P. and R. A. Yawn: 1989, "Preterm Birth Prevention in a Rural Practice," *Journal of the American Medical Association* 262, pp. 230–33.

Yazigi, R. A. et al.: 1991, "Demonstration of Specific Binding of Cocaine to Human Spermatozia," *Journal of the American Medical Association* 266, pp. 1956–59.

Zuckerman, B. et al.: 1989, 'Effects of Maternal Marijuana and Cocaine Use on Fetal Growth,' *New England Journal of Medicine* 320, pp. 762–68.

Legal Cases

Albala v. City of New York, 434 N.Y.S.2d 400, 1981.

Application of the President and Directors of Georgetown College Inc., 331 F.2d 1000 (D.C. Cir.), cert. denied 337 U.S. 978, 1964.

Addington v. Texas, 441 U.S. 418, 1979.

Beal v. Doe, 432 U.S. 438, 1977.

Becker v. Schwartz, 46 N.Y.2d 401, 386 N.E.2d 807, 413 N.Y.S.2d 895, 1978.

Bellis v. U.S., 417 U.S. 85, 1974.

Bergstresser v. Mitchell, 577 F.2d 22, 1978.

Bowden v. State, 256 Ark. 820, 510 S.W.2d 879, 1974.

Breithaupt v. Abram, 352 U.S. 432, 1957.

Buck v. Bell, 274 U.S. 200, 1927.

City of Akron v. Center for Reproductive Health, 462 U.S. 416, 1983.

Colautti v. Franklin, 439 U.S. 379, 1979.

Commonwealth v. Daniel I. Cass, 392 Mass. 799, 467 N.E. Rptr. 1324, 1984.

Commonwealth v. Pelligrini, No. 87970 (Mass. Sup. Ct. 1990).

Curlender v. Bio-Science Laboratories, 106 Cal. App. 3d 811, 165 Cal. Rptr. 477, 1980.

Dennis v. Walker, 284 F. Supp. 413, 1968.

DeShaney v. Winnebago County Department of Social Services, 851 U.S. 1071, 1989.

Farwell v. Keaton, 396 Mich. 281, 240 N.W.2d 217, 1976.

First National Bank v. Bellotti, 435 U.S. 765, 1978.

Gibson v. Gibson, 3 Cal.3d 914, 479 P.2d 648, 92 Cal. Rptr. 288, 1971.

Goldberg v. Ruskin, 499 N.E.2d 406, 1986.

Goller v. White, 20 Wis.2d 402, 122 N.W.2d 193, 1963.

Grayned v. City of Rockford, 408 U.S. 104, 1971.

Griswold v. Connecticut, 381 U.S. 479, 1965.

Harris v. McRae, 448 U.S. 297, 1980.

Hastings v. Hastings, 33 N.J. 247, 163 A.2d 147, 1960.

Hayes v. Shelby Memorial Hospital, 726 F.2d 1543, 1984.

In re Baby X, 97 Mich. App. 111, 293 N.W.2d 736, 1980.

In re Infant Doe, No. GU 8204-004A (Monroe County Circuit Court, 1982).

In re Philip B., 92 Cal. App. 3d 796, *cert denied* 445 U.S. 949, 1980.

In re Ruiz, 500 N.E.2d 935, 1986.

In re Steven S., 126 Cal. App.3d 23, 178 Cal. Rptr. 525, 1981.

International Union, United Automobile, Aerospace and Agricultural Implement Workers of America, et al. v. Johnson Controls, Inc., 886 F.2d 871 (7th Cir., 1989), 499 U.S. 187 (1991).

Jacobsen v. Massachusetts, 197 U.S. 11, 1905.

Jefferson v. Griffin Spalding County Hospital Authority, 247 Ga. 86, 274 S.E.2d 457, 1981.

Jennifer Johnson v. State of Florida, 578 So.2d 419, 602 So.2d 1288 (1991).

Jorgensen v. Meade Johnson Laboratories, Inc., 483 F.2d 237, 1973.

Keeler v. Superior Court of Amador County, 2 Cal.3d 619, 87 Cal. Rptr. 481, 470 P.2d 617, 1970.

Little v. Little, 576 S.E.2d 493, 1979.

Loving v. Virginia, 388 U.S. 1, 1967.

Maher v. Roe, 432 U.S. 464, 1977.

McFall v. Shimp, No. 78-17711 In Equity (C.P. Allegheny County, PA, 1978).

NAACP v. Button, 371 U.S. 415, 1963.

Natanson v. Kline, 186 Kan. 393, 350 P.2d 670, 1960.

Park v. Chessin, 400 N.Y.S. 110, 1977.

People v. Morabite, 580 NYS2d 843, 1992.

People v. Stewart, No. M508197 (San Diego Municipal Court, 1987), E. L. Miller, Jr. and R. C. Phillips: "Points and Authorities in Opposition to Defendant's Demurrer and Motion to Dismiss."

Pierce v. Society of Sisters, 268 U.S. 510, 1925.

Planned Parenthood of Central Missouri v. Danforth, 438 U.S. 52. 1976.

Presley v. Newport Hospital, 117 R.I. 177, 365 A.2d 748, 1976.

Procanik v. Cillo, 97 N.J. 339, 478 A.2d 755, 1984.

Raleigh Fitkin-Paul Morgan Memorial Hospital v. Anderson, 42 N.J. 421, 201 A.2d 537 (per curiam), *cert. denied*, 377 U.S. 985, 1964.

Renslow v. Mennonite Hospital, 67 Ill.2d 348, 367 N.E.2d 1250, 1977.

Reyes v. Superior Court of the State of California, 141 Cal. Rptr. 912, 1977.

Rochin v. California, 342 U.S. 165, 1952.

Roe v. Wade, 410 U.S. 113, 1973.

Roller v. Roller, 37 Wash. 242, 79 P. 788, 1905.

Schloendorff v. Society of N.Y. Hospitals, 211 N.Y. 125, 105 N.E. 92, 1914.

Schmerber v. California, 384 U.S. 757, 1966.

Smith v. Brennan, 31 N.J. 353, 157 A.2d 497, 1960.

Smyth v. Ames, 169 U.S. 466, 1898.

Snyder v. Massachusetts, 291 U.S. 97, 1934.

Stallman v. Youngquist, No. 6457 (Ill. Sup. Ct., 1988).

State v. Allen, 291 S.E.2d 459, 1982.

State v. Bremer, No. 90-3227-FH (Mich, Cit. Ct. 1991).

State v. Gray, 584 N.E.2d 710 (Ohio 1992).

State v. Inzar, Nos. 90CRS6960 & 90CRS6961 (N.C. Cuper. Ct. 1991).

State v. Richards, 585 S.W.2d 505, 1979.

Strunk v. Strunk, 445 S.E.2d 145, 35 A.L.R.3d 683, 1969.

Tarasoff v. Board of Regents of the University of California, 17 Cal.3d 425, 551 P.2d 334, 131 Cal. Rptr. 14, 1976.

Turpin v. Sortini, 31 Cal.3d 220, 182 Cal. Rptr. 337, 643 P.2d 954, 1982.

U.S. v. Crowder, 543 F.2d 312, 1972.

Webster v. Reproductive Health Services, 492 U.S. 490, 1989.

Williams v. Zbaraz, 448 U.S. 358, 1980.

Winston v. Lee, 470 U.S. 753, 1985.

Womack v. Buckhorn, 384 Mich. 718, 187 N.W.2d 218, 1976.

Wright v. Olin Corp., 697 F.2d 1172, 1982.

Zepeda v. Zepeda, 41 Ill. App. 2d 240, 190 N.E.2d 849, *cert. denied* 1964, 379 U.S. 945, 1964.

Index